In Our Hearts
We Were Giants

The Ovitz Family, Antwerp, 1949.

Back row, left to right: Sarah, Azriel, his wife Leah, daughter Batia, Moshe Moskowitz (Elizabeth's husband), Unidentified woman, Batia (Avram's daughter), her mother Dora. *Front row, left to right:* Micki, Franziska, Perla, Elizabeth, Rozika, Frieda, Avram, Shimshon.

In Our Hearts We Were Giants

The Remarkable Story of the Lilliput Troupe—
A Dwarf Family's Survival of the Holocaust

YEHUDA KOREN
and
EILAT NEGEV

CARROLL & GRAF PUBLISHERS
NEW YORK

IN OUR HEARTS WE WERE GIANTS
The Remarkable Story of the Lilliput Troupe—
A Dwarf Family's Survival of the Holocaust

Carroll & Graf Publishers
An Imprint of Avalon Publishing Group Inc.
245 West 17th Street · 11th Floor
New York, NY 10011

First Carroll & Graf edition 2004

Library of Congress Cataloging-in-Publication Data is available.

ISBN: 0-7867-1365-8

Endpaper photo: A rare photo of the Lilliput Troupe before the war. Left to right:
Elizabeth (drums), Rozika, Perla, Frieda, Franziska, Micki. Avram, the master of
ceremony, is absent from the photo. (Courtesy of the Ovitz family)

Design by Simon M. Sullivan

Printed in the United States of America
Distributed by Publishers Group West

To our mothers, Sarah and Rachel

Contents

PROLOGUE

There's a long pause after the chime echoes inside. No ray of light sneaks from under the door, no muffled noises disturb the quiet afternoon.

Two peepholes, one above the other, catch the eye. The lower is just thirty inches above the ground. Until not long ago, Perla Ovitz would drag herself to the door and, peeking out, try to guess by the look of the trousers or the dress hem if the person on the other side was friend or foe. Nowadays, confined to her bedroom, she's too weak to make the journey. Her vigorous voice erupts from a loudspeaker in the hallway; it demands identification. Then there's a buzz, and you can push the heavy brown door open. You blink in the dusky corridor. You're not sure how to continue, for fear of slipping or bumping into concealed furniture, or, worse, stumbling over your hostess. She's under three feet tall. Her voice is your compass, guiding you forward. You grope blindly toward a diminutive silhouette in the doorway of the dimly lit room. She waits at the threshold in a full-length, majestic crimson dress and allows her visitor to tiptoe past. You step carefully inside. Then, she waddles in.

It is her bedroom. The legs of the double bed have been sawn off and although it is practically lying on the floor, a small stool stands next to it, to enable her climb into sleep. Beyond a kindergarten table and chairs is a child-sized washbasin. From your towering angle, there's not much difference in her height if she's standing up or sitting on the edge of the bed. Your first impulse is to shrink down, so as not to dwarf her with your presence. She nods toward the normal-sized sofa beside her bed. You take care to keep your feet on the ground, as crossing your legs will place your shoes in front of her face.

The raven-black hair of the ageless doll-like lady is carefully combed back and held in place by a velvet bow, in old-fashioned Hollywood style. She's theatrically made up—her cheeks are rouged, her nails are lacquered shiny red. She wears earrings, a necklace, rings. *As long as you breathe, you should look your best. I don't want people to pity me.* It's a motto she is fond of repeating.

She enchants with her dazzling smile, and her bubbly talk is studded with unexpected aphorisms. *A beaten dog dreads even the kindest people*, for instance, is how she excuses her cautiousness. She spends most of her time sitting on her petite chair, or reclining, dressed, on her covered bed, as these days she can stand no more than a minute or two unaided.

She's on her own most of the day, and needs everything to be easily accessible—a packet of chocolate cookies and a plastic box of sliced apples lie on the bed should she get hungry. A thermos of water waits within reach.

She can't move without her cane, which serves as an extended hand, to pull, press, push. Tiny stools scattered through the house allow her to rest at any time in her movements around her rooms. All the light switches have been lowered to her height.

The kitchen has a knee-high stove, and a special mechanism allows her to open the refrigerator door with a push of her cane. All the food is stored on the bottom shelf.

Vases that stand as tall as her hold abundant bouquets of silk and plastic flowers in her favorite colors: sharp violets, soft pinks. A heavy red curtain at the wide entrance to the living room is pulled to both sides and gathered in thick cords, as if a show were about to begin. Forty-five years have passed since Perla Ovitz took her last bow, but the stage stays with her still. When all her family still surrounded her, she loved the lights; she even flooded herself with them offstage, at home. Now, trapped alone in the big empty apartment, she seeks the economy and safety of dimmed lamps and half shadows.

Perla's memories, though, remain vivid—in their glories and their horrors. Hers is a true story of seven dwarfs. It's a story, however, that delivers Perla and her brothers and sisters not into the arms of a benevolent Snow White, but into the grip of a beast. It's a story that ultimately takes them into some of the darkest corners of hell that human beings have ever experienced. And it's a story that they survived.

ONE

Transylvania, 1868

The story begins with giants.

In long-gone days, it is said, in hilly northern Transylvania, the Dolhai Valley was strewn with tribes of giants. For ages upon ages since the creation, they lived and prospered and roamed the earth. Then came the deluge, and they all fled to the peaks of the mountains. There, one by one, they perished, and when the waters receded, only two had survived: a giant and his daughter, Roza Rozalina. Her eyes black as coal, her hair as red as flame and as long as the sadness of the fir trees, sorrowfully she wandered through the valley.

"Father," she sighed, "I'm withering with loneliness. Will I ever find a mate?" She headed toward the Iza River and, daydreaming, strolled along the bank. All of a sudden, she spotted tiny creatures ploughing between the grass blades. Roza Rozalina was astonished: never had she seen creatures so similar to her, and yet so small. She picked up a handful and nestled them in her apron. These moving toylike creatures would rescue her from boredom, she thought. She examined them closely. One in particular caught her eye. He was handsome as the moon and appeared to be less frightened than the others. Her cheeks blushed as she felt the pangs of love.

When she showed her catch to her father, he was alarmed: "Alas, my daughter, our time is up! These tiny creatures will inherit the earth. Return them immediately to their place!" But Roza Rozalina was incapable of obeying. Soaked in tears, she begged the Almighty to tie her fate to that of the small, handsome brave one. And the Almighty shrunk her a little, and stretched him a lot, until they became in size like twins. Eventually their descendants filled the land. They named the place Rozavlea, after their giant, ancestral mother.

In that sleepy little Romanian village, the ancient legend has been passed on from one generation to the next. Every August, the roughly seven thousand peasants who live there celebrate the festival of Roza Rozalina, with the schoolchildren each year staging the story. And in this same village, so proud of its legendary giantess matriarch, a real dwarf was born in 1868.

It was the third pregnancy for Frieda Ovitz, and having already given birth to a healthy daughter and son, she was distressed to discover that her baby had stopped moving inside her. In that remote part of the world, she had recourse only to prayer or an amulet, or the hope of a miracle. Being an Orthodox Jewish woman, she sought the advice of her rabbi.

"Your child will live," he assured her, as he glanced at her belly from behind the table that separated them, "but he won't grow tall." Heartbroken, Frieda and her husband, Leib, decided to try halting destiny by naming their newborn son Shimshon Eizik, after Samson, the biblical giant. The first years passed without apparent complications, and the parents began to believe they had been spared. But when the child reached the age of seven, even they had to admit that he had long since stopped growing. They probed each other's memory, they asked their elders. As far back as anyone could remember, in all their family history there had never been anyone who had not grown tall. Little Shimshon Eizik was shuttled between doctors, healers, and sages; he was prescribed medications and charms, spells and potions. But to no avail—they added not a millimeter to his stature. Frieda gave birth to two more boys; to her relief, both of them continued growing normally.

The peasants of rural Rozavlea, which, like the rest of Transylvania, belonged to the Austro-Hungarian Empire, were wretchedly poor, with limited options. But a three-foot-tall youth like Shimshon Eizik could not even hope to lift an ax or cut a tree or push a plough, and to him every farm animal was an immense and menacing monster. Realizing their son would never be able to support himself by physical labor, Frieda and Leib Ovitz invested in Shimshon's schooling. They furnished him with tutors, and the bright, good-natured boy excelled in his studies.

As a teenager, Shimshon Eizik tried to come to terms with his lot. The sages of the Halacha, the ancient Jewish code of law, knew that the sight of human malformations could evoke scorn and derision. Shimshon Eizik thus found solace in the Hallachic imperative that if one sees a black man, a red man, or an albino, a giant, a crooked-faced man, or a dwarf, one should say, "Blessed be God, who alters man." In this way, the negative response to disfigurement was channeled instead into admiration for God's diverse powers of creation. Traditionally the blessing was spoken only on one's first encounter with the deformed person, as it was meant to overcome the initial repulsion and enable the speaker to treat the "altered" man as an equal.

But when Shimshon Eizik read further into the holy texts, he was upset to learn that they defined a dwarf as a cripple and thus disqualified the small-statured man from certain functions that normal-bodied men were allowed to perform. Even if born to a line of holy priests, a dwarf was, for instance, never allowed to serve in the temple. So Shimshon Eizik sadly realized that in spite of an apparent tolerance for anomalies, Judaism tended to exalt those blessed with a perfect body.

Furthermore, Jewish folktales often portrayed dwarfism as a punishment for some wrongdoing or sin. Sometimes, too, it represented the lesser of two evils. In one old tale, a childless couple frequents the cemetery to beseech God for offspring. One day, in the midst of their weeping and pleas, an angel descends to them from heaven. "God has heard your prayer, and granted your wish," the angel tells them, "but you must choose: you can have either a son who will grow no larger than a pea, or a tall, healthy daughter who will leave you and convert to Christianity at the age of thirteen." The couple does not hesitate: "Let him be as small as a pea."

Dwarfs, however, could also serve as symbols of distinction and merit, as in the case of Rabbi Gadiel, who has been immortalized by S. Y. Agnon. A kind of Jewish "Agnus Dei," Gadiel the Dwarf heroically sacrificed himself to save his community from blood-libel—the accusation that his congregation had murdered a Christian child to acquire blood for the baking of the unleavened Passover bread. Nonetheless, such heroism aside, before the advent of modern genetics, the third-century Talmud sternly warned that "giants should not marry each other, as they will give birth to a flagpole, and midgets should not couple, as they will produce a thumb."

So, tiny in stature—no taller than a boy of five—but a lively and self-confident eighteen-year-old, Shimshon Eizik Ovitz was searching for a normal-sized bride. In a deeply religious society that valued learning, Shimshon's excellence in rabbinical studies and his piety compensated for his physical deficiency. He could offer his bride the prospects of a good livelihood, along with the community respect he enjoyed as an educated person. Nevertheless, the choices were meager, as only about two hundred Jews lived in Rozavlea, and no more than a few thousand in the neighboring villages, the Jews then totaling just 20 percent of the population. After much searching, the local matchmaker suggested eighteen-year-old Brana Fruchter, from the nearby village of Moisei. As usual in a prearranged marriage, Brana did not have much say in the matter.

About the time of his marriage to Brana, Shimshon Eizik decided to discontinue his studies. By then not only had he succeeded in overcoming any feelings of shame and unease for his own body, which created a stir wherever he went, but he had also learned how to manipulate public curiosity and to transform mockery into admiration. His audience would soon forget his size and shape and become captivated instead by his quick tongue and charisma.

Playing to his advantage the old traditions that the Jewish communities of the region had preserved, Shimshon harnessed his eloquence to his odd but magnetic appearance and slipped easily into the cultural role of *Badchan*, a merrymaker, a colorful, virtually indispensable figure at wedding festivals, which provided the harsh life of the rural Jewry with its most joyful moments. Life, in fact, stood still when the community celebrated nuptials, which were often as lavish as carnivals and which gave the peasantry a rare chance to let their hair down in an acceptable way. Throughout the festivities, the *Badchan* would entertain the guests with drollery, riddles, and anecdotes.

A complex enterprise involving hundreds of guests and celebrating the creation of a new family, the wedding was an event that called for perfection: opulent food, impeccable service, the choicest tableware, ravishing clothes, the finest orchestra—and a knowledgable, clever, masterful *Badchan*. No matter that these conservative, superstitious Transylvanian communities feared the "evil eye," which could damage the health of expected offspring; Shimshon Eizik Ovitz's deformity did not deter potential clients from hiring him. For his skills had made him famous throughout the region, and beyond.

Months before the wedding, the fathers would book him for the week. They would negotiate his fee, cover his travel expenses, and arrange his lodgings. In the weeks leading up to the wedding, Ovitz would prepare for the occasion by gathering information about the newlyweds, their parents, and the community dignitaries. He would then write songs and ditties based on family histories, assorted facts and anecdotes, rumors and gossip—all of his versification aiming at a good laugh. At the occasion itself, dressed smartly in a black suit and hat and carrying a small cane, Ovitz would appear in the decorated courtyard. Before the guests arrived, his assistant, who always traveled with him, would lift him to a chair standing on a table that would serve as his podium. From there, as master of ceremonies, he would do as he was expected: he would make his audience shed tears one moment, roar with laughter the next. With his ditties he would encourage both the bride and her all-female entourage to weep, for his verses offered them a cathartic antidote to the fears and apprehensions of an uncertain future:

> *Cry out your eyes, O graceful bride,*
> *Your diamond tears enhance your charm.*

Now is the time to wail out loud
As soon you'll become a wife.

With sympathy for both the young bride and groom, each leaving a familiar, secure childhood home to live with a person practically unknown to them, Ovitz would remind them in his sermon of their respective conjugal roles and responsibilities. But the tension would be broken immediately after the taking of vows and declaration of man and wife, as then Ovitz would put on his funny face. Working hard to create a jovial mood, he would encourage the guests to dance until they dropped. From time to time he would announce a special guest and offer a witty verse about him—perhaps in praise of the gift he had brought. As a jester, Ovitz was allowed to toss little barbs at the community's hypocrites and misers.

Shimshon Eizik Ovitz was an earnest jester. He amused his audience with puns and limericks based on familiar quotes from Talmudic thought. He gauged the mood of the wedding guests and told the orchestra what tunes to play. He showered witticisms upon the grandmothers of the brides as they whirled in their customary dance. He kept spirits high and the revelry going nonstop, until the early hours of the morning. When he could, he would grab a moment to rest and slump into his chair, for Ovitz's small feet and short legs provided only meager support.

The morally strict Jewish society in Eastern Europe at the end of the nineteenth century allowed entertainment only on certain holidays and festivals; the theater was banned as indecent. The wandering *Badchans* were in essence the pioneering actors of the

Jewish world, the founders of the Yiddish theater. They enjoyed great popularity, as they ministered to a basic human need: release. Years later, when Jewish orthodoxy had lost its grip, Ovitz's children would follow in his footsteps by establishing their own vaudeville troupe, which would take the entertainment first offered in religious ceremonies onto the stages of theater halls, all for the sake of pure fun.

On November 2, 1886, Shimshon Eizik Ovitz was lost in prayer when he heard the first cry from the bedroom. Peszele Fogel, the midwife, emerged and announced that he had a daughter. She was named Rozika. When the toddler began walking, she swayed from side to side like a duck, and Shimshon Eizik Ovitz recognized the dreaded sign all too well. On January 27, 1889, Franziska was born, and she too proved to be a dwarf like her father and sister. If Shimshon and Brana feared the mark of heredity would strike their progeny again and again, they nevertheless bore it and obeyed the biblical command that they procreate. A daughter, Mancie, and a son, Judah, followed Franziska, but they both died in their first year and took the secret of their future growth to their tombs.

Ovitz, meanwhile, began to drift from his career as a *Badchan*. In all his merrymaking, Ovitz would impress his audience as much with his Talmudic wisdom as with his wit, so that before and after the wedding celebrations, various guests would approach him with their religious and personal dilemmas. Many of the region's Jewish communities were so small they could not afford a rabbi, and the scholarly Ovitz filled the gap. He molded himself into the rabbinic role. He dressed and behaved like a sage; he groomed his beard to look respectable. (In fairy tales, dwarfs grow long beards, but in real life most of them decline to do so, as it makes them look even shorter.)

So it was that Ovitz moved into his new role as the esteemed wandering rabbi of Maramures County. For a week or two, he would settle in a small village, conduct prayers, and preach. For its part, the community would provide him with lodgings and furnish a consulting room. He frequently had to deal with questions regarding the kashruth, or dietary laws; in particular, the separation of meat and milk, for what housewife did not agonize over the dictum that she pour away a bucket of precious milk if she suspected a speck of meat had somehow fallen inside?

While giants were traditionally deemed to be stupid—all body and no brains—dwarfs, whatever the mixed biblical and rabbinic opinions, were popularly believed to have been born with great wisdom and magical powers, as godly compensation for what they had been deprived of in inches. Shimshon Eizik Ovitz benefited from this folk belief. He rapidly became famous for his spiritual powers, and people flocked to see him wherever he went.

Surrounded by people who believed in miracles, the charismatic Ovitz added amulets, spells, and charms to his repertoire. He would lay hands on the head of a sick child and recite a prayer. For an infertile woman, he would inscribe a blessing in ancient Hebrew letters on a piece of parchment with instructions that it be worn at all times. Often he provided the services of a lay psychologist by listening to the laments of wives with matrimonial problems and advising them how to restore peace—and straying husbands—to the household.

Ovitz was paid handsomely for his opinion and advice, especially by businessmen who consulted him regularly before signing new deals. He himself had a good head for business; he invested his earnings in property and land. Official Maramures County documents attest to Shimshon Eizik Ovitz's popularity, prosperity, and social mobility: first registered as a "cantor," he appears in later years as a "wizard," and finally, estimably, as a "landlord."

But great healer that Ovitz was, he was powerless when his own wife, Brana, fell ill and died of tuberculosis in the winter of 1901 at the age of thirty-three. Since he spent most of his time traveling to make a living, he could not take proper care of his two teenage daughters. Nor could he simply leave them to their own devices. Furthermore, the community expected this well-known religious authority to find a new wife.

Barely had the usual thirty days of mourning passed when the matchmakers began knocking at the door. Ovitz refused to consider widows and divorcees, as they were burdened with their own children, but he did find Batia-Bertha Husz, a girl from a distant village only two years older than his daughter Rozika, much to his liking.

What might have persuaded a pair of loving parents to give their pretty, healthy, eighteen-year-old daughter to a crippled widower not only almost twice her age but also with two teenage dwarf daughters? Shimshon Eizik Ovitz's reputation as a prosperous healer and spiritual superman must have worked for him. To head off the anticipated gossip about Ovitz's preference for a young virgin, everyone was told that the bride was already an old maid of twenty-four.

Beginning a fresh chapter in his life, Shimshon no doubt hoped that his hereditary luck might also change. It didn't. On September 26, 1903, Avram was born, a dwarf. Born in June 1905, a baby girl, named Frieda after Shimshon's mother, proved to be a dwarf as well. With the birth of their third child, in August 1907, the Ovitzes had reason to believe the spell had finally lifted: Sarah grew healthy and tall. Then, in July 1909, came Micki, a dwarf. Two years later, the pendulum again swung in the other direction, Leah being normal-sized; but their sixth child, Elizabeth, born in April 1914, was not. Three years later the normal-sized Arie arrived. And on January 10, 1921, the youngest of them all was born.

Choking, suffocating, she emerged with the umbilical cord tied around her neck. The despairing midwife took her away from the exhausted mother, and, placing her quietly aside, waited for her to die. At first, Batia Ovitz didn't understand. She asked to see the baby, and when the midwife ignored her, she became alarmed. "Let her rest in peace," advised the midwife, hinting consolingly at the baby's critical condition. "This child must live! Bring her to me!" ordered Batia, forcing herself upright. The midwife obeyed. Batia hugged the baby, and that's when she noticed its jaws were locked. She bent its head back, and inserting her index finger into the tiny mouth, she almost tore it open. The baby responded with a deep cough.

Piroska Ovitz—her Yiddish name, Perla, would reflect her pearl-like size and beauty—liked to blame her mother for her big mouth. In Perla's infancy, it was hard to tell whether or not she would join her three normally growing siblings, but early signs seemed to indicate that she would escape the six dwarfs' fate. She didn't. Shimshon Eizik's genetic trait once more asserted its dominance, as it had in the other six of his ten children. Perla, the seventh, made the Ovitzes the largest recorded dwarf family in the world.

Ovitz built a new home for his large clan. He rented the old shed in the backyard to the new village doctor, so they now had a physician at hand. Although their house stood next to the synagogue, Ovitz and his seven dwarfs found it difficult to cross the muddy earth in the long, cold winters to attend daily prayers. When they did manage, they unavoidably created a great deal of fuss, for in order to see the cantor and the Holy Ark, they all had to be raised onto small stools placed on the bench.

To make things easier on them all, Ovitz converted one of his rooms into an everyday prayer room. As one of the community philanthropists, he would eventually donate part of his land and money to help renovate the synagogue, which he would attend mainly on the high holidays. He meanwhile continued his travels, while Batia at home took care of the ten children. Since Batia treated her husband's two daughters from his first wife as her own, Perla grew up without not knowing that Rozika and Franziska had a different mother: *As they were miniatures, I didn't realize they were almost mother's age. They helped her a lot to raise us.*

In September 1923, Shimshon Eizik Ovitz attended a wedding in a faraway village. Immediately after the meal, his body temperature soared; he began sweating and vomiting. His assistant and coachman, Simon Slomowitz, rushed him home. Ovitz was wracked with pain. The fish he had eaten was poisonous. He died after a week of agony, at four in the afternoon on Sunday, September 16. He was fifty-five years old.

Only a few tombstones from the extinct Jewish community of Rozavlea have survived in the abandoned cemetery. Miraculously, one of them marks the grave of Shimshon Eizik Ovitz. The fading Hebrew inscription reads: "Here lies an honest, virtuous, learned man, a charitable benefactor of the poor, all of whose deeds were for the honor of God."

TWO

Rozavlea, 1923

F or a widower with ten children, the matchmaker could still find a spouse. But there was no chance that, at thirty-nine, the newly widowed Batia Ovitz would find a man willing to take on the burden of providing for her and her children, five of them under fourteen, seven of them dwarfs.

The family struggled to rearrange itself. Avram, who had just turned twenty, stepped into his father's shoes. He had already accompanied Shimshon Eizik on his travels as his apprentice. Avram had not merely observed his father perform the roles of rabbi and *Badchan*; he had also, on occasion, mounted the table and joined Shimshon Eizik in rousing the crowd. He and his father shared the same small frame, and their double-bill dwarf act had been a success.

As both the new provider and the head of the family, Avram Ovitz strove to maintain his father's contacts in the villages scattered through the region with the aid of the ever-loyal Simon Slomowitz, his father's coachman and traveling assistant. Gradually gaining confidence, Avram began to compose his own witty lines and develop his own style of performance. All this experience would prove to be useful later on, when he was writing the acts for the renowned Lilliput Troupe.

Perla, who was only eighteen months old when her father died, had no memory of him. As a child, the only man she called "papa" was her brother Avram. No one at home corrected her; perhaps out of pity, her siblings wished to postpone the bitter truth of her orphanage as long as possible. Avram took charge of her education; Avram tested her in her studies. When she wanted sweets, she turned to Avram for money. By the time she reached the age of six, she had grown to the same height as Avram, but this did not strike her as odd.

One day, while Perla was helping a girlfriend who lived across the street with her homework, Perla began bragging about the generosity of her father. The girl's mother overheard Perla's boasts and felt obligated to correct her. "You really can't call him father—he's your brother!" she said to Perla. "He is *too* my father—he gives me all my things. Everybody's got a father, and so do I!" Perla contended, but the neighbor wouldn't let it drop. "Actually, you don't have any father! He's dead!"

Perla rushed home. Sobbing, she told her sisters what the neighbor had said. "She's lying!" she cried. "Come and tell her she's wrong!" As Perla's sisters hugged her and tried to console her, it started to dawn on her that the neighbor might have been speaking the truth. Then, for the first time, her sisters told her the story of her real father, Shimshon Eizik. For years to come, Perla had to bite her tongue to keep the word "papa" from slipping out when she addressed her brother Avram.

The Ovitz clan buzzed with beelike cheerfulness. Each member played a specific part in the household, and Batia orchestrated them all. The normal-height teenagers Sarah and

Leah took care of the day-to-day physical tasks, like washing and cooking, or scrubbing on a wooden plank the basketfuls of laundry that they'd carry to the Iza River. For years they also did the sewing, until Elizabeth and Perla were old enough and skilled enough to make clothes for their sisters. The dwarfs refused to wear children's clothes: *They looked ridiculous on us. People tend to view dwarfs as children anyway, and we wished to look respectable.* The age span between the oldest and youngest dwarf sisters was thirty-five years, but since all five of them were almost the same height and size, they could all wear identical clothes. In their all-blue or all-pink dresses, they were often mistakenly thought to be twins or triplets. The five female dwarfs also combed each other's hair and painted shiny varnish on each other's nails. They never wore high-heeled shoes, which, besides being difficult to stand on, lent them no support and made no real difference in their height. *Shoes had to be custom-made for us anyway, because of our unusually broad soles.*

The interior of their wooden home, which was painted white, resembled a doll's house. Decorated with a great deal of handmade lace and tapestry, it was furnished with low washbasins, beds with sawed-off legs, tiny chairs, and many stools. The four normal-height members had to adjust, although there was also furniture suitable for them and for the occasional guests. The dwarfs had to be careful using the toilet in the backyard outhouse. A smaller wooden tier made just for them narrowed the hole in the privy bench so that they wouldn't fall through.

The Ovitzes had everything they needed in their small paradise. The front garden was full of flowers, and the backyard was an orchard: apples, plums, peaches, pears, grapes, hazelnuts. They raised chickens and geese and kept a few cows in the shed. While they had to rely on hired help to pick the fruit, milk the cows, and pump water from the large stone well in front of the house, they were able to bake their own bread, smoke their own geese, churn their own butter, and make their own jam.

The Ovitz house stood on Rozavlea's main street. Relatives of Shimshon Eizik Ovitz—the three brothers and one sister—lived nearby with their families. The two younger brothers, Israel-Meir and Lazar, were both artistically inclined, and Uncle Lazar and five of his ten sons formed a klezmer troupe that played at weddings. Influenced by local Gypsy bands, the now-famous klezmers—the Hebrew-Yiddish word actually means "musicians"—had been playing folk tunes, dance music, and Hassidic melodies all over Europe for centuries. They were popular not only in the Jewish communities, but also among the non-Jewish town dignitaries and the bourgeoisie, who preferred the Jewish klezmers to their Gypsy counterparts, since the Gypsy music was considered coarse.

"The heart is like a violin: you harp on the strings, and melancholy tunes pour out," goes a Yiddish proverb. The fiddler—in well-known paintings, Chagall has depicted him gliding with his instrument over village rooftops—was the klezmer band's leader. Next in importance was the clarinet player, whose music, which could at once make eyes water and feet tap, while the bassist provided rhythmic and harmonic underpinnings. As the band's primary purpose was to crowd the floor with dancers, the beat of the percussionists was firm and steady. Instead of a piano, larger bands also had an accordion, as well as a cymbal.

Like all klezmers, Lazar Ovitz and his sons were natural musicians with no formal musical education. Unable to read music, they were spontaneous, skilled improvisers who mastered their instruments through instinct and played with emotion. In the 1920s, around five thousand klezmers in eastern Europe were vying for public attention. Competition was so intense that sometimes a band would pay parents to perform at a wedding and then hope to make some small profit from the tips they'd get for playing favorite tunes. Despite the meager earnings, klezmers stuck to their trade, for it was also a passion, even when it had to be financed through manual labor—Lazar Ovitz and Sons, for instance, were horse traders. While both the *Badchan* and klezmers made their living from weddings, they enjoyed different levels of esteem. Because Jewish culture valued the word more than the tune, the *Badchan* earned more respect for his learning and verbal facility than the klezmers, whose joie de vivre was aligned with a fecklessness considered low-class.

The musicians in most klezmer bands did not come together by chance. Usually they were carrying on a family trade, with talents and melodies they had inherited from parents and older relatives. This is how Rozika and Franziska came to play the violin; they picked up the music and mastery from their uncle and neighbor Lazar. In pious families, however, it was unheard-of for young women to travel alone, so the two sister violinists accompanied their brother Avram on his trips to weddings in the region. The three Ovitz dwarfs soon became a major attraction, the girls exciting audiences with their child-sized violins and winning applause when they sang in their high-pitched voices. Thus began a family pattern. Each child would learn to play an instrument, and at sixteen would join the musical troupe of the Ovitzes.

Being surrounded by six brothers and sisters her own height made it easier for Perla to come to terms with her dwarfism. *Like every child, I expected to add a few centimeters every year and grow*

like a flower. But when I saw the others, I realized I'd never grow tall. It saved me from feeling inferior and helped me accept myself as I am. In my dreams, my legs and arms don't lengthen, and I've never fantasized about a good fairy coming to double my height. Being a dwarf is no punishment. The difference in height does not diminish my pleasures. Our life is as worthwhile as anyone else's.

On December 1, 1918—two years before Perla's birth—Romania annexed Transylvania from Hungary as part of the Great War's peace agreements. The official language of Transylvania thus became Romanian, and all public Hungarian cultural institutions were eradicated. But like most Transylvanian Jews, the Ovitzes prided themselves on their historical connections with Hungary and maintained their cultural alliance to Hungary at home. Perla picked up the language and old songs by listening to her sisters. She had a musical ear and a good singing voice. *From infancy, I imitated my sisters and sang from morning to night, giving everyone a headache. Our tenant doctor continually bribed me with chocolates to shut me up.*

Perla was a bright child. She'd begun reading even before she started to attend the local primary school, which was just a few houses down the road. Although she could manage the short distance well enough, she often found herself in the arms of teachers and classmates hoping not so much to spare her legs as to have fun leaping around with a living doll in their embrace. Nobody bothered to ask Perla for her permission, and she did not protest, for she did not want to lose their company. She especially liked to play hide-and-seek with her neighbor Arie Tessler. Whenever he caught her, he would spontaneously swing her in victory around the room. "I have always believed she was my age and only recently learned to my surprise that she is in fact six years older than me. Her tiny build fooled me," recalls Arie.

In school plays, Perla was often cast as a baby in a cradle—a role that she did not seem at all to mind. She certainly didn't mind being spared the daily humiliation of blackboard arithmetic exercises, since she could not reach the board. She was also exempt from gymnastics, and she avoided the schoolyard during recess, for fear of being knocked down by the full-size children. Instead, she used the time to do her homework, an activity that enhanced her popularity among her classmates, as she willingly let them copy her notebooks. *They all needed me for their studies, so they never mocked me, and treated me with respect.* In return for her help, they escorted Perla home. They would carry her books and guard her from dogs—all of which, from Perla's perspective, looked huge and threatening. A dog, no matter how friendly, could tip her over just by brushing against her or trying to lick her face.

One day between classes, Perla was standing alone in the empty schoolroom staring at a large map of Romania. In her hand she held the teacher's pointer, which was longer than she was tall. She was unaware that a supervisor had stepped inside until he thundered, "What are you doing here, little girl?" For a moment she was dumbfounded, but she soon composed herself. "I'm studying. I know the map by heart and can point wherever you want, even with my back to the wall," she boasted. He challenged her to find Cluj, then watched in disbelief as Perla turned around and, magicianlike, lifted the pointer over her shoulder and hit the town on its dot. Amazed, he asked for more towns, and then mountains. Each time, the tip of her pointer landed on the exact spot. The act made her famous in school and she repeated it again and again. Not once did she reveal even a flicker of stage nerves.

Perla's family enjoyed happy times when, one after the other, three of the female dwarfs got married. The first was Rozika, the oldest and already an old maid of forty when, on May 2, 1927, she married her twenty-eight-year-old cousin, Marcus Ovitz. The twelve-year gap in their ages didn't show, since, like most dwarfs, she looked much younger than her years. The next to wed was Franziska—she married Marcel Leibovitz—and then Frieda exchanged vows with Ignaz (Izo) Edenburg, an electrician from the nearby town of Sighet. The village gossips, who couldn't get over the fact that all three grooms were healthy men of normal height, concluded that they must have been drawn to the family fortune.

Because the three newly wedded wives refused to leave their kin, their husbands had no choice but to move in. Each couple had a room of its own, but the new spouses were expected to earn their keep by helping the family dwarfs with daily chores. This arrangement would apply to all future weddings as well. Some spouses would adjust. Others would find it a strain and divorce. "My uncles and aunts, the seven dwarfs, were so attached to each other they were like a mythological creature, one body and seven heads," explains Perla's nephew Shimshon Ovitz.

Summer departs early in Transylvania, and September is often a capricious month. The sunshine is deceptive, and the chilly air behind its beams can be dangerous. One such September day in 1927, a neighbor of Batia Ovitz implored her to share the last chance for a swim in the river. It was Friday, and although Batia had nearly finished preparing the Sabbath meal, she did not feel inclined to join in the adventure. But her friend insisted, and Batia gave in. The two women headed toward the Iza, its banks serene and its water glimmering with temptation. Batia Ovitz was almost glad that she had overcome her misgivings as she braved the river's gray-green water. She barely noticed the chill in the light September wind. Then, suddenly, she felt a stab in her chest. She screamed. Leaning on her frightened friend, she struggled her way home. The doctor was called in; he diagnosed tuberculosis.

For almost three years, Batia Ovitz lay bedridden in her home. Every day, when Perla returned from school, she would rush to her mother's bed and, to make her happy, recite her lessons. *But I was not allowed to cuddle with her, like I was used to. Let mother rest, I was always told, and sent from the room.* Once the door was shut, her mother would cough out blood.

On February 8, 1930, a Saturday evening, the Ovitz house was filled with gloomy-faced people. *I asked my sisters why they were all dressed in black and what all the strangers were doing. I was told they came to take Mummy to the doctor. I was puzzled as to why they needed so many people to accompany her. My sisters didn't answer. I thought they were crying because of her illness.*

Nine-year-old Perla was not taken to her mother's funeral. For weeks, the entire family evaded her questions. Perla, in her mother's inexplicable absence, refused to eat. Rapidly she lost weight. Her sisters finally had to lock her like a goose between their knees and force food down her throat. Eavesdropping one day, Perla heard anxious whispers from the next room: "If she goes on much longer with her hunger strike," they said, "very soon she'll join Mother." Perla could not contain her happiness. She pushed the door open and pleaded, "Please let me join Mummy." The whispers resumed, and then her sister Sarah turned her way: "Promise not to cry." Perla nodded. "Mother has gone," said Sarah. "So let's go where she is," urged Perla.

The sad truth began to sink in on Perla only when her sisters couldn't stop sobbing.

THREE

Rozavlea, 1930

H is name was Hershel Weisel, but he was known in the region as Hershel der Langer (Hershel the Tall One), for he was a giant. In his boatlike shoes, he stood seven feet, two inches tall, and with his wild beard, protruding teeth, and thundering voice, he might have been feared as a monster. Instead, he was a laughingstock. Unable to find a job because of his massive size, he was reduced to begging. To earn extra money, he toured the villages with his normal-height wife, and Long and Short, as they were called, leapt around like dancing bears, to the applause and ridicule of all.

Batia Ovitz feared that a lone dwarf would be twice as helpless as such a giant. Her children's only strength, she believed, lay in numbers. On her deathbed, she imparted to them a rule to guide them through life, a rule that in fact would eventually save them: "Through thick and thin, never separate. Stick together, guard each other, and live for one another." She exhorted them to cultivate a common skill so that they could earn their living together, with no need to rely on the kindness

of strangers—to find a profession in which they would be neither isolated nor ostracized, but rather welcomed; a profession
in which they would flourish.

The stage seemed to be the perfect choice; for would they not
there be applauded, courted, honored? Three of the dwarfs had
already been in the wedding-show business, and they could
continue to try their luck with a klezmer band. But that option
would leave out the remaining four, so it was rejected. On the
other hand, establishing their own wedding band also presented problems: some klezmer bands featured one woman, or
maybe two, but a group of five female and two male musicians
would have been too much for the more conservative revelers
to allow. And in any event, prospective in-laws might well be
reluctant to book an all-deformed band for their children's great
day. Furthermore, the small, weak lungs of the Ovitzes did not
permit them to play any wind instruments—an essential for
weddings. Even if they could, playing energetic dance music for
endless hours on their broad, crooked feet would be an intoler-
able strain. Lastly, the socioeconomic status of klezmers was
already low, and the Ovitzes suspected that as dwarfs they
would be doubly discriminated against.

Because they deviate from the norm, dwarfs, like many such
groups, have always had a problem earning a living. Yet, historically, they have generally fared better than sufferers from other
major deformities. The public has, of course, always been interested in the diversity of creation and in oddities of nature: an ele-
phant man arouses aversion and pity; a giant evokes astonishment;
a girl with three legs prompts apprehension. But dwarfs make
people smile. Unlike "freaks"—historically labeled *mirabilia mon-
strorum* or "monstrous wonders"—dwarfs are *mirabilia hominum*:
"human wonders," maybe because every adult was once a child

and so finds it easy to identify with the plight of a small person in a world dominated by tall people and big objects. Then too, the diminutive stature of dwarfs kindles a parental instinct. Indeed, dwarfs have often been treated like children, picked up like babies, and spoken to in patronizing tones. Perhaps, in the disturbing disproportion between a dwarf's normal-sized head and short limbs, is perceived the symbol of an eternal child.

Dwarfs had their golden age in ancient Egypt. There dwarfs were honored and venerated like gods, and in fact one of them was a god, whom the Egyptians named Bes. His realm was midwifery, and he also looked after misfits neglected by the other gods.

Pharaoh Pepi the First (2600 BC) enjoyed the company of Danga, his dwarf jester, who sharpened his perception of the relativity of size and supremacy: "I am the gods' Danga," Pepi observed, "for they must find me as ridiculous as I find my Danga." Augustus Caesar too was deeply attached to his dwarf Lucius, so much so that upon Lucius's death, Augustus had his statue sculpted and inserted with precious stones for eyes. Court dwarfs played their handicap to their advantage; they survived by making others laugh, often through pranks and foolery, and frequently with astonishing wit. Only they could speak critically and frankly to the pharaoh, king, or tsar without having their heads severed from their bodies. Only Bahalul, the dwarf of Caliph Haroun al Rashid, could have insulted his master so obnoxiously, with practical jokes and verbal forays, all while pretending be an idiot.

No palace has been complete without dwarfs. Those at the

Viennese court were described by the nineteenth-century British Lady Montague as "devils bedaubed with diamonds." Royal families exchanged dwarfs as presents; King Charles the Ninth, for example, happily received four from the king of Poland, Sigismund Augustus, and three from Maximilian the Second of Germany. Notably, thirty-four dwarfs served in Rome as waiters, and objects of curiosity, in a banquet given by Cardinal Vitelli in 1566. A century later at the court of Charles the First, the Stuart king presented a dwarf named Geoffrey Hudson as a wedding gift to his queen: when she cut into the crust of a large pie baked in honor of the occasion, the dwarf jumped out. With even greater fanfare, Valakoff, the favorite dwarf of Peter the Great, was presented to the female dwarf of Princess Prescovie Theodorovna in 1710. The Russian tsar invited seventy-two dwarfs to the special party, and then allowed the newlyweds to spend their wedding night in his royal bedchamber. On a more practical level, the endearing quality of an adult intelligence locked inside a child's body made male dwarfs safe companions for little princes, while female dwarfs attended princesses. In regal court paintings, the dwarfs are often found standing next to dogs or monkeys, no doubt because they were perceived to fill roles similar to those of the royal pets. In the first third of the twentieth century, the court-dwarf tradition had not fully expired: once when Perla Ovitz performed in Bucharest, she and her family were invited to the palace of King Karol the Second. *We gave a special performance, the king sitting on his throne surrounded by his entourage. They all applauded fervently, and we bowed to the floor. The king beckoned us to approach, and we gathered around him. He fondled us, as if deciding if we were real people or mechanical dolls.*

Still, for the most part, by the end of the nineteenth century, the court-dwarf fashion had fizzled. Life in the service of nobility had nonetheless left its mark in dwarfs' stage names, which included a Princess Martha, Princess Elizabeth, and Princess Pauline. At a bit less than two feet tall, Princess Pauline is the shortest woman listed in the *Guinness Book of World Records*. For their part, male dwarfs honored themselves with military ranks, like the great American showman General Mite, as well as his famous colleague and the star of the Ringling Brothers and Barnum & Bailey Circus, General Tom Thumb, who entertained Queen Victoria at Buckingham Palace.

Unlike giants or other people with physical deformities, performing dwarfs borrowed not only the titles of the nobility but also their style of dress: dashingly elegant gowns, spectacular hats, lots of fake jewelry. Their regal appearance and imperial manner were so convincing that they sometimes confused the public, especially as certain kings and generals were also strikingly short: Attila the Hun, Charles the Third, Vladislaw the First of Poland. Napoleon himself was no giant. As royalty tended to marry within the family, they had a higher than normal rate of bodily deformations—a phenomenon made eloquently clear in Velasquez's paintings.

Vittorio Emmanuele the Third, king of Italy, was so embarrassed by his height of four feet, three inches that he was never seen without his high heels. To compensate for his heredity, he married the giant Princess Elena of Montenegro, who stood nearly two feet taller than him. Wherever Perla and the other dwarfs traveled, people inquired whether they were Vittorio Emmanuele's relatives: *Vittorio Emmanuele was the most famous European dwarf of the time, and we were a very famous troupe, so everyone thought there had to be a family connection.*

Of course, dwarfs' lives were not always or even usually gilded. More often than not, dwarfs were abused and mistreated, as in the salons of aristocratic Roman ladies, who commanded them to run about naked. They appeared naked, as well, at Roman festivals, where they were tossed into the arena either to fight one other or to serve as prey for wild beasts. Queensland, Australia, has provided its own modern manifestation of such cruelty, with a sadistic game called "dwarf bowling," in which the human bowling balls are lifted in one arm and thrown against the pins. Only recently has "dwarf bowling" been banned.

At the end of the nineteenth century, the Darwinian concept of evolution sparked excitement not only among scientists but also among the public at large. So it was that staring at freaks or evolutionary anomalies came to be regarded as "an educational experience." From 1840 to 1940, in fairground tents all over Europe, "freak shows" flourished. Spectators rushed in droves to see disfigured and malformed people doing mundane tasks that should have challenged them: an armless lady making tea, a legless man riding a bicycle—or a dwarf mastering a musical instrument.

Already the objects of public curiosity, dwarfs felt that they might as well make a living at it. From the beginning they were part of these freak shows, along with fire-eaters, bearded women, and legless men. Dwarfs with some artistic talent sang and danced; others entertained by juggling or performing impressive physical feats that might have overpowered even a normal-sized man. Those suffering from severe abnormalities and distorted bodies were often displayed in closed tents or cages, simply to provoke revulsion.

When a dwarf wished to be appreciated for his real talent and true artistry as a performer (as opposed to his dwarfism), it generally proved to be impossible. Frank Delfino, who started his showbiz career in the Midget Village at Chicago's 1933 World's

Fair, hoped to gain recognition as a virtuoso violinist. He insisted that no mention be made of his deformity in publicizing his concerts, but to no avail; his impresarios billed him as "the world's smallest violinist." Although he would appear in films like *Planet of the Apes* and *The Incredible Shrinking Woman*, he became better known for the role he played in McDonald's hamburger commercials until the age of eighty.

Traditionally, many dwarfs have performed in circuses as clowns and acrobats, often mounted on ponies or elephants. Nearly every circus used to employ a troupe of dwarfs—in Russia today, there are still six all-dwarf circuses. The most famous Jewish circus dwarf was Zoltan Hirsch, half of the duo Gérard and Zoli. Born in Hungary in 1885, Zoli was the only short person in his family—a condition due to rickets. A wandering circus that had settled in his town caught his imagination, and he spent his days among the performers. He found wearing a top hat, smoking jacket, oversized silk tie, and shiny black shoes far more appealing than being a blacksmith, his destined profession. In a career that took him from Russia to England, South Africa, and Latin America, he everywhere enjoyed celebrity status. He also appeared in films and published an autobiography, appropriately titled *The Great Life of a Small Man*.

Dwarfs found their stage was not only in tents or fairgrounds. At the end of the nineteenth century, Berlin was entranced by Fatmah and Smaum, sibling dwarfs from Ceylon. They appeared daily between two and ten o'clock in Hagenbeck's Ceylon Teahouse. When Fatmah died at sixteen, her brother switched to sports, and performed at the Berlin Wintergarten and Zirkus Busch. In 1904, Samuel W. Gumpertz founded a midget city in Coney Island's Dreamland. He gathered three hundred dwarfs from the United States and various fairs and circuses around the world and offered them both a steady salary and residency in his "Lilliputia," named after Lilliput, the land of the little people in Jonathan Swift's *Gulliver's Travels*. Lilliputia was built as a replica of fifteenth-century Nuremberg; every building was proportionally scaled to the height of the four-foot (and shorter) inhabitants. They had their own parliament, theater, shops, cafés, restaurants, post office, and barber shop, as well as diminutive horses and chickens. Reflecting Gumpertz's fine eye for detail, the laundryman was a Chinese dwarf. On Lilliputia's beach stood a miniature lifeguard tower. The midget city's fire department responded hourly to false alarms, with midget firemen rushing through the narrow streets with their hoses. Visitors could walk around the miniature town and, peep-show-like, watch the dwarfs go about their daily routine. When the park was closed at night, the dwarfs were free to follow their own pursuits.

Gumpertz's idea caught on quickly. In 1913, Leo Singer established his own version, Lilliputstadt, in Vienna's famous Prater amusement park. Similar dwarfs' towns were subsequently built in Berlin, Paris, Budapest, Chicago, and San Francisco. Carl Schaefer's Märchenstadt Lilliput toured several German cities. The outbreak of the Great War ended such tours in Europe but the undaunted Singer sailed with fifty of his dwarfs on a world tour that passed through Asia, Australia, and South America before landing in the United States. The dwarfs performed from coast to coast and were President Harding's guests at the White House. A few decades later, in 1939, Singer would supply Hollywood with 124 dwarfs for the filming of *The Wizard of Oz*.

Since they had economic value, dwarf actors were relatively well cared for by their impresarios. They counted themselves lucky to be holding safe, decently paid jobs, and to be living among peers who could be supportive of them in their many moments of frustration. It is estimated that in pre–World War II Europe alone, at least 1,500 dwarfs made a living out of show business. Seventy-one different impresarios represented them, Leo Singer himself employing twenty-five agents who scoured remote European villages for dwarfs and sometimes purchased even tiny ten- or eleven-year-olds from their parents.

Somehow, Singer's agents never reached Rozavlea, but if they had knocked on the Ovitz door, it would have been slammed in their faces. *Circus was not for us, as we didn't have the physical strength or inclination. We abhorred the idea of being animals in a human zoo, of people crowding us for hours, pointing their fingers and saying, "Look, she's cleaning the windows." We never wanted to make a living out of exhibiting our deformity. We always wanted to be taken seriously as professional actors.* The Ovitzes conducted their lives communally; every step they took was discussed and every decision they made was debated in a family council. After much discussion, they determined that the only acceptable career for them lay in an improvement upon the klezmer idea, but not simply as an all-dwarf band. At the time there were other all-dwarf bands in Europe, but they were invariably just one act in a whole vaudeville show. The Ovitzes wanted a show of their own.

With the experience he had gained writing gags as a merrymaker, Avram Ovitz began scripting them for his sisters and brother. Whereas klezmers offered sets of dance music, the Ovitzes put together a program of love songs and local hits. *Onstage it was all romance, because we knew that is what people crave in real life*. And the audience went mellow when Perla, rocking from side to side sang:

> *Nobody loves you*
> *as much as I love you*
> *Nobody hugs you*
> *the way I do*
> *The flowers are blooming just for you*
> *and it's all because I love you.*

She always preferred the tragic love ballads, and sixty years on, her voice still carries the emotion with which she sang:

> *Since you left me and went away,*
> *I've been waiting in vain*
> *Although you'll never return.*

Not everything being either roses or thorns, the Ovitzes tailored their two-hour program to fit all moods and tastes. Between the songs—which they performed in five languages—they kept their audiences roaring with laughter with broad jokes and hilarious stand-up scenes. From the Hassidic branch of their family, they had inherited both the dictum "Serve the Lord with joy," and the notion that music, song, and dance were superior to words of prayer as expressions of faith. For the Hassidim, to live in joy was a virtue, and to yield to melancholy was anathema. To kindle the spirit and rise to a state of joyous ecstasy, the Hassidic faithful shook their torsos and clapped their hands with fervor during prayer. With similar enthusiasm the Ovitzes made gifts of their talents to praise God and bring joy to the community, at the same time that they made money out of laughter.

Still, they had to weigh the propriety of singing secular hits like "I left my heart in Hawaii," though they could find justification in the Cabala for performing current pop tunes. The *Nizozoth*, or divine sparks, says the Cabala fell down from the Spheres of Holiness and were scattered throughout all the universe—even into non-Jewish music. Through the singing of songs and performance of such non-Jewish music, those sparks are again released, to be lifted up and purified.

Determined to make music, the Ovitzes set out to buy instruments that would suit their stature: the two oldest sisters, Rozika and Franziska, already had their quarter-size violins, and for the raven-haired, dramatic Frieda, a local craftsman made a cymbal with shortened legs. Micki played both a half-sized cello and a small accordion, while the energetic Elizabeth took on the drums, the only regular-sized instrument in their band. And Perla got a tiny, four-string pink guitar that looked like a toy. Perla, however, would not immediately join her family on its performance tours—as she was barely ten, she would first have to finish four more years of schooling. Of the seven, only Avram— singer, actor, and their master of ceremonies—performed without a musical instrument.

For the Ovitzes, as for all performers, costumes were of the utmost importance. Mistresses of the sewing machine, the sisters stitched together fluffy, silky evening gowns in bright, cheerful colors, all of them identical in cut and design, with bows and lace to accent them, and with sequins, little pearls, and spangles to make them shimmer in the light. The men wore white jackets and bow ties. Hair presented a problem, for in Orthodox Judaism hair is considered seductive. Every married Jewish Orthodox woman in Rozavlea shaved her head completely and then covered it with a shawl to demonstrate her modesty. Since childhood, the Ovitz girls had witnessed the monthly visits of a rough, bony woman with whom their mother would lock herself in the bedroom. Shyly she would then lift part of her scarf to reveal any new growth of hair, and the woman would shave it away. After covering the freshly shorn area again with her scarf, their mother would bare another patch of hair to her visitor's razor. Such a custom would not serve Batia's five performing daughters. They needed their beautiful, voluminous hair to enhance their presence onstage. Likewise, during performances, Avram and Micki exempted themselves from the prescript that Jewish men cover their heads at all times with a hat or a skullcap. Fortunately, the dwarfs' diminutive size placed them beyond the strict Orthodox Jewish code of dress and appearance, as did their profession. Because their livelihood depended on their dress and looks, the Jewish community accepted their aberrant immodesty.

"The Lilliput Troupe" seemed an obvious choice as both name and commercial identity for the Ovitzes. Since it was a family business, they decided not to hire a professional manager. Avram, already the head of the family, took responsibility for marketing and contracts. Backstage, Sarah assumed the duties of the wardrobe mistress: she laid out the costumes for each scene, and helped her dwarf sisters undress and change when they rushed from the stage between scenes. Izo Edenburg, Frieda's husband, worked as a stagehand and arranged for transportation. Leah stayed behind at the family farmhouse in Rozavlea, where she attended to the animals and crops, and kept the house ready for the troupe on its return from long, exhausting tours. She also ably dealt with the accounting and bookkeeping for the family enterprise.

The only sibling who did not participate in the family business was Arie. He had a good singing voice, but he chose to lead a life of his own. A tall, handsome man with a talent for handicrafts, he became a first-rate tailor and moved to the town of Satu Mare. Leaving the family would turn out to be his doom.

FOUR

On the Road, 1931–1940

O n Sunday mornings, Simon Slomowitz would stop horse and carriage at the Ovitzes' door. Then he and Izo Edenburg would pile the cymbal, the set of drums, and the cello, all of them sealed in their crates, onto the carriage and tie them securely with a rope. After that, they would add to the load a large box of props, two suitcases packed with neatly folded costumes, and a carton filled with food for the journey: smoked goose thigh, fruit and vegetables from Leah's garden, a jug of cider made from the Ovitzes' own apples, dry cake, and round loaves of bread. Then the seven Lilliput Troupers would step out from their one-story house and gather around the carriage. One by one they'd wait to be lifted up onto the carriage by the strong arms of Slomowitz and Edenburg. Wrapped in bulky overcoats, the dwarfs would huddle together on the benches, the women guarding their elaborate coiffures against the damp and dusty wind in colorful scarves.

In the absence of buses and paved roads, Slomowitz supplied the only shuttle service between the village of Rozavlea and Sighet, which was twenty-two miles away. Because few villagers had business in the town, Slomowitz found himself generally underemployed, so he was able to work regularly at the Ovitz home as a handyman. When the dwarfs formed their troupe and began traveling, he became their loyal, reliable coachman as well. Even as a young man, Slomowitz had spent much of his time with the Ovitzes, since he had assisted their father, Rabbi Shimshon Eizik. "They made him feel needed and important, and he stayed well beyond his working hours. More than feeling pity for their helplessness, he enjoyed their cheerfulness, the music, and the cultivated atmosphere," recalls his son Mordechai Slomowitz. It didn't hurt that, for years, Simon had been—and was still—in love with the beautiful, coquettish Frieda, despite the fact that she was married to Izo and that he himself had a wife, Chaya, and seven children. Chaya Slomowitz deeply resented her husband's absences from home for days on end, but she refrained from protesting too much, as her family's livelihood depended so completely on the Ovitzes.

The first performances of the Lilliput Troupe were local, in Maramures County. Handwritten posters announced their arrival in the isolated villages, and money changed hands at the door, just before the show started. Not many artists bothered to tour this wretched, godforsaken region, so the local talent from Rozavlea quenched the deep thirst of the villagers for amusement. The troupe's success was in fact instantaneous, although they soon realized they would not be able to make a steady living off a population of 175,000, many of them peasants too poor to afford the price of a ticket.

However small the Ovitzes' stature, the Lilliput Troupe began thinking big—as their father had. The tales of Shimshon Eizik's far-flung travels, of the fame they had brought him and the fortune he had gained, had become legend to his children; and in the legend they found a model: like a small army, they set out to conquer the nearby districts one by one with their entertainments. Starting with appearances in shabby village halls, they moved on to town theaters and cinemas. Success followed upon success. The troupe's confidence grew, and so did their reputation. With the news of their spectacular show traveling fast, they soon found themselves performing all over Romania, Hungary, and Czechoslovakia.

They traveled mostly by train. Since Rozavlea had no railway station, the troupe had to first endure the bumpy three-and-a-half-hour ride by carriage to the depot in Sighet—while the Ovitzes could have easily afforded a move to Sighet, they preferred the safety and intimacy of their pastoral village. Each concert tour lasted several weeks. The troupe would stop in one town for a few days, where they'd present two or three performances each day, usually to loud applause and full houses, and then move on to another stop. Life on the road is difficult for any actor, but for them it was ferociously exhausting. Outside the security of their home, its every detail tailored to their smallness, they continually struggled in alien territory that was fraught with obstacles.

Indeed, they could not make a move without the help of their entourage. They had to be lifted like babies from the platform into the train wagon and then raised up to the seat. In restaurants, they needed a hand to climb onto a chair. Performing halls and hotels confronted them with endless stairs. They had to carry their small wooden stools with them in their travels in order to reach hotel beds and washbasins, or simply to take a moment's rest.

The troupe's tour schedule was coordinated with local festivals, market days, and annual fairs; their program was adjusted to the audience, country, and event. The Ovitzes were fluent in several languages—Hungarian, Romanian, German, Yiddish—and could sing in a few more. They could perform on an improvised platform under the sky as easily as on a proscenium stage in a hall lit by crystal chandeliers. The Ovitzes made only one exception regarding their engagements. They would not perform at weddings. Not as professional artists: *An artist should keep his standards—the moment you lower them you'll never get them back.* When invited as guests to family weddings, they would, of course, often be asked to entertain the crowd; with considerable reluctance they would agree.

Orthodox Jews were in fact not permitted to enjoy show business in any form. Still, when Issac Peri—now an Israeli historian of Romanian Jewry—was seven, he could not resist. Everyone in Tirgu-Mures was talking excitedly about the Lilliputs—"The dwarfs are coming, the dwarfs are coming"—except Issac's father. A very religious man, the leader of his town's congregation, he would not allow his son, even should Issac dare to ask, to attend such a circus. Desperate to see the amazing dwarfs, Issac snuck into the open-air theater. A man in the audience placed him on his knees so that little Issac could see. His father never learned his secret. At another performance, Arie Tessler, Perla's childhood playmate, was astonished to see the girl he used to swing around the room now standing majestically onstage and singing grandly in the company of her family. He recalled: "They swept everyone off their feet with their jokes and songs. One scene has stuck with me. I was standing by the postal manager, one of the more educated and respected people in our village—throughout the show he was very enthusiastic. Suddenly he shouted the name of a Russian song, something having to do with heartache, and when Perla sang it he cried like a baby until the end."

Every song the Ovitzes performed was greeted with a storm of applause, and master of ceremonies Avram would have to beg for quiet. At the end of the show the dwarfs were commonly hailed with flowers; often money was thrown onto the stage. Once when Perla, beaming, turned, about to make her bow to the audience, she was struck in the chest by something sharp and heavy. It nearly knocked her down, but fortunately it had not hit her face. When she recovered her breath, Perla picked up the object from the floor: it was a banknote, tied around a heavy coin so that it would fly across the hall and land on the stage. From then on, Avram warned audiences to be cautious when expressing enthusiasm and advised them to place their gifts on the apron of the stage—not to hurl them and place the Lilliputs in peril. At evening's end, the troupe would collect bouquets, coins, notes, chocolates, and even small bottles of perfume. The appreciation was mutual. *We were very friendly toward our audience. An actor should be warm, not conceited, though not everyone can restrain his arrogance.* As a promotional gift, the Ovitzes had cards printed with a picture of all seven dwarfs and autographed "Souvenir from the Lilliput Troupe." Decades later the cards, carefully preserved in photo albums kept by devoted fans, would emerge from oblivion.

In every town they performed in, the Lilliput Troupe would be invited into the homes of the affluent Jews, just as their peers in past generations had been feted in the castles of kings and nobles. Tables loaded with kosher delicacies would overwhelm the dwarfs, for their frugal upbringing had accustomed them neither to lavish banquets nor to a bohemian life. They refrained both from drinking in taverns with their fans, and from dining in fancy restaurants after a show. When the stage lights darkened, they preferred to return quickly to their hotel, where seven dwarfs and their three-man entourage would squeeze themselves into three plain rooms. Nor would they indulge in extravagant shopping sprees, not even when touring the big cities. In any case, they wouldn't find clothes or shoes in their sizes on the shelves. The Ovitz sisters had a lifelong passion for cosmetics, however, and they also loved to visit fabric shops, where they would buy endless yards of silk and satin for their gowns.

The Ovitzes embarked on their entertainment career in the early 1930s; their timing was good. Dwarfism had by then reached the height of its popularity, and an all-dwarf family band performing on miniature musical instruments was an irresistible novelty with great commercial value. Importantly, too, by the 1930s dwarfs had become objects of curiosity not just onstage but also in respectable academic circles, where the border between the freak show and the lecture hall commonly got blurred. The topic of dwarfism gained popularity among physicians as much for its clinical interest as for its quaint appeal.

Doctors working side by side with freak-show impresarios broke professional taboos by issuing medical certificates that described in detail the patient's aberrations. These certificates, read aloud at the freak shows, were offered as proof of authenticity to enhance the commercial value of the miserable human exhibits. Dwarfs were also hunted down by doctors at fairgrounds and amusement parks, then transported to medical schools for research. Many dwarfs simply hired themselves out for academic research, which for the most part involved endless measurement of every inch of their bodies. Head size commanded particular interest among advocates of the pseudoscience of phrenology.

The findings of such researches were often presented to full houses in medical and anthropological societies around Europe, sometimes with the human guinea pig onstage.

It wasn't just living dwarfs that intrigued the doctors; their skeletons did too, and they were mounted for the public in permanent museum displays. In his performances, the legendary Owen Farrel—a dwarf strong enough to lift four grown men, two sitting astride each arm—would lie down on the ground and allow a cart to be driven over his chest. He sold his body in advance to a surgeon for a weekly pension, to be paid him until his death. To this day his tiny skeleton is displayed at the Hunterian Museum in Glasgow. Especially terrible is the case of Caroline Crachami, described in the book *The Smallest of all Persons Mentioned in the Records of Littleness* by Gaby Wood. Allegedly born in Sicily but raised in Dublin, Caroline was always frail—she weighed barely one pound at birth—and suffered from a persistent cough at an early age. A certain Dr. Gilligan persuaded her parents to allow him to take her to London, supposedly for the benefit of a better climate. He then exhibited the one-foot-seven-inch-tall girl not only in London but also in Liverpool, Birmingham, and Oxford, everywhere advertising her as "the smallest person on earth." This "Sicilian Fairy" had an "unearthly voice," which enchanted royalty and the aristocracy. And for an extra shilling, gentleman visitors could line up to touch and fondle her. In 1824, after one such evening in which she met more than two hundred guests, Caroline collapsed. She was not quite nine years old at her death. When her grieving father arrived at the doctor's clinic in London to take his daughter back to Ireland for a family burial, he discovered he was a week too late. Gilligan had already sold the child's body to the Royal College of Surgeons for skeletonization for five hundred shillings. In addition to the body, he threw in Caroline's miniature two-inch-long shoes, a pair of socks, a tiny ruby ring, and her thimble.

Caroline Crachami is exhibit 227 at London's Hunterian Museum. The room next to her exhibits the skeleton of Charles Byrne (a.k.a. O'Brien), also from Ireland. A giant well over seven feet tall, Byrne left his impoverished land to earn a living as a story-teller spinning out tales of "bliss and blood" in the exhibition halls of affluent London. There, in 1783, he met the surgeon John Hunter, who convinced the city's new twenty-two-year-old sensation to sign documents permitting the doctor to dissect him after death, in order to conduct valuable scientific research. Dr. Hunter was convinced that Byrne would soon die because of his height, and indeed the giant man perished shortly after signing the con-tract. Byrne, though, was tormented by the idea of his flesh being boiled from his bones, so he paid an undertaker to ensure that his corpse would be sunk in the Thames with leaden weights. Informed of Byrne's escape plan, Hunter outbribed the undertaker by a few hundred shillings: the corpse was snatched from the grave and transfered to the Royal College of Surgeons. The kettle in which it was boiled is the property of the museum. The Royal Col-lege's skeletonization technique would be repeated often in the pathological laboratories of Nazi doctors during World War II.

In Arie Tessler's memory—he saw the Ovitzes perform on several occasions—the dwarfish stature of the Lilliput Troupe was their primary attraction. "Still, people don't dress up, spend money on a ticket, and sit for a couple of hours just because the performers are dwarfs. If they had been lousy musicians, everyone would have booed them off the stage after five minutes. Their long career speaks for itself." Indeed, even as the Ovitz family accumulated fame and fortune, they did not slow down. Because they could not predict how long their good health and success would last, they worked tirelessly and conducted their finances cautiously. They invested heavily in gold and jewelry, which they took care to stash away. They also brought fragrances from afar to the village and fascinated neighbors with their stories of distant wonders. Although the Lilliput Troupe performed only in adjacent countries, Rozavleans to this day boast that the Ovitzes' renowned tours took them "all over the world."

The Ovitzes were quick to appreciate the potential of a new invention: radio. Izo Edenburg used his electrical training to install an antenna on the roof of their house in Rozavlea so that they could listen to distant stations and keep up-to-date with the latest developments in popular music—and thus expand their repertoire. Since the dwarfs could not read notes, they had to learn their music by ear. They would gather around the big brown Telefunken, first humming, then adding their voices, and finally accompanying the radio on their musical instruments.

In the mid-1930s, the whole village was astounded when a big, dark car stopped in front of the Ovitz house. An Italian model, it was spacious enough to easily accommodate the whole troupe, as well as their costumes, props, and musical instruments. To have a car then meant more than it does to own a private jet today. Edenburg looked dashing driving it, and, the Rozavleans fought for the privilege of washing and polishing it. An ex-Rozavlean, Benjamin Samuelson recalled that "being able to be even close to a car was so rare, it was like a privilege." He was seven years old at the time, and was always puzzled by how they all fit in that car. One day he was sitting with his friends on the riverbank in Rozavlea, "when we had the stroke of luck.

They allowed us to wash their car. This was an unbelievable experience, an honor we didn't expect, but took full advantage of. We were being asked, even encouraged, to touch that car. This state of grace lasted for a few years. Whenever they came back to town, the car would be taken to my river, where my friends and I would wash it for them."

The automobile made such an impression on the villagers that even now, more than six decades later, merely mentioning the name Ovitz elicits an instant smile from the few old peasants still living in Rozavlea, along with a comment such as, "Ah, they had the first and only car in the whole region. Up to then, we never had a carriage without horses." They can still describe the auto in minutest detail, and they still wonder how, of all people, it was the weakest of the weak who had come to own such a marvel.

FIVE

Hungary, 1940

Circus performer Lya Graf had traveled far to pursue success. Full of hope, the exquisite twenty-year-old dwarf had taken a boat from Germany to New York, where she was immediately snatched up by the Ringling Brothers and Barnum & Bailey Circus.

The circus's publicity man thought hard to come up with a gimmick that would garner public attention for the new discovery. He took Lya to Washington, and on June 1, 1933, he tiptoed with her up the stairs of the Senate building. They were heading for the Senate Banking and Currency Committee room, where J. P. Morgan, the leading American financier of his time, was due to testify, when the publicity man spotted his prey. He plopped Lya onto Morgan's lap, and as quickly as he snapped his fingers, the press photographer, who was in on the stunt, snapped a picture. The blazing flash dissolved, and the whole room fell silent. The sixty-six-year-old Morgan was famous both for his lack of humor and for his aversion to physical contact. That morning he was especially out of sorts because of the

Senate hearing. Yet after a moment's bewilderment, and to the considerable surprise of all, his scowl turned into a wide smile. The following day, all the major American newspapers carried the photograph of the enchanting, wavy-haired blonde dwarf and the powerful, bald multimillionaire. "Morgan, and even Wall Street as a whole, profited adventurously from the encounter. From that day forward until his death a decade later, he was in the public mind no longer a grasping devil, whose greed and ruthlessness had helped bring the nation to near ruin, but rather, a benign old dodderer," the *American Heritage Magazine* would later comment.

The shy and sensitive Lya Graf, however, gained little she valued from the "adventurous encounter." The exposure and attention that the photo brought her proved to be too much for her to handle. Unable to bear the prospect of becoming a celebrity freak, a dwarf on exhibition, instead of being recognized as an artist, she returned to her native Germany two years later. In 1937, she was arrested by the Gestapo. Not only did her dwarfism get her categorized as "useless for society," but she was also half Jewish. In 1941, she was transported to Auschwitz, where she soon died.

The Ovitzes were not aware that the earth was trembling under the feet of Jews throughout Europe. They were oblivious to Hitler's rise to power, the Nuremberg laws, Kristallnacht, concentration camps. Not even the outbreak of a world war, and the subsequent cancellation of their performances in Nazi-occupied Czechoslovakia, awakened them to the disturbing new reality. Like many other Jews in Transylvania, they simply did not feel personally connected to the events unfolding in distant Germany. They continued to do what they had to do to make a living. They performed. Their admirers, after all, were waiting for them.

So was history. It did not take long for events to catch up with the Ovitzes. During the twenty-two years of Romanian rule over Transylvania, Hungary had never abandoned its hopes of retrieving its former province. The right moment arrived in June 1940. The Soviets issued Romania an ultimatum demanding the return of Bessarabia; Hungary, for its part, called for the restitution of Transylvania. As Hitler was secretly planning to invade Russia in "Operation Barbarossa" and thus needed both Hungary and Romania as allies, he could not risk the possibility of military confrontation between the two countries. On August 30, 1940, German foreign minister Joachim von Ribbentrop and his Italian counterpart, Count Galeazzo Ciano, dictated their arbitration terms: Romania was to cede northern Transylvania, which had a population of two and a half million.

The months prior to this agreement had seen the collapse of law and order in Romania, and with it the rise of a new wave of anti-Semitism. The Romanian government had long been antipathetic to the Jews, so the Ovitzes, like all Jews in the region, welcomed what they perceived as a return to the golden era of Austro-Hungarian rule. What they failed to realize was that the current Hungarian regime was itself anti-Semitic.

On September 13, 1940, the transfer of government was completed, but within a few days, the flowers of hope proved to have sharp thorns. Hungary quickly implemented anti-Jewish measures. All Jewish newspapers were shut down, along with social and sports clubs. Jews were expelled from secondary schools and universities. Civil servants, doctors, lawyers, teachers, and other white-collar professionals lost their jobs. Jewish businesses were confiscated, with only a lucky few able to hand over their keys to non-Jewish partners and thus maintain at least a partial livelihood.

Performances by Jewish artists were restricted to Jewish audiences. But most Jews, financially impoverished and emotionally ravaged, had neither the inclination nor the money for song and dance. Their careers in crisis, the Ovitzes traveled to Budapest, now their capital, on a mission that dared not fail: their application for the newly required Hungarian identity cards. They stormed the government office. Radiating the natural charm and theatrical self-confidence they'd gained through years of celebrity, in full feather, the seven contagiously cheerful dwarfs so dazzled the officials with their fairy-tale presence, publicity photos, and bubbly chitchat that they never were asked the one essential question. The word "Jew" did not appear on their freshly issued official identity cards.

So the dwarfs could go back on the road—but not, to be sure, as if the world were waging no war: for nearly four years, they lived in racial disguise and constantly ran the risk of arrest for breaking Hungarian laws that forbade them as Jews to perform for non-Jewish audiences. They stopped speaking Yiddish in public; they pricked up their ears for gossip. Rumors, whispers, hints of apprehension, could quickly cut short a commitment in any town or village. If they were booked for a Friday evening or a Saturday matinee—the Jewish Sabbath—one or another of the troupe would play ill, a doctor would be summoned to the hotel to fill out a certificate, and a large apology notice would be posted on the doors of the performance hall. The disappointed audience would be promised an extra performance on Sunday.

The Ovitzes still felt relatively safe in their own village. Their home remained a popular venue for the celebration of the Jewish festivals, and villagers who had not been invited would glue themselves enviously to the windows. On hot summer days, if they were not on tour, the Ovitz women, as always, would take their small wooden stools out into the shade of the garden's fruit trees, and in the cool afternoon hours they would move to the pavement where they could see and be seen by their neighbors. All would stop to greet the sisters and to share gossip.

According to one of their neighbors, Rosa Stauber, in this period "people in the village would wear rustic clothes, sheepskin jackets, makeshift boots, and the children ran in the mud barefoot. And there were the Ovitzes in the latest fashion—city clothes, delicate, flowery dresses, black lacquered shoes. They were the only women in the village with manicured nails, red lipstick, powdered cheeks, and eyelashes painted black. It was an attraction—a free show. They were so beautiful and artistic and sweet-smelling, like elegant dolls." The village children would sneak up on the Ovitz men, quickly measure themselves against them, and shout "I'm taller! I'm taller!" to their friends— a practice that Avram and Micki tolerated as an innocent game. On Saturdays after the prayer service, the Ovitzes would stroll down the peaceful main street of Rozavlea, as the villagers who survived the war's impending horrors recall: a procession of seven strolling dwarfs brought up in the rear by the family's taller members. The seven celebrities would exchange benevolent smiles and waves of the hand with the village people. If they detected any mockery, the dwarfs tried not to show it.

According to statistics for this period, the marriage rate among the general population was approximately 75 percent; however, wedding bells rang for only 30 percent of people with restricted growth. The Ovitz family managed much better: five of the seven dwarfs ended up married, all of them to normal-height spouses who moved into and became part of the Lilliput household. Perla Ovitz had a whole set of suitors, and was confident of eventually marrying. *But I never went hunting. I didn't need to—they were all after me. Men were attracted to us because we had pretty faces and good manners. The fact that I was small didn't bother them. Some men prefer dolls. Height and body size are no sign of health or fertility; some rings have huge worthless stones, others have tiny precious ones. Just as diamonds can be small, so were we.* She met some of her suitors after performances. They would buy tickets to successive shows, never once take their eyes off her, and sometimes dare to make the next move by squatting at the artists' entrance. Feeling too young to make a romantic commitment and not ready to leave her family or to desert the stage, Perla consistently responded to her suitors with rejections. Her brother Micki, a bachelor in his thirties, never reconciled himself to being single, though it is generally more difficult for women than men to accept miniature partners. Time and again, Micki or members of his family would try to persuade a girl to marry him. They all declined with a diplomacy that veiled deep offense.

Dwarfs, of course, can have normal-sized children; statistics show the chance of passing on dwarfism to be 50 percent. One American dwarf couple, Robert and Judith Skinner, a little less than two feet, three inches tall each, managed to have fourteen normal-sized children. None of the female Ovitz dwarfs, however, ever conceived. Their doctors had in fact advised them not to, as their pelvises were too narrow for safe delivery. Married to the tall and full-bodied Dora Katz, Avram Ovitz did father one child, Batia. She was born in 1936; she developed normally.

In the summer of 1941, the Hungarian authorities rounded up 35,000 Jews who had settled in Transylvania after 1919 and could not prove their Hungarian origins. They were deported to the Hungarian-occupied parts of Galicia, where, they were led to believe, they would be resettled on deserted farms. Soon after, on August 27 and 28, 1941, 23,600 of them were massacred. A man from Sighet did escape. Hit by a bullet, he fell into the freshly dug mass grave and was covered by corpses. He managed eventually to crawl out from under the dead bodies of his countrymen and at great peril returned to Sighet. Trembling, he described the atrocities he had witnessed to the Jewish community leaders. Few believed him; most branded him insane. Still, his testimony passed from mouth to ear—but even those who responded to it more with serious concern than with instinctive skepticism took solace in the fact that they were true Hungarians and had lived in the region for generations. The government would not visit such horrors upon them.

The massacre at Kamenets-Podolsk was the first large-scale murder in what would emerge as the Nazis' "final solution." On January 20, 1942, the systematic implementation of the program in all countries under German rule would be laid out at the notorious Wannsee Conference in Berlin. Soon after would begin the herding of millions of European Jews into the cattle cars of trains that would deliver them to death camps or to their execution in the slaughter pits. But the Hungarian government was, in fact, delaying the deportation of its Jews.

At their home in Rozavlea, the Ovitzes continued to enjoy familiar routines as well as some unexpected happy events. Moshe Moskowitz, the manager of a Jewish theater in Cluj, became a frequent visitor. He had seen the Lilliputs perform numerous times and knew their repertoire by heart. His enthusiasm for their program prompted him to propose the possibility of a merger. Not only did the Ovitzes decline—out of concern that they'd lose their independence and fear that they'd see their income cut in half—but Moskowitz, who had come to take them over, found the tables turned. He had fallen in love with Elizabeth and, as a result, became the Lilliputs' new manager.

In her memoirs, Elizabeth Ovitz claims she was a romantic seventeen-year-old when the tall, mature Moskowitz proposed to her. Her recently discovered birth certificate shows, however, that she was actually twenty-eight at the time, the same age as her prospective husband—her miniature size and childlike looks had made it possible for her to subtract eleven years from her age without suspicion. She married Moskowitz on November 6, 1942. But she was truly an Ovitz. Throughout their career, the dedicated, industrious Lilliput Troupe had hardly ever turned down a job offer; on occasion, to fulfill several conflicting requests, they would split into performing duos, trios, or solos. So it was that Elizabeth, on her first weekend as a married woman, set out with her sister Leah as chaperone to honor a solo star engagement at the doctors' ball in Sighet. Her husband stayed at home. It was almost morning when Elizabeth returned, and she found him awake and furious. But the newlyweds had no time to explore the ramifications of their first matrimonial quarrel, since a week later they were forced to part.

In 1941, the Hungarian army began conscripting all Jewish males between the ages of eighteen and forty-eight into military labor camps at the Ukrainian front. There the Jewish recruits disarmed land mines, paved roads, constructed bridges, built fortifications, and dug in copper mines. Under deliberately harsh conditions, many of the men died from exhaustion, starvation, and torture. The aim of the general conscription was not only to gain manpower but to forestall the possibility of Jewish resistance to future brutal measures by the Nazis. In the process, Hungarian Jewish families and communities were brought to the brink of starvation. The Ovitz family soon lost four men to the conscription: brother Arie, who left behind his young, pregnant wife, Magda; Azriel, Leah's husband, who would not witness the birth of his first son; Izo, torn away from his beloved Frieda; and Moshe, separated from his wife of only ten days. The Ovitz dwarfs had two new worries: the fate of their loved ones, and the management of their daily life without essential help. Not the least of their new difficulties was the loss of ready transport, as only Izo Edenburg could drive the deluxe car on which they had become so dependent.

The Transylvanian Jews had lost control of their daily lives and were suffering from collective anxiety-based paralysis. Although hundreds of Polish Jewish refugees, who had witnessed firsthand Nazi murders and massacres, had fled to Transylvania with terrifying tales, very few of the Ovitzes' neighbors responded by fleeing as fast as they could into deepest Romania. In any event, given the dwarfs' physical helplessness, this was an option they could not seriously contemplate.

By the start of 1944, more than four million European Jews had already been murdered; hundreds of thousands more were still penned up in ghettos and concentration camps. Nevertheless, despite their new hardships, the Ovitzes managed to maintain their careers. Remarkably, they continued to book even extended tours that would take them hundreds of miles away from their village. Like many others, they imagined the war would soon be over—that the flames would die out before they themselves would be burned.

On Sunday night, March 19, 1944, the Ovitzes retired to their hotel rooms in Szolnok, Hungary, after a well-received show at the National Theater. They had just started a new concert tour, with three more weeks of performances before their return to Rozavlea for Passover. They were exhausted, and all but Micki soon fell asleep. Lying awake in bed, he was listening to the soft night sounds, when suddenly he heard loud music blaring through the hotel walls. Its rhythm persistent, its beat heavy, he began drumming out its tempo on the blanket with his fingers. When it showed no signs of stopping, however, he became irritated. Banging on the wall was not his style, so he grumpily got dressed and went down to the lobby to complain.

SIX

Maramures, Easter 1944

The same sounds were spilling triumphantly into the dimly lit lobby. Micki Ovitz was puzzled. "There's no news on the radio, but rumors say the German army has invaded," explained the receptionist. Micki realized the game was up. He clambered back up the stairs and banged on his sisters' doors. It took some time before they opened. Micki's news stopped their grumbling at the early hour.

Some of the hotel guests had already gathered for breakfast in the dining room when the seven Lilliputs, their sister Sarah, and their stagehand assembled in the lobby with their luggage. They fought hard to conceal their panic while Avram Ovitz paid the bill and apologized for their untimely checkout. News of a sudden illness back home, he said, as he slipped the cashier a few folded notes.

Two taxis got them to the railway station, where a crowd full of equally anxious passengers blocked the aisles with stacks of baggage. Hordes of gendarmes and armed soldiers marched up and down the hall. The Lilliputs settled themselves into a corner. In the past, Avram, head of the troupe and family, had always gone to the booth to purchase their tickets, but it occurred to them that times had suddenly changed—and a ticket agent could arbitrarily determine their fate. They decided that the coquettish, assertive Elizabeth would get the best results. Tall sister Sarah paved her way.

"Papers!" grumped the man behind the barred window. Elizabeth stepped out of the line while Sarah hurried back to the group to collect the identity cards. The cashier was too busy to notice there was no face in the window when Elizabeth's tiny hand, her short, puffy fingers capped by shiny crimson nails, laid the pile of documents on the counter. With some suspicion he flipped through the pages, then mumbled that only one train was going in their direction and already the demand for tickets was close to exceeding availability, even for eligible passengers. Elizabeth suspected that eligible meant non-Jews, and had to remind herself that the Ovitzes' cards did not indicate their Jewish origins. She stretched up on her tiptoes and told the agent, "Our husbands are at the front, fighting for the fatherland." To see a hero's wife, the agent had to bend forward, and even then he could glimpse only the top of her shiny black hair. "And do you have enough money for nine tickets?" he asked in a tone reserved for children. Swallowing her pride, Elizabeth handed him the pile of notes she had taken from Avram's wallet.

Elizabeth's smile of relief was signal enough for the Lilliputs to pick up their baggage and prepare to move. As they headed toward the train platform, they tried to avoid bumping into the tense-faced gendarmes. To their horror, a patrol spotted them and strolled over. The Lilliputs froze; the gendarmes gathered around them. It took a minute before the Lilliputs realized the soldiers were not after their papers but were looking for a laugh.

Promptly, the dwarfs complied, with an account of their performances and standing ovations. Avram provided a juicy joke and proffered the gendarmes an open invitation: "Whenever you see our posters, tell the cashier you're our guests—he'll let you in free." Once again, they had won over their audience, and the gendarmes, like VIP escorts, cleared the Lilliputs a path to the platform, lifted them up onto the train, and passed them on to their car. Throughout the journey, the Ovitzes trembled at every railway stop. Twelve hours after they boarded, they were home.

The Ovitzes' fears were not unjustified. The Russian front had tightened by March 1944, and Hitler had stopped trusting his Hungarian allies, who were seeking a way to break from the Nazi embrace. The invasion of Hungary—named "Operation Margarita 1"—ended four and a half years of relative safety for the Hungarian Jews. Until then, the Hungarian government had rejected Germany's directive that all Jews be deported to the death camps. Following the invasion, the new Fascist government was eager to make Hungary *Judenrein*—free of Jews.

For the first time in their lives, the Ovitzes felt overpowered by circumstances. They canceled all their scheduled shows, and did not venture out to perform even in the vicinity of Rozavlea. Shutting themselves inside their house in anxiety, they waited for the persecutive fog to clear. Anti-Jewish decrees were issued daily. By national order, every Jew aged six and up had to wear the yellow Star of David. Elizabeth and Perla fashioned dozens of yellow stars and meticulously stitched them to coats and jackets. Perla would nurse her pain long afterward: *We felt like walking dartboards, available for stabbing or a shot in the heart.* Jews were not allowed to leave their towns and villages. All their valuables—gold, silver, jewelry, carpets, furs—had to be surrendered to local authorities. Affluent Jews were summoned to the police station, where every last gem was interrogated, beaten, and tortured out of them. Christians were threatened with severe punishment for hiding valuables for Jewish neighbors.

Nevertheless, many Jews attempted to find hiding places for their possessions. Some of the Ovitzes' friends crept in the dead of night to the isolated cemetery on the far bank of the river and there dug a pit for their valuables in the heavy soil. For the Ovitzes—with Arie, Azriel, Izo, and Moshe away in the labor camps—this was not an option. Fortunately, though known to be rich, they were somehow escaping police scrutiny. Certain that in the inevitable house search their wooden floors would be torn up, the walls hammered open, and the upholstery slashed, they searched the courtyard for other alternatives, but nothing seemed safe enough. Then their eyes fell on the family car, which had been standing idle for two years. They carefully wrapped their gold and jewelry in cloth before cramming it into a tin box. In the dark of night, their small size now an advantage, Avram and Micki crawled beneath the car, scooped out a hole in the ground, and stashed away the box.

Special Hungarian police squads and local clerks called at every Jewish household to record the names and ages of all the tenants and to obtain a full description of the house with a list of its facilities and contents. As it was a time of emergency, and as the officials left carbon copies of their documents with the residents, the Ovitzes found it reasonable to assume the survey was being done for their benefit. In fact the documents provided authorities with a ready means to track down anyone trying to run away or hide. They also proved very useful in the efficient seizure of Jewish property and its distribution to the neighbors.

To foster isolation from the outside world, the government

ordered all Jews to surrender their radios. The Ovitzes dared to hang on to their big brown wood-paneled Telefunken: listening to it furtively, they prayed for news of a German defeat. Since no one else in the village owned a set, the Ovitzes were quickly informed on. They counted themselves lucky, however, for though the radio was confiscated they were not punished for the offense.

On Friday evening, April 7, 1944, the Ovitzes sat down for their Passover seder. More emotionally than ever before, they read the Haggadah. Profoundly moved by its account of the Hebrew enslavement in Egypt, they prayed that God would repeat their ancestors' miraculous exodus, when the waters of the Red Sea parted to provide them a path to freedom and then converged to drown the enemy that pursued them. They tried to take solace, too, in the possibility that Maramures, a remote Hungarian province far from the central government in Budapest, might be spared. They did not know that just a few hours earlier, the interior minister had signed a decree ordering the ghettoization of all Hungarian Jews, its implementation to begin in the county closest to the Russian front: Maramures.

The Ovitzes celebrated the seven days of Passover in ignorant bliss. Then on Saturday, April 15, before they'd had a chance to put away the festive plates and cutlery for the next year, they heard the chilling announcement in the street. "We were ordered to pack our suitcases and move to the synagogue," remembers their cousin, Regina Ovitz. "We were in shock; we couldn't decide what to do first. We thought that since the Red Army was approaching, we were being taken away from the border for a temporary stay in a safer part of Hungary. The pessimists among us concluded we were being sent to labor camps. No one thought about dying."

The Jews of Rozavlea rolled pots and pans in blankets, as they could not be sure of kosher conditions wherever they were going. They selected their best clothes, gathered necessary supplies, and packed the food left over from Passover. Expecting to continue their professions, the men bundled up their tools: an awl, an ax, a hammer, a saw. Reasoning that in a strange new place the Maramures Jews would welcome the pleasure of entertainment and find in it a source of unity as well as a remembrance of bygone days, the Ovitzes packed the instruments they could most easily carry: Rozika and Franziska's violins, Perla's guitar, Elizabeth's small drum. They locked away the bulky cello, cymbal, and big drum. Of course, they also packed their favorite stage costumes and makeup kits. After hastily watering their garden and scattering food for the chickens and cows, they asked their longtime neighbor to keep an eye on the place.

At the entrance to every pious Jewish home, a small holy scroll with a metal shell—a mezuzah—is nailed to the right doorpost, above one's head, so that it can be touched for its blessing upon entering and leaving. In general the Ovitzes had fitted everything down to their scale, but they had exempted the mezuzah, as they did not wish to debase it. Now, on the brink of a lengthy journey, they carefully observed the ritual. One by one, they lifted their right hands up toward the mezuzah and kissed their fingers in prayer. They were about to lock the door when the gendarme supervising their departure stretched out his hand. "Don't bother," he said. "I'll keep the keys."

The synagogue could hardly contain the village's 650 Jews with their baggage. The Ovitzes tried to make themselves safe in a corner by erecting a fence with their luggage; otherwise, they might have been crushed. The doors of the synagogue had been sealed and Hungarian militia surrounded the building so that no one could flee. As the hours passed, the heat and stench became suffocating. Rozika and Franziska fainted, and the village doctor was brought in. "It's too crowded for the dwarfs here; it may put their lives in danger," he told the officer in charge. The black rooster feather in his helmet bobbing, the officer consulted his superior and returned with a reprieve. The Ovitzes gathered up their belongings. They did not have to carry their baggage far, as their house stood next to the synagogue.

That night, there was a bang on the Ovitzes' door. With great apprehension they answered it—and discovered a rowdy group of tipsy gendarmes standing before them with guns, bayonets, and bottles. The frightened dwarfs stood aside to let them in. The men in uniform slumped onto the red velvet sofa: "Let's have some fun!" they demanded. Bewildered, the Lilliput Troupe took out their instruments, arranged themselves in a corner, and hesitantly started to play and sing. The drunken gendarmes joined in. Clapping ecstatically, they commanded the dwarfs to play their favorite songs again and again. Occasionally one of the officers would pull himself up and, swaying heavily, lift Elizabeth or Perla away from her instrument and try to dance. *Not long before they had been a paying audience; now they had us for free. They wanted us to drink with them, but we explained we'd be too sick to play. They were away from home, longing for a woman, so again and again they demanded love serenades. I was in no mood for romance, all I wanted was to cry, but we had no choice. When they left at dawn, we were shattered, humiliated. We couldn't stop thinking, what does our whole miserable community, suffocating in the next-door synagogue, think of the merry sounds coming from our home?* And every night of the following week, the scene was repeated. The dwarfs felt vulnerable without the barriers of the proscenium arch, the stage lights, the curtains.

But they realized that once again their deformity was playing to their advantage.

A new order was issued. All the Jews of Rozavlea, including the Ovitzes, were directed to march the seven and a half miles to the village of Dragomiresti. The militia allowed only small children, the elderly, and invalids to use carts instead of walking. A villager who had worked on the Ovitz farm offered the Lilliputs his carriage. On arrival in Dragomiresti, Rozavlea's Jews joined those from thirteen other villages. Their total now 3,500, they were herded into a closed section of the village. The more fortunate arrivals were quartered with twenty other ghetto-dwellers into one flat. The less fortunate made sheds, barns, and stables their makeshift dwellings, or else they simply slept outdoors. The Ovitzes managed to squeeze themselves into the flat of a family friend. Everyone in the ghetto lived under a curfew that was lifted one hour each day for purchasing essentials. Residents of the ghetto returning late to their homes incurred beatings—a real fear for the dwarfs, because of their difficulty walking—so Leah, Sarah, and sister-in-law Dora served as the legs for all. Each day they rushed frantically to meet the needs of their survial.

In an effort to avoid any resistance, the Hungarian militia— aided by German officers—segregated the leaders of the different Jewish communities from the other villagers and detained them in separate quarters. To break the general spirit, the militia issued decrees, most humiliatingly the mandate that the Jewish men shave their beards and cut off their earlocks, which they had religiously groomed since early manhood. The Ovitz men were spared this disgrace, since on professional grounds they had never grown beards.

Most of the non-Jewish villagers in Maramures turned their

backs on their Jewish acquaintances, who had often employed Gentiles to do rural work. Indeed, some of them welcomed the plight of the dispossessed and immediately began plundering their property. A small minority, with altruism and empathy, took the time and trouble to visit their former employers or neighbors and on occasion to bring them food. According to Haim Pearl, "They sometimes traveled for hours carrying vegetables, fruits, eggs, oil, and flour from the deserted Jewish farms. My uncle was seventy-six, a rich landowner, and his peasants kept coming to the ghetto to consult him about sowing and cultivating the land for the coming season. When they saw their dignified master, pale, exhausted, and beardless, crouched with his bundle on the floor like a pauper, they burst into tears, and drew us into weeping along with them." Still, with every day spent in the ghetto, more of its inmates became convinced that they would survive to see the next—in part because the Hungarian militia nurtured the notion by disseminating false information.

On Sunday, May 14, in the evening, all men between the ages of eleven and sixty were ordered to assemble in the schoolyard, which had been turned into a horse stable. It was full of excrement. A handful of German officers was present, but the operation was executed wholly by Hungarian gendarmes. Dozens of them stood on the bridge leading to the compound to create a wall of bludgeons, with which they battered the captives as, terrified, they were forced to cross the bridge. Some tried to escape and fell into the water, to roars of laughter and cheers from the local villagers. When dawn broke, the militiamen herded women and children over to the school. And the exodus continued.

As Perla Ovitz remembers it, the dwarfs were wearing three layers of clothing, because they wanted to carry as much with them as they could, yet not be too heavy to move. A reporter and a photographer were covering the local exodus, and as always, the dwarfs stole the show. To get a good laugh, the creative photographer put a soldier next to them, for size comparison.

The photo that appeared in the next day's newspaper showed the Ovitzes dragging themselves along on their walking sticks and preparing to mount a horse cart. Although it was a hot day in May, the dwarfs are wrapped in overcoats and scarves as if it were the dead of winter. They look calm enough. Rozika and Franziska have even managed a smile when they spotted the media. Unheeding to the tragedy of it all, the obtuse news editor titled the story "Jewish Dwarfs at the Ghetto."

The caption reads: "The family arrives at the compound with its baggage. The soldier next to them seems like a giant, but actually he is of medium height."

As the photos indicate, the Ovitz dwarfs were put on a cart, as were Dora and Leah. Sarah had been ordered by a gendarme to dismount and walk. She was immediately swallowed up in the crowd. Frantic and tearful, her sisters spotted one of the officers who had passed several nights at their home. Pleading their helplessness without the aid of their full-size sister, they begged him to restore her to the cart. Thanks to her grass-green coat, they could see her from afar, and they retrieved her before she got totally lost in the human colonnade that was wriggling up the hill toward the train station at Viseul de Jos. Propelled forward by blows from the gendarmes, they were not allowed a moment's rest during the fifteen-mile march. The climb was steep and the sun was scorching. They were deathly thirsty. They stumbled; some fell. Villagers running alongside the doomed convoy waited for their chance to dash forward and snatch a fallen blanket, a rolling kettle, a sack of potatoes.

They had walked nine hours and it was already twilight when

they reached the station. They beheld in silhouette a never-ending line of freight wagons, their doors wide open, waiting to swallow them up. In a frenzy now, the soldiers used the butts of their rifles and waved their bayonets to get the exhausted Jews into the wagons. The air resonated with alarm. Mothers were screaming and children sobbing as families were torn apart in the commotion.

Swept up into the chaos, gripped by panic, dozens of the Ovitzes' friends and relatives, including Uncle Lazar the klezmer, and his sons and grandchildren, were desperately trying to find each other. The cart carrying the Ovitzes halted at a distance from the station. The coachman helped the dwarfs down and then left them on their own. The swarm soon pulled them forward to the freight train. They lifted their eyes. The floor of the wagon was higher than their heads; they could not possibly mount it. Clinging to their belongings, they tried to shield themselves as people stepped, tripped, or climbed over them to get into the train. It was Simon Slomowitz, their handyman, who suddenly saw their distress. His wife and children behind him, he pushed aside the crowd and made his way toward the Ovitzes. One by one he lifted them into the wagon and then tended to his own family. They all huddled together in a corner of the wagon. A German officer counted all the occupants and wrote the total number in chalk on the door. The inside of the wagon went dark. The doors of all the wagons in the train, around forty of them, slammed shut. Then they were crawling out of the station.

The wagons were intended for transporting cattle, so there was no light. The single small hatch in the ceiling let in hardly any air—and certainly not enough for the eighty frightened people packed into each wagon with their suitcases, boxes, and bundles. The space was so tight that they had to stand for end-less hours and could sit only in turns. To spare their weak legs, though, the Lilliputs were allowed to crouch together on a small island on the floor. But pressed on every side by scores of people who towered and swayed above them, they were robbed of the scant air that came through the hatch. They fainted often throughout the journey.

As no one had any idea how long the journey would last, each family rationed the meager food they had brought with them. In the hot, steamy wagon, Mordechai Slomowitz, together with his five younger siblings, began crying for water. "Father added some vinegar to the bottle to keep us from drinking too much and wasting the precious fluid," he remem-bers. Some people were yelling, some were praying; others were simply too numb to react. The unbearable stench of urine and excrement filled the wagon. A single bucket served as the toilet for the entire car. It was too wide for the Ovitzes to use; com-passion prompted someone to offer the use of his child's chamber pot.

When the train left the station, the Ovitzes had thought they were heading east. But the train stopped so often, and so fre-quently reversed or altered its route after waiting for hours on a side track, that they soon lost their sense of both time and direc-tion. Each day a brief stop in an empty field, with no road signs or local residents to disclose their location, allowed them to breathe, stretch, and attend to their bowels—but always at gun-point. Before they were granted permission to climb down from the train, they were warned that if any one of them ran away, the entire wagonload of people would be shot. The Ovitzes did not dare leave the train. They traveled for three days and nights, famished and dehydrated, sweating and suffocating, huddled together on the floor. At last, the train came to a final halt.

The door slid noisily open. The cool night air caressed their faces, revived their souls. For a moment.

SEVEN

Auschwitz-Birkenau, May 1944

Asecond deep breath filled the weary travelers with a sickening stench—a mixture of scorch and smoke. Before they could define the foul odors, they were deafened by shrieks and roars, and the loud barking of dogs. Beams of light from powerful projectors made them blink; they stood paralyzed at the wagon doors. The ramp beneath them was teeming with vicious dogs and helmeted soldiers. Men in odd striped jackets leaped onto the wagon and began pushing the bewildered occupants downward. "Leave your luggage on the wagon, you'll get it later!" they were told in Yiddish. Simon Slomowitz was the first to jump down from the train; then, cradling the dwarfs in his arms one by one, he lowered them to the ground. Their layers of clothing made them bulky and awkward to hold.

A soldier passing along the ramp was shouting, *"Zwillinge heraus! Zwillinge heraustreten!"* which sounded bizarre: "Twins step out!" Other soldiers were hollering, "Men to the left, women and children to the right!" as they split the crowd in two. "Five in a row" was the next command. With his nineteen-year-old son, Mordechai, Simon Slomowitz helplessly watched his wife, Chaya, and his five younger children drift away. Everything was happening too quickly for the Ovitzes to follow. Shoved aside, they clung desperately to each other in a tight ring: the seven dwarfs, their two tall sisters, sister-in-law Dora, and the two children. The strange, immobile coil of twelve bodies of dramatically varying sizes attracted the attention of the SS men. In a moment, the Lilliputs were surrounded by troopers.

Turning to look back at her husband and son, Chaya Slomowitz saw that the Ovitzes had been enveloped by soldiers' helmets. For a few seconds Chaya stood stock-still. Then, despite the grudge she harbored against the Lilliputs—and quite contrarily to her own nature—she gathered her children behind her and, in one of those inexplicable acts of human courage, fought her way back through the crowd to the Ovitzes.

Oddly enough, in all the distress and confusion, the Lilliputs had regained some of their composure, no doubt because the soldiers were not harassing them the way they were the others. "We're all one family, from the same village," said Mrs. Slomowitz firmly, although her only connection to the Ovitzes was through her husband, their coachman and handyman. The Lilliputs said nothing. They had no idea where they were or where the future would take them, but if Mrs. Slomowitz wished to link her destiny to theirs, so be it. An officer allowed Mrs. Slomowitz to join the Lilliputs' circle; encouraged, she played her trump again. "My husband and son are over there, with the men. Can they join us, too?" Surprisingly, the officer complied. A soldier was sent to fetch Simon and Mordechai. Now they were twenty.

Granted such consideration by the German officer, the Lilliputs had regained some of their confidence, enough so that they began to behave like stage stars who had been besieged not by SS troopers but by ardent fans. Micki Ovitz felt enough at ease to draw from an inner pocket in his coat a pack of fan cards autographed "Souvenir from the Lilliput Troupe," which he handed around to the SS men. Two other neighbors from Roza-vlea, Gitel-Leah Fischman and her daughter, stopped to peer at the surreal scene. "Don't tell me you're another of their rela-tives!" sneered the amused officer. Before the Fischmans could reply, Micki Ovitz jumped to the rescue. Pointing out at the exquisite twenty-year-old Bassie, he announced, "Not yet, but she'll soon be. She's my fiancée!" The officer did not pursue the point. "Step aside," he commanded all of them, "and don't move until *Hauptsturmführer* Dr. Mengele arrives!" After instructing a soldier to guard the group of now twenty-two detainees, he added, "No one is allowed to take them away until Dr. Mengele sorts things out!" Another soldier jumped on his bicycle and rode away. It was past midnight, the morning of Friday, May 19th, 1944.

Standing at the edge of the ramp, the Ovitzes and their entourage watched as the backs of their uncles and aunts, cousins and friends, all the neighbors from Rozavlea, disappeared in their march toward the building with two chimneys that seemed to ceaselessly pour out flames and smoke. "What's that fire all about?" asked Perla Ovitz. A man in a striped jacket looked at her with revulsion and said: "Don't you know where you are? This is no bakery—this is Auschwitz, *Kever Yisroel,* the Grave of Israel, and you'll soon end up in the ovens, too!" He spoke not out of malice but from furious despair. Reduced to a mere shadow of a man, he was a Polish Jew who had been in hell for too long, and was indignant at the new arrivals' ignorance, of what their brethren have been through for the last few years.

Suddenly, each flame looked like a human being, flying up and dissolving in the air. We went numb, then started thinking about the unknown man we were waiting for—if this was a graveyard, what was a doctor doing here?

Josef Mengele was known in his Bavarian hometown— Günzburg—for his musical and dramatic talents. In his teens he wrote a play based on fairy tales; its success earned profits that were donated to local orphanages. However, his father, a well-off engineer and industrialist, expected his eldest son Josef to take over the family business, a prosperous agricultural-equipment factory. In high school Josef was more ambitious than brilliant. According to his school friend Julius Deisbach, Mengele did not want simply to succeed, but to "stand out from the crowd," and he once told Julius he would one day find his name in encyclopedias. It was a charismatic science teacher who shifted Josef's interest from the arts to the natural sciences: throughout his life, Mengele instinctively bowed to authority figures.

In 1930, Mengele enrolled as an anthropology and medical student at the University of Munich, where he became intrigued by the burgeoning field of heredity and eugenics. Mengele's doctoral advisor was Professor Theodor Mollison, who liked to boast that he could tell a Jew just by looking at his photograph. In 1935, Mengele received a Ph.D. in Anthropology from the Munich University for his thesis entitled "Racial Morphological Research on the Lower Jaw Section of Four Racial Groups." He later moved to Frankfurt, to Prof. von Verschuer, and in 1938 received his medical degree with a dissertation on cleft palate in children.

Mollison's enthusiastic letter of recommendation won Mengele a highly coveted position as a research assistant at the Institute for Heredity, Biology, and Racial Purity at the University of Frankfurt. In the words of Mengele biographers Gerald Posner and John Ware, "Mengele was now at the epicenter of Nazi philosophical and scientific thinking, which held that it was possible to select, engineer, refine and ultimately purify the race." He became the favorite student of Professor Freiherr Otmar von Verschuer, a renowned geneticist and ardent admirer of Hitler. Mengele assisted his mentor by writing expert opinions on legal paternity issues. (In a court case that accused a young man of violating the Nuremberg laws by having an affair with a German woman, Mengele argued that the man was a Jew and, therefore, guilty. The court, however, chose to believe the neighbors' account that the man's natural father was German. Upset by the decision, von Verschuer complained to the minister of justice about courts that preferred domestic gossip to serious scientific research.)

Mengele was particularly fascinated by the genetics of dominant abnormalities, and began his quest by looking at himself in the mirror. He had a structural tooth problem, and his two doctorate theses dealt with the palate and jaws. Having a dimple on the chin, and a flat round disc on his ear cartilage, which he was embarrassed about, inspired a paper on the hereditary transmission of Fistulae Auris—a condition that is characterized by an abnormal opening in the ear cartilage and that is coincident with chin dimples.

In 1937, Mengele joined the Nazi party, and a year later, the SS. Also in 1937, he was awarded a second doctorate for his work "Genealogical Studies in the Cases of Cleft Lip-Jaw-Palate," in which he claimed that these dental irregularities were hereditary and tended to appear with other hereditary abnormalities, like idiocy and dwarfism—and in which Robert Lifton sees a prefiguration of Mengele's genetic research at Auschwitz.

This work, along with similar research on harelip, was listed in the 1938 edition of the prestigious *Index Medicus*, and von Verschuer enjoined Mengele to participate in his research on twins. Mengele's academic career was flourishing, but it was interrupted in June 1940 when he was drafted into the army and the Waffen-SS.

Mengele's two years of service, mostly at the Russian front, earned him four decorations, including the Iron Cross First and Second Class, and a wound that withdrew him from the battlefield. Reassigned to the *Reichsarzt S.S. und Polizei* at the Berlin headquarters of the Race and Resettlement Office, which was responsible for concentration-camp medical experiments, Mengele was able to resume his close relationship with von Verschuer, as he had himself recently moved to Berlin to take up his new post as the director of the Kaiser Wilhelm Institute of Anthropology, Heredity, and Eugenics.

Professor von Verschuer's monumental research on twins had suffered a setback because of the war, which had diminished the supply of cases for his studies. Thus he suggested that Mengele apply for a position at Auschwitz, where they would have continual access to human specimens. On May 30, 1943, now thirty-two years old, Mengele arrived in Birkenau, about two miles from Auschwitz. Birkenau had begun operating in February 1942; Auschwitz was no longer large enough to deal with the mass of socially and racially undesirable peoples.

Appointed chief physician of the Gypsy family camp, Mengele was responsible for camp hygiene, and, in rotation with other doctors, for selecting which of the new Birkenau arrivals on the ramp should be sent to their immediate deaths and which should be assigned to slave labor. His enthusiasm, ambition, charisma, and cruelty set him apart from the other death-camp doctors. Mengele's first task after his arrival at Birkenau was to crush a typhus epidemic that had contaminated a third of the inmates of the women's camp. When two SS guards also caught the disease, the camp command took extreme measures. In her book *Prisoner of Fear*, Ella Lingens-Reiner, a former inmate-doctor from Vienna who worked with Mengele, reports that for want of a vacant disinfected barrack, Mengele sent an entire barrack of 498 women—most of them Jewish women from Greece—to the gas chambers and then had the emptied barrack disinfected. The next step in Mengele's decontamination method was to disinfect the women in the adjacent barrack and then transfer them to the first disinfected barrack—this process of "musical barracks" being continued until all the women had been disinfected.

At the service of Professor Von Verschuer, Mengele was, of course, collecting twins during his time at Birkenau, but he was also using his long, diligent shifts on the ramp to discover unusual and striking human mutations. Like a demonic impresario casting the ultimate freak show, he plucked out from the masses hunchbacks, pinheads, hermaphrodites, giants, dwarfs, extraordinarily obese men, grotesquely corpulent women, and anyone else suffering from a growth disorder. Sara Nomberg-Przytyk, an inmate in the Birkenau infirmary, recalls that "Mengele loved to single out those who had not been created in God's image. He once brought a woman to our area who had two noses; another time a girl of about ten who had sheep's wool on her head instead of hair; on another occasion, he brought a woman who had donkey ears."

On the night the Lilliputs arrived at Birkenau, Mengele was fast asleep in his room at nearby SS headquarters. All the troopers on duty at the ramp, however, knew well his passion for freaks, and to gain favor with the illustrious physician, they were always on the lookout for new specimens to add to his "human circus." While a lone dwarf did not provide reason enough to knock on Mengele's door in the middle of the night, seven dwarfs, along with their tall, normal-sized siblings, seemed to be good cause for disturbance.

Professor von Verschuer had always emphasized that heredity could best be researched on complete families, so when Mengele learned that a large family with dwarf traits had just arrived, he did not waste a moment. Nor did the Ovitzes waste their chance to dazzle him. Crowding around him, they answered his questions eagerly, in a chorus. They told him about Rabbi Shimshon Eizik and his two tall wives, Brana and Batia; they told him about the births of ten children, seven of them dwarfs, and about their marriages to husbands and wives, and told him about in-laws, fiancées, cousins. And Mengele was indeed dazzled: "I now have work for twenty years," he said joyfully.

Unable to suppress her feelings, Perla involuntarily slapped her cheek and muttered, "Oh my God!"

Mengele turned to her: "Yes? Anything wrong?" he inquired.

With the eyes of her family trained on her like bullets, she didn't dare utter another word. *He was polite and curious, but as he is only interested in dwarfism and our family tree, I thought to myself, I won't survive him, not in this place.* Preoccupied with his precious find, Mengele turned and whispered some orders to the officer in charge, then disappeared. He had to find suitable accommodation for the group.

Mengele was a choosy collector. After a brief look, he'd often reject as "uninteresting" specimens of twins and dwarfs, and without a second's further thought send them on to their deaths.

Had the Ovitzes arrived separately at Birkenau, most of them almost certainly—and surely normal-sized Leah, Sarah, and the children—would have been killed. Their desirability lay in their number and in their anomaly as an entire family. Batia Ovitz's admonition that her children stay together was once again proving to be wise.

Together the Ovitz family slumped onto the ground. Though dead tired, they were too afraid to doze off. The ramp was now empty. Groups of men in striped jackets were throwing the piles of ownerless luggage into trucks. Only three hours had passed since their arrival, and all the noisy confusion, all the anguish and hysteria, had yielded to a heavy, dull silence. Nearly all the passengers on the night train into Birkenau were now dead, and already their bodies—more than three thousand of them—had been dragged from the gas chambers and fed to the cremato-rium. Of the Dragomiresti transport of 3,500 people, fewer than four hundred would survive the night. They had been selected for forced labor and were going through various stages of admittance: having all their body hair shorn, taking a bru-tally cold shower, quickly donning striped prison clothing; then a hastened march to the barracks. It was nearly dawn when the train rolled back outside the camp, to clear the rails for the next in line.

A black army truck pulled up to the hushed group of the Ovitzes. Simon Slomowitz and his son helped everyone get up onto the bed of the truck. They were all sitting on the metal floor, so they couldn't see where they were going. The truck stopped. Their bones creaking, they dismounted, and an officer led them into a building. A pungent odor assaulted them. Hooks with numbers were attached to the walls; there were wooden benches to sit on. They were the only ones inside, all

twenty-two of them. "Take off your clothes!" the officer bel-
lowed. Then, in the anxious silence, everyone looked to the
seven Lilliputs for guidance. "We are Orthodox Jews and can't
undress together, men and women, brothers in front of sisters,"
pleaded Avram Ovitz. The officer was impatient. They knew
they had better not argue. Averting their eyes from each other,
they shed layer after layer of their clothes. Judah Slomowitz was
eleven at the time: "I had never seen a naked woman before and
I was bewildered and intrigued with so many of them around
me: my mother, my sisters, the dwarf ladies. It excited me to
embarrassment. I couldn't help myself, and burst out laughing."

A heavy door opened and the wave of heat that escaped
assailed their faces. They had barely crossed the threshold when
the door slammed behind them. *It was almost dark and we stood
in what looked like a large washing room, waiting for something to
happen. We looked up to the ceiling to see why the water was not
coming. Suddenly we smelt gas. We gasped heavily, some of us
fainting on the floor. With our last breath we cried out. Minutes
passed, or maybe just seconds, then we heard an angry voice from
outside: "Where is my dwarf family?!" The door opened, and we saw
Dr. Mengele standing there. He ordered us carried out, and had cold
water poured on us to revive us.* Those minutes or seconds
indelibly etched the imminence of death on the memory of
sister Elizabeth and the three Slomowitz sons, Mordechai,
Joseph, and Judah. They all testified separately that they were
beginning to be gassed—and that everyone would have died if
Mengele had not suddenly reappeared.

Nevertheless, the story's verification with specialists and rel-
evant documentary evidence suggests it is unlikely any gassing
was scheduled for the Ovitz group that day. The gas chambers
were designed to kill between five hundred and two thousand

people at once, depending on the size of the hall. Zyklon B was effective only in a room temperature of 27 degrees Celsius, which was achieved by cramping a mass of people into inadequate space. Gas chambers were simply not operated for twenty-two people; small groups were shot. Furthermore, according to the camp's rigid safety orders, the SS personnel had to wear gas masks when operating Zyklon B. Although the victims died within fifteen minutes, the SS men routinely waited half an hour before turning on the powerful fans that dispersed the gas from inside the chamber. Only then were the doors opened. The operators themselves did not enter; instead, Jewish inmates from the *Sonderkommando* were sent in to drag out the bodies for cremation.

Consequently, if the Ovitz group had been consigned to a gas chamber, once the extermination process had begun, it could not have been halted, as by then it would have been impossible to open the doors. What seems more likely is that the Lilliputs had been taken to the camp sauna for disinfection, where the water poured over heated stones would have produced much steam and fumes as well as temperatures intense enough to open wounds and cause someone to faint. The sauna would have had a particularly traumatic effect on both small children and fragile dwarfs—an effect that might easily have created the impression of being gassed.

In any case, the twenty-two members of the Ovitz group returned to the dressing room, where they lay on the benches until they regained their senses. They were exempted from the sauna's second phase, in which they would have been forcibly shoved into the next hall to shower in ice-cold water and then to towel-dry with ten people to one flimsy towel. They were also spared the invasive search of all bodily orifices for gold or jewelry. Contrary to standard procedure, the Ovitzes were given their own clothes back, after they'd been disinfected. It was a practical move on the part of Mengele, a seasoned laboratory scientist, who cared for his human subjects the way he did his lab rats, according to their particular needs. And Mengele realized they needed their own, specially sewn clothing. To dress them in clothes that had been stockpiled after being stripped from some of the hundreds of thousands of children murdered in Auschwitz-Birkenau simply would not do: though Lilliputian in height, the Ovitzes had the bodies of adults, with breasts and curves and wide bottoms.

Finally, the long night ending, a truck drove the twelve Ovitzes and their recently extended family to the *Familienlager*—the Family Camp. Situated not far from Auschwitz-Birkenau's main gate, the "Family Camp" had been opened in September 1943 for Czech Jews who were transported from the Theresienstadt concentration camp in their homeland. Its purpose, similar to that of Theresienstadt, was to offer Czech families as evidence that would refute reports of mass extermination in Auschwitz-Birkenau in the event of a Red Cross inspection.

The residents in the "Family Camp" were not sexually segregated, unlike the 100,000-plus inmates of Auschwitz, where the fundamental rule regarding separation of males and females was so strictly enforced that even a pair of three-year-old mixed-sex twins being kept alive for experimental purposes was separated and held in different camps. Although the "Family Camp" did not fall under Mengele's medical supervision, he managed to find space there for the dwarfs, who, to their profound relief, were thus able to stay together. Mengele's attention, however, did not spare the dwarfs Auschwitz-Birkenau's institutional tattoo. Though painful, tattooing was welcomed by inmates, as it indicated that they had, for the time being at least, escaped execution. The administration at Auschwitz-Birkenau, the only Nazi concentration camp that tattooed its prisoners, kept extremely meticulous inventory lists and each day recorded any change in the number of prisoners. Deaths among inmates due to torture, disease, exposure, and generally harsh conditions could total as many as several hundred in a single day, and the only way to identify a corpse, and thus strike it from the list, was by the number tattooed on the left forearm.

On that same fateful Friday, May 19, the seven Lilliput males were tattooed. The Ovitzes and the Slomowitzes were tattooed in succession by age and family relation. The first to stretch out his arm was Simon Slomowitz—in blue ink the needle etched the number A-1438 into his skin. Then his sons, Mordechai, Joseph, and Judah. The Ovitzes followed: first, forty-year-old Avram; next, thirty-five-year-old Micki; and finally, fourteen-month-old Shimshon, Leah's baby, whose small arm was almost totally covered by the number A-1444. Their names and numbers were recorded and a copy of the list was sent to the head office of the Auschwitz-Birkenau camp: inventory item 148855 notes that seven Jews from Hungary, among them twin brothers, were admitted to the camp after selection and given numbers A-1438 to A-1444. The bureaucratic error by which the two dwarfs were classified as twins probably originated in their connection to Mengele, who had selected them for his experiments, most of which involved twins.

Three days later, the women and girls in the Ovitz group were tattooed, though not in any particular order. Perla, the youngest dwarf, stood first in line and received the number A-5087. Next came her eldest sister, Rozika, and then, in succession, Frieda, Franziska, Elizabeth, Sarah, and Leah. Avram's wife, Dora, embraced her eight-year-old Batia while the child bore the pain that came with A-5094. Dora then extended her own arm, and Gitel-Leah Fischman and her daughter Bassie followed. Seventeen-year-old Fanny Slomowitz became A-5098. Her mother, Chaya, and two sisters, Helene and Serene, were the last to bear the ordeal. *Some of us fainted during the ordeal, and our arms were so swollen that they ached the rest of the week.*

On that same day, Monday, May 22, 1944, a train from Satu Mare stopped at the ramp. Among the passengers was Magda, the twenty-four-year-old wife of Arie Ovitz, along with her parents and four-month-old baby, Batia. When the anti-Jewish decrees were issued in March 1944, the Lilliputs had cabled Magda and begged her to join the rest of the family in Rozavlea, as Arie had been inducted into a Hungarian army labor camp. Nor had the Ovitzes yet seen Arie and Magda's baby girl, named after their mother. Magda had cabled back that she could not leave her parents. The Lilliputs had then invited Magda's parents as well, but they did not want to leave their home. Now the four of them stood together on the ramp at Birkenau: without the Lilliputs; without a chance for survival. *Not a day has passed since without the tormenting thought that if we had all come together to Birkenau, they would have survived.*

Above left: Lya Graf fan card, Germany, 1930s. (Unknown source)
Above right: The duo Gerard and Zoli, Hungary, late 1930s.
(Courtesy of Szilagyi Gyorgy, Budapest)

Alexander Katan with his son Alphons, 1935, in Leeuwarden,
Holland. (Courtesy of Alphons Katan)

Zoli with 13 tall men, Hungary, late 1930s. (Courtesy of Szilagyi Gyorgy, Budapest)

Left: Frieda (on the left) with husband Izo Edenburg and Perla, at home in Rozavlea, February 1941.
Above: Elizabeth in Rozavlea, April 1941.

Wedding photo of
brother Arie Ovitz
and his wife Magda
early 1940s.

SUVENIR DE TRUPA LILIPUT

Souvenir from the Lilliput Troupe: the Lilliputs' fan card of the kind that Micki handed out upon arrival at Auschwitz-Birkenau. (Courtesy of Gitta Drattler-Budimsky)

TÖRPE ZSIDÓK A GETTÓBAN

The Ovitz family in the ghetto of Dragomiresti, Spring 1944.

Portrait of Celine, the French Gypsy who was Mengele's victim, painted in Auschwitz by Dina Gottlieb. (Courtesy of Dina Gottlieb-Babbitt)

Top: Medical document, signed by Mengele, instructing that blood will be taken from Avram Ovitz, June 28, 1944. **Bottom:** Blood test of Perla Ovitz, same date.

Medical order to take blood for syphilis test from Simon Slomowitz and his three boys, plus Avram and Micki Ovitz, August 16, 1944.

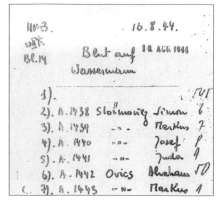

Blood tests for Chaya (Helene) Slomowitz and two of her daughters, plus Leah (Lina) Ovitz and Dora Ovitz (wife of Avram). All five women were of normal height. August 1944.

Mengele's experimental subjects—twin children—leaving Auschwitz, January 1945. Bespectacled Ludovit Feld is in the foreground. (Courtesy of the Auschwitz State Museum)

Rozavlea, Transylvania, 1927.
Top row, left to right: Leah, Simon Slomowitz (their coachman and handyman), Sarah, unidentified cousin. **Middle row:** Arie, Frieda, their mother Batia Ovitz, Avram, Micki. **Bottom:** Perla, Elizabeth. (Courtesy of the Ovitz family. Unless otherwise noted, all illustrations are courtesy of the Ovitz family.)

Wedding photo: May 2, 1927, wedding of Rozika and her husband, Markus Ovitz.

Four Ovitz sisters: Rozavlea, 1930s.
Top row: Rozika, Franziska. **Bottom row:** Elizabeth, Frieda.

Micki in a cabaret-style publicity photo, 1930s.

Izo Edenburg: Frieda's husband and the family driver, in Sighet, mid-1930s.

EIGHT

Auschwitz-Birkenau, June 1944

The month of June saw the height of the carnage.

Since April 1944, the camp headquarters had been feverishly preparing for the arrival of Hungarian Jewry. The crematoria had been thoroughly renovated, and the chimneys reinforced with iron hoops. An improved platform enabled the trains to disembark closer to the gas chambers. The Ovitz transport in mid-May was among the first to arrive. From then on, several times a day, a freight train hauling forty wagons, each one crammed with eighty people, unloaded its human cargo at Birkenau.

The thirty-six furnaces in the four crematoria couldn't burn all the corpses, and many of them had to be incinerated in open pits. According to the official records of the Auschwitz State Museum, over four hundred thousand Hungarian Jews were murdered in the course of sixty days. Their belongings— clothes, shoes, kitchen utensils, toiletries, spectacles, toys— piled up in huge mountains outside the storage blocks; eventually they would be shipped to Germany to ease the lot of the populace. Of every ten people who stepped down onto the ramp that had received the Ovitzes, nine were sent directly to the gas chambers. Their names went unregistered; their arms were not tattooed.

While the Ovitzes sensed they were enjoying special treatment, they could not determine precisely why. The shortage of manpower in German industry and the high expenses incurred by the war had been delaying the program for the total extermination of the Jews. Most of the new arrivals at the camp—the 10 percent spared the gas chambers—now provided slave labor in branches of well-known German factories that had been built near Auschwitz. Others quarried rocks or farmed the nearby fields or helped to maintain the camp by cleaning sewage or carting corpses. The work, of course, was not so much a liberation as a brief, tortured interval before certain death. It was in any case obvious to the dwarfs that they were not being kept alive so they could join the workforce. But perhaps they might be expected to entertain the exhausted laborers, so as to raise their morale. They could only wonder and speculate as they waited, idle, in the barrack.

All the inmates were quartered in barracks originally designed as stables for the German army. Each stable, blueprinted for the shelter and care of fifty-two horses, had been modified to house more than five hundred prisoners under inhuman conditions. Each prisoner was allotted a bunk—or wooden plank—less than sixteen inches wide. Only a line of narrow hatches admitted scarce rays of light. The roof leaked, and the floor—or rather, the dank ground—swarmed with rats.

Two small rooms that flanked the entrance to each barrack had been designed for the exclusive use of the "block elder"—a veteran prisoner in charge of enforcing the daily routine in his or her respective barrack. Concerned that his dwarfs might end up trampled by the mass of full-size inmates in a grossly over-crowded barrack, Mengele appropriated one of those small rooms for the Ovitzes and their entourage. Whereas Birkenau inmates slept two or three to a ragged blanket in their single set of clothes on thin, louse-infected mattresses stuffed with saw-dust, the Lilliputs enjoyed individual wool blankets, sheets, and even pillows. "The dwarfs slept on the lower berth, and even this was too high for them to mount," remembers Joseph Slo-mowitz, who was thirteen at the time. "We had to help them up and down. Our parents and the tall Ovitzes slept on the middle berth, and we children climbed up to the top one."

Every morning in Birkenau began with a nightmare: the *Appell*, a roll call. It forced all inmates to rush outside at four o'clock and stand at attention for hours in rows of ten while they were counted over and over again. Motionless, clad in their rags, they stood exposed to heat, cold, rain, snow: their torture knew no season. At the end of the day, after eleven hours of hard labor, they went through the same process again—and on occasion, at midnight; whenever the SS chose. Those who col-lapsed were dispatched to the gas chamber. It was obvious that none of the seven dwarfs could survive a single *Appell*, and Mengele not only exempted the dwarfs from the ordeal, but also extended the privilege to their entire "family." All of them were counted in their room, to help them maintain their physical and mental condition. For Mengele had plans for them.

The inmates' thin striped uniforms offered no protection against the harsh weather at Birkenau, and they were otherwise dirty, torn, ridden with lice. Their ill-fitting wooden clogs caused painful abscesses. On the other hand, as the Lilliput group had been allowed to keep its own clothing, Perla could wrap herself warmly in the brown sheepskin coat she had brought from Rozavlea. On it, she stitched the required identification sign—a red triangle topped with a yellow stripe. The dwarfs took meticulous care of their clothes, because they knew it would be difficult to replace them. Elizabeth especially cherished her antelope shoes. When the seams ripped open she sewed them by hand and she kept on repairing them until they became tattered past hope. As a result, she was granted a visit to "Kanada"—the Auschwitz storerooms, named for a dreamland of wealth and comfort—where she was allowed to select a suitable pair of children's shoes. The dwarfs enjoyed another privilege, too—not because some shred of altruism on Mengele's part prompted it but because his research required it: they were not forced to shear their hair.

Nor were they subjected to corporal punishment. Flogging inmates until their torn flesh bled or hanging them by their hands was common practice in Auschwitz. Likewise, the arbitrary selection of prisoners for the gas chambers and the random shooting of inmates were daily routines. In a world of shaven heads and ragged striped uniforms, the Lilliputs' hair and clothes were a shield of protection, for the SS instantly recognized the dwarfs as Mengele's wards and therefore exceptions to SS rules. The Lilliputs received no special treatment at mealtimes, however, and the death camp's food was vile. In the morning, the barrack usually received a barrel of darkish, cold, unsweetened and diluted coffee substitute, though sometimes it was treated to a mixture of water and herbs that was supposed to pass for tea. Lunch was either a watery soup made with potatoes and cabbage leaves, or roots, the sort normally fed cattle, that had been boiled in a huge vat of water. The quantities were meager, not that Perla would have wanted more. She found the soups nauseating, rancid with the smell of rotten vegetables and more suspicious substances—some sort of poison, she feared. *Once when they poured us soup, I saw worms crawling in the bowl. There were bits of glass, buttons, things looking like teeth and little fingers of children.* Dinner offered no more than a piece of stale bread and water. The contaminated water caused severe diarrhea, so even in the summer heat the dwarfs refused to drink it. They were constantly thirsty.

The inmates' barracks had no sanitation facilities. Instead, the roughly ten thousand "Family Camp" residents had to manage with the 270 faucets and 174 toilet holes in the sanitation barrack, which they were allowed to visit twice a day. As the time allotted for these visits was extremely short, the inmates were always fighting for places. On the rare occasions that they were allowed to shower, the inmates had to undress in the barrack and then ride naked to the cold-water showers in open trucks, no matter how wet or bitterly frigid the weather. As a result, many inmates caught pneumonia, which worked as effectively—if less efficiently than a bullet or gas—in their extermination. The dwarfs, however, benefited from Mengele's well-known obsession with hygiene. *He was manicured, immaculately clean, and always wore white cotton gloves. He demanded that we wash every day. He knew we would be crushed and frozen in the latrines, and ordered that a colorful curtain be hung in a corner of our room. There was a warehouse full of little chamber pots that parents had taken for their babies on the long train journey. The babies were all killed, and Dr. Mengele furnished us with one of the pots, as well as an aluminum bowl to wash in. Simon Slomowitz would bring a bucket of water from the washrooms, and we would wash each other with the help of Sarah and Leah. Sometimes we used the undrinkable tea to shampoo our hair. It was important to be*

clean, to keep the lice away from our hair and bodies. Dr. Mengele
ordered us to stay away from people, so as not to become contami-
nated. Obedience was the first lesson we learned in the camp. You
had to know how to behave in that place: not to be a spoilt child and
desire something you could not have.

Every day the Lilliputs meticulously groomed themselves.
They scrubbed and brushed themselves and each other for
hours in preparation for their summons to Mengele's cabinet.
They dressed up in their finery. They powdered their faces and
rouged their cheeks. Makeup had always been essential to the
Lilliputs, and they'd had the forethought to ferret some away in
their pockets when they boarded the train to Auschwitz. So now
they could stroke in a black line along the lids of their eyes, and
they could pout their lips and color them red.

The first time that the Lilliputs were summoned to the *Revier*—
the clinic—and the doctors in white gowns examined them,
they thought it was a routine admission procedure. But the
examinations continued. Each day they returned again to the
clinic, and it soon dawned on them that they had been receiving
special treatment from Dr. Mengele for some medical purpose.
Josef Mengele was only one of dozens of doctors who performed criminal experiments on the inmates at Auschwitz-
Birkenau. Whereas German law protected laboratory animals, it
had established no limitations whatever in regard to research
and experimentation on human guinea pigs. Like all the doctors
in the death camps, Dr. Hans Münch, whose laboratory for the
Waffen-SS's Institute of Hygiene was located in Auschwitz's
notorious block 10, had free rein with the prisoners. "The

working conditions were ideal. The laboratories were excellently equipped, and the cream of academia was present—people with an international reputation. I could carry out experiments on human beings usually only possible on rabbits."

Mengele felt no compunction about experiments conducted upon the Jews. He argued that since all Jews were doomed to die anyway, he caused them no worse harm through his research and, indeed, made constructive scientific use of their now otherwise worthless lives. When Mengele met his son Rolf in Brazil in 1977, he told him that he had wanted to help people in the camp, and that the twins—as he referred to all his experimental subjects in the camp—"owed their lives to him." Some of the experiments were commissioned by the army. Inmates would be injected with poisonous substances, for instance, in order to discover what methods and means soldiers might be using to get themselves disqualified from service on the eastern front. German pharmaceutical companies and medical specialists took advantage of the unlimited pool of subjects to test any new substance or procedure that captured their eugenic interest, such as efficient, cheap methods to implement mass sterilization, and to eliminate the mentally, genetically, or racially unfit. So it was that thousands of young prisoners suffered radiation, repeated injections with various chemical substances, operations without anaesthetics, castrations. Those who did not die in the name of German science often ended up gruesomely maimed.

Grants that Professor von Verschuer's Kaiser Wilhelm Institute received from Germany's main research foundation, the Deutsche Forschungsgemeinschaft, financed Mengele's research at Auschwitz-Birkenau, initially on specific proteins and eye color. Such funding likewise furnished Mengele's laboratory with the latest and most sophisticated medical-technology equipment. Acting on the instructions of his supervisor, von Verschuer, Mengele dispatched to the Kaiser Wilhelm Institute blood samples, limbs, and eyeballs in different colors. Mengele had whole families of Gypsies killed specifically for their eyeballs.

According to Professor Benno Müller-Hill, from the Institute of Genetics, University of Cologne, "The goals of the research project of Mengele and von Verschuer were to decipher genetic differences of Jews, Gypsies and others in resistance to various infectious diseases, and to assemble as much material as possible from genetically affected twins or families." Dr. Jan Cespiva, a former Auschwitz inmate testifying against Mengele in 1963 before the public prosecutor in Frankfurt, stated, "I was able to see with my own eyes how he infected twins with typhus in the sickroom of the Gypsy camp, in order to observe whether the twins reacted in the same way or differently. A short time after being infected, they were sent to the gas chambers." To Professor Berthold Epstein, a distinguished Jewish pediatrician imprisoned at the camp, Mengele confided that his only goal in the war was to stay alive and use his work at Birkenau as a springboard toward a professorship. So he was looking for an insurance policy, in the shape of a scientific treatise that would confirm his professional stature and the indispensability of his research at Auschwitz-Birkenau. "We are enemies—you will not get out of here," Mengele bluntly told Epstein. "If you perform scientific work for me and I publish it in my name, you will prolong your own life." As a result, Epstein extensively researched a deadly gangrene of the face and mouth. He conducted the research on Gypsy children and adolescents.

The ambitious Mengele was not long content with his position at Birkenau as von Verschuer's assistant. He wanted a research niche of his own. In the spring of 1944, with Birkenau preparing for the massive influx of Jews soon due from Hungary, he saw his chance. During his first year in the camp, he had restricted his experiments to a few dozen cases, most of them sets of twins that he had discovered among the Gypsies and Czech Jews in Birkenau's separate sub-camps. But now, with the imminent arrival of hundreds of thousands of Jews, research vistas of unlimited scope and variety were about to open up for him.

According to monumental research assembled by Danuta Czech for the Auschwitz State Museum, the category "twins selected and admitted to the camp" is first recorded in registry documents on May 17, 1944—just two days before the Lilliput Troupe's arrival. Importantly, the term "twin" in the records does not simply signify multiple births; rather, it refers to any child or adult selected by Mengele for his experiments. On the first day of his hunt, he found 39 promising human specimens. In a fortnight, he had added 192 more, and by the end of July he had collected 300: 177 females and 123 males, mostly twins, with ages ranging from infancy to senectitude. As Olga Lengyel, one of the Jewish doctors whom Mengele forced to assist him, recollects the day he discovered the Lilliput Troupe, May 19, "he was beside himself with joy."

Eighty-five years earlier, an Austrian monk named Gregor Mendel was experimenting with peas that he grew in a greenhouse in the Augustinian Abbey of St. Thomas in Brünn (now Brno, the Czech Republic). In 1865, Mendel, who was also interested in various human deformations, published an article in an obscure scientific journal summing up his experiments. While, as is well known, he was the first to suggest the existence of genes and the principle of genetic heredity, his findings were essentially ignored for three decades. Nevertheless, in the period after 1900 (a good fifteen years after Mendel's death) his botanical research would emerge, transformed, as the monster of eugenics. Fused with social Darwinist ideology and its version of "survival of the fittest," Mendelian genetics would culminate for Mengele in his exploration of heredity factors through experiments on human anomalies, as well as in his selection, on eugenic premises, of internees for the gas ovens at Birkenau—as it happens, a mere 120 miles from Mendel's solitary room.

Working within a particular utilitarian tradition, eugenic scientists claimed that heredity accounted for most physical and social ailments. Distinguishing between "good" and "bad" genes, they set out to root out the bad ones—through sterilization. By 1920, twenty-five American states had legalized the sterilization of such undesirables as the criminally insane, and the mentally ill or handicapped, and others considered genetically inferior. But all told, the American laws were applied to a relatively modest degree. While modeling its own program of compulsory sterilization on both American and Scandinavian precedents, Nazi Germany pioneered the zealous implementation of such a program. In June 1933, the Law for the Protection of Hereditary Health established the criteria for compulsory sterilization. Among those to be sterilized: the mentally retarded, manic-depressives, schizophrenics, epileptics, the hereditarily blind and deaf, and alcoholics, along with people suffering from grave bodily malformations or arrested growth. Once the law was implemented, a total of roughly four hundred thousand German citizens fell victim to it.

By law, starting in 1933, all doctors, nurses, and midwives had to report any patient, and every newborn child, who evinced deformations of head or spine. More aggressively, under a policy initiated in 1938, the state authorized the killing of all children suffering from severe physical or mental problems and in October 1939, this euthanasia policy was extended to include adults. The adult program, known as "T4," put to death around one hundred thousand people. It also categorized approximately another twenty thousand Germans as subjects possessing bodily malformations grave enough to merit euthanasia, but no statistics exist that indicate how many were actually killed. Deformed people with homes and families were relatively safe; those institutionalized were at the mercy of caretakers and doctors. For instance, Dr. Hans Grebe, Mengele's colleague at the Kaiser Wilhelm Institute, told Professor Benno Müller-Hill that his research on dwarfism in 1942 and 1943 became impossible and had to be abandoned because so many of the subjects in governmental institutions had disappeared.

So it was that all the diversities of creation and wonders of nature that had drawn crowds of parents and children to Sunday fairs, to Lilliput-cities, the Vienna Prater, and the Berlin zoo, had become outcasts. Once greeted with flowers and besieged for autographs, these entertainers and performers were now declared a social burden, a genetic error that the state set out systematically to erase.

Mengele had at least three clinics in Birkenau—in the men's camp, the women's camp, and the Gypsy camp—and several laboratories supplied him with medical services. Before fleeing Birkenau in January 1945, he hastily packed into a trunk what research data, documents, and specimens he could. The rest he

set on fire. It's a small victory of history, that in a place so dedicated to destruction, nonetheless, after the liberation of
Auschwitz, in the registry book of the X-ray clinic and in laboratory report forms on samples of blood, saliva, urine, and
feces, several thousand lab results were found intact. Of these
results, seventy-five pertained to the Lilliput group.

The earliest surviving Lilliput lab records are dated June 28,
1944—a very busy day, evidently, as all twenty-two of the group
were taken to Mengele's clinic in block 32 of the Gypsy camp. To
Joseph Slomowitz, it looked like any ordinary clinic—the staff in
white gowns, stethoscopes dangling on doctors' chests, files containing each subject's personal data and test results. The Slomowitz family, all of normal height, of course had no blood
connection to the Ovitzes, but they had conned Mengele into
believing that they were kin. Thus they were always taken along
with the Ovitzes to the clinics, and on their medical forms, all the
Slomowitzes are categorized as dwarfs. That they were all also so
tall puzzled Mengele. Fearful that Mengele would discover the
truth and send the family to the ovens, the Slomowitzes drew his
attention to their youngest, Serene. She was seven, but the Slomowitzes told Mengele that she was thirteen and had stopped
growing. Since they had no identity papers, Mengele had no way
to verify the information. And on the premise that Serene was
indeed a dwarf, he extracted bone marrow from the spines of the
entire family in an attempt to ascertain why all but Serene had
grown tall. The pain they endured was terrible.

On each visit to Mengele's clinic, all those summoned from
the Lilliput group waited on a bench in the corridor as one by
one they were called in. Even the youngest children had to face
Mengele's syringe alone. These examinations lasted for hours,
and no one could return to the barrack until all of them had

been questioned, probed, and tested. Perla soon noticed that at the end of each day Mengele would prepare the schedule for the next; then, every evening, the block elder would come to the Ovitzes' room and call out from a list the numbers of those in the group who were summoned for the next day's test. If it was to be done in the nearby barrack, they would walk there, but otherwise an ambulance would fetch them. *Every few days the doctors drew blood. The night before, we had to fast. It was a big syringe, the amount they took was enormous, and being feeble from hunger, we often fainted. That didn't stop Mengele. He had us lie down, and when we came to our senses they resumed siphoning our blood. The nurses and doctors were prisoners too, but they didn't try to make it easier on us. They punctured us carelessly, and blood spurted. We often felt nausea, and vomited a lot. When we returned to our barrack, we would slump on the wooden tier, but before we had time to recover, we would be summoned for a new cycle.*

In the 1940s, medicine was obsessed with blood and its constituents. It was generally believed that blood plasma retained all traces of illness and contained all genetic traits. German scientists therefore considered blood a key to the differentiation between superior and inferior races. This premise accounts for the particular ordeal of Shimshon Ovitz. Born prematurely, Shimshon was still markedly smaller than normal at a year old. Both his parents were of normal height, but his mother had had a dwarf father and had seven dwarf siblings: thus, Mengele was extremely eager to learn Shimshon's genetic destiny. Shimshon intrigued Mengele more than any other member of the group, and he showed the infant no mercy. Because the veins in Shimshon's arms were too narrow for extractions, Mengele had blood drawn from Shimshon's fingers and from behind his ears. The stabs of the needle left his soft skin black and blue. To extract enough blood to fill a single tube seemed to take an eternity. Often Shimshon fainted; his aunt Perla would give him her own precious sugar cube, which she received to revive her after the blood-taking. Once, Shimshon's aunts later told him, the test tube fell to the floor and, smashing, splattered blood all over the examination room. The staff doctor was terrified, as he knew that Mengele was impatient for results and that the extraction of another tubeful of blood was impossible. The only possible solution to the dilemma seemed to be to extract blood from his mother, Leah, instead, and present it as Shimshon's own. Although she had already supplied her quota, Leah again had the rubber band squeezed tight around her arm; she fainted as the blood flowed.

Frequent extractions of blood often proved to be fatal to weakened, hungry, and exhausted victims. Hani Schick, who came from the town of Sighet, arrived at Auschwitz-Birkenau ten days after the Ovitzes with her husband, five-year-old son, Otto, and twins Joseph and Hedi, who had just turned one. Her husband was selected for death, and Hani would have met the same fate had it not been for Mengele, who noticed the twin babies clutched in her arms. He took them in tow. The twins and Hani were examined and weighed. Large quantities of blood were drawn from the two babies, under Mengele's supervision. On July 4, a staff doctor drew 200 milliliters of blood from each of them and the next day, Joseph died in his mother's arms. The body of one-year-old inmate number A-12087 was laid outside the barrack; the death-cart picked it up and took it to the crematorium in the morning. Eleven days later, inmate number A-7044 joined her twin brother. For eight months, Hani Schick managed to hide her son Otto in the sick women's barrack. Two weeks after the liberation, the child died of a liver infection.

Jewish gynecologist Dr. Gisella Perl, also from Sighet, was

forced to work on Mengele's team. In her book *I Was a Doctor in Auschwitz*, she recalls that "the healthy, the talented, the beautiful, were ruthlessly exterminated, but everything abnormal was a source of constant amusement and enjoyment to our jailers, because only when comparing themselves with these freaks could they feel superior. There were days, though, when the midgets served other purposes than entertainment. Often, altogether too often, Mengele took great amounts of blood from their veins, in order to play around with it in the laboratories reserved for German 'scientists.' The poor midgets grew paler and weaker as time went on, although Dr. Mengele paid generously for the blood he took, by giving them a double ration of bread on such days. The ordinary bread ration, the same we received, was insufficient even for midgets. I shall never forget the little lady midget who told me one day that the double bread ration made her so happy that she did not even mind the cruel, painful and sickening process which made her earn it."

As an SS officer who enjoyed three-course dinners of, say, thick tomato soup, half a fried chicken, and a scoop of vanilla ice cream, Mengele was totally detached from the deprivation and hunger that his dwarf specimens daily suffered. Whenever he saw them, he would exclaim, "Surely you've enough to stuff yourself with!"—or something to that effect. Hungry as they were, the dwarfs never dared to complain. Most Auschwitz inmates showed grave symptoms of emaciation, and Mengele did try to improve the diet for his specimens. Still, milk soup, a slice of white bread, a teaspoon of beet-jam, a slice of cheese, and a piece of sausage—indulgences that other inmates could not even dream of—hardly improved it enough. The Ovitzes were constantly, severely fatigued from the loss of blood. *He gave us some porridge, baby food, but we had passed the age and hunger drove us crazy. The children were always crying for food. One of the Slomowitz boys said, "You're small, you don't need to eat much, give me your portion, I have to grow." He constantly threatened to tell Dr. Mengele the secret of us not really being family if we didn't give him our food. One day, I had had enough and grabbed his hand, pulled him out of the barrack, and pointed up at the smoking chimney at the end of the camp. "Go tell Dr. Mengele, that's where he'll immediately send you and your family!" That reduced him to silence.*

Analysis of the surviving lab reports shows that Mengele divided the Lilliput group into subsections. On different dates, he would summon different combinations of their members: the males and not the females on one day, the dwarfs and not the normal-sized ones on another, or only mothers and children on still another. *He made never-ending comparisons. He drew blood from our older dwarf sisters who were born to another mother, comparing it to ours to see if we were really from the same father. He compared our blood to that of our tall sisters to see in what way it was different—he couldn't stop wondering how such a high quota of dwarfs could be produced from two tall mothers and one dwarf father.*

With no special forms available for his experiments, in the meantime Mengele used the standard medical forms issued by the "Hygienic Bacteriologic Laboratories of the Waffen-SS" for the soldiers' sick parade. By the entry for "SS rank and number," he filled in the name of the prisoner and his or her Birkenau number; by the entry for "clinical diagnosis," he wrote *Zwerge* (dwarf); and by the entry for "address of transmitting office," he indicated the sub-camp and barrack where the Lilliput group was sequestered. He personally signed each form with his flamboyant signature, followed by his full rank. The forms indicate that the Lilliput blood samples were sent to the laboratory of the

SS-Hygiene-Institute in block 10 of Auschwitz. Far from recording any effort to break the genetic code for dwarfism, the surviving forms reflect, instead, the routine health-care procedures of the 1940s. The laboratory checked the blood for Takata-Ara and Rest-NaCl as well as vitamin C, in order to trace kidney problems, liver function, and typhus. "Looking at the remaining medical tests done on the dwarfs, it seems that although Mengele acted according to the practices of his time, he had no idea what he was looking for. Hence the repeated tests and the large amounts of blood he took," observes Professor Raphael Falk of the Hebrew University's Department of Genetics. Any sophisticated tests had to be performed at the Kaiser Wilhelm Institute in Berlin. Elizabeth Ovitz recalled that she once saw in Mengele's clinic a box of big, new syringes that had arrived from Berlin; the inscription on the outside of the box read "The Protected Jewish Hungarian Dwarf Inmates." Her account is confirmed by Professor von Verschuer himself, reporting to the Deutsche Forschungsgemeinschaft that "blood samples are being sent to my laboratory for analysis" by "my post-doctoral assistant, M.D. Ph.D. Dr. Mengele." Whenever a lab form returned with the stamp "Blood Homolyzed Condition Not Separable," blood had to be taken again. The medical forms show that because of laboratory failure, Elizabeth Ovitz had to give blood for a Wassermann test three times in ten days. It's hard to comprehend why Mengele insisted on looking for syphilis in the children as well, including eleven-year-old Judah, nine-year-old Helene, eight-year-old Batia, and even baby Shimshon. They, as well as the adults, all proved negative.

NINE

Auschwitz-Birkenau, July 1944

From the first instant, from the first frame, the story of Snow White and the Seven Dwarfs had enchanted Dina Gottlieb. The first-ever full-length animation film became a box office hit at the same historical moment that anti-Semitic laws began to bar Jews from public places in German-occupied Prague. The fragile, blonde, blue-eyed art student Dina Gottlieb knew the Disney film virtually by heart. She had seen it six times, and each time she had risked her life to view it. For each time she had removed her yellow star to slip into the cinema. In September 1943, Dina and her mother were sent to Auschwitz-Birkenau, where they were placed in the Czechoslovakian Family Camp. In an effort to mask the horrors of the place from their children, the Czech Jews set up a barrack for playing and studying. Dina volunteered to decorate the walls of this bizarre island of insanity: "I painted a meadow with some trees, and was about to insert cows or sheep when I noticed that all the children had gathered behind me. I turned and asked which they wanted, and in a chorus they all shouted, 'Snow White and the Seven Dwarfs!' " Dina duly painted a graceful Snow White dancing with Dopey and surrounded by clapping dwarfs, one of whom played an accordion. The large, brightly colored fresco inspired the children to write and stage their own version of the fairy tale. They named it "Snow White in Auschwitz."

The fresco inside block 31 drew the attention of an SS doctor, who reported it to Mengele. Certain she was going to be gassed or shot, Dina Gottlieb was terrified when she was summoned to Mengele's office. As she recalls it, Mengele was leaning behind a tripod and looking through a camera at a group of Gypsies standing in front of it. He beckoned her to approach and take a look. But he knew that ultimately he would not be satisfied with the quality of the color in the photographs; he never was. Might she be able to more accurately record the skin tones in paint? he wondered. She said she would try.

Dina was supplied with paint and brushes, and the gates of the Gypsy camp were opened to her for models. As she walked around, she observed scenes of daily life that seemed almost normal: children chasing each other in a game of tag, old women chatting, a young man playing a guitar. It was the sad beauty of a young French Gypsy woman, however, that captured Dina's artistic eye. She found an interpreter and learned that the young woman's name was Céline, that she was twenty, the same age as Dina herself, and had just lost her two-month-old daughter due to the lack of milk. "Tell her that Dr. Mengele asked me to make some portraits," Dina instructed the interpreter. "I want to paint her. Can she come tomorrow to his office?" She could, and did. Every morning at seven, when Dina arrived, her subject was already there waiting. "I worked very slowly, hoping to gain time for Céline to get back on her feet. With her grieving face, I painted her as a Madonna veiled in a blue scarf. My workroom was next to Mengele's office, and occasionally he would drop by to inspect the progress. Once, he pulled up Céline's blue scarf—rare conduct for Mengele since he preferred to avoid touching prisoners. He demanded that the Gypsy's ears be emphasized, as part of his racial research." Céline was suffering from severe diarrhea: she could not digest the camp's coarse, dry black bread. Coaxing a slice of white bread each day out of Mengele, Dina passed it on to Céline secretly. The two young women became friends. They found ways to overcome the language barrier. They laughed together; Céline taught Dina a French song. After a fortnight, Mengele declared the painting complete. Dina would never see Céline again.

Not happy with Gottlieb's apparent preference for good-looking Gypsies, Mengele himself chose Dina's next set of models, a selection of elderly women and men. She got the impression that the doctor wanted simply to acquire visual documentation to support his racial theory, as Dina's series of eleven Gypsy portraits were intended to illustrate the book that Mengele was hoping to write. When she had completed the final portrait, Mengele seated himself in front of Gottlieb, folded his hands in his lap, and asked her to draw him. "I picked up a pencil and looked into his eyes—they belonged to a dead man. The squeak of the chalk on paper was the only sound in the room. He broke the silence, teasingly asking if I noticed anything special about him, something only his wife would know. I hesitated before I dared to point at the mark on his left ear. It was a flat, round disk on his cartilage. Mengele smiled with approval."

In the workroom next to Dina's, a female Polish prisoner took the handprints and fingerprints of all the inmates selected by Mengele for his experiments. Dina, for her part, sketched their skulls, ears, noses, mouths, hands, and feet. She nearly fainted, though, when she was instructed to draw a heart that had been split in two and stored in a jar of formaldehyde; the heart's owner had been shot in an attempt to escape. For Dina, it was often distressing work. "Then one day, I saw a column of dwarfs trotting toward me, like a film scene. There were seven; I could not believe my eyes. It was as if all my animated dwarfs—Dopey, Grumpy, Sneezy and all the rest—had descended from the mural in the children's barrack and come to life. But I was no Snow White, and they were real. I could not help smiling in response to the dwarfs, and to the magic number of seven—there was something optimistic and encouraging about such fragile beings managing to survive here."

On Saturday, July 1, Perla, Avram, and Micki Ovitz were driven to the X-ray clinic in the main camp of Auschwitz. Perla was extremely worried: why had she been summoned again, after having had seven X-rays taken just three days earlier, together with her sisters Rozika, Franziska, and Elizabeth? Had the X-rays revealed something suspicious? She listened to her body, and tried to discern if she was experiencing some unusual aches or discomfort. And if she was ill, would she be treated for the disease or dispatched to the gas ovens?

Mengele always insisted on rigorous medical procedures. Hungry as the dwarfs were, they had to fast before most of their blood tests, and before every abdominal X-ray they were given laxatives to purge their withered bowels. All night they'd be running to the chamber pot in the corner of their room. The clinic registry book shows that on July 1, at the end of a busy day, the three Ovitzes were scheduled for one of those extended X-ray sessions that could last for hours. While they sat naked on the black swivel chair, the giant machine was repeatedly adjusted to their size. All the other inmates listed in the register had a single X-ray—an arm, ribs, a leg, a shoulder—but the Ovitzes were subjected to ten different shots each. Starting with the head and proceeding to the chest, pelvis, hands, and feet, their entire bodies were X-rayed. A few days later, Mengele laid the X-ray negatives on Dina Gottlieb's desk and gave her transparent tracing paper. She pasted the negatives to the window to get more light; she followed the contours with her pencil. She immediately noticed the tiny fingers and thought that they belonged to children. Mengele, however, pointed out to her the different bone structure: the fingers had an extra bone that could be detected only in X-rays. This bone, Mengele explained, protruded at the age of eighteen months in individuals born to dwarfism and thus enabled physicians to make an early diagnosis of the condition. In those same few days, and as more passed by, Perla heard nothing from Mengele, and so Perla convinced herself that her new set of X-rays had turned up nothing clinically wrong.

Equipped with the most sophisticated gear of the time, a photographic workshop and studio were operating in block 28 of the main camp at Auschwitz. For the most part, the photos that were processed there depicted political prisoners, although Mengele also took advantage of the studio and workshop to compile a photographic record of his research subjects. One of the photographers, Polish prisoner Wilhelm Brosse, had started working with Mengele at the end of 1943. The first subjects that he photographed were Gypsies with gangrenous faces; twins, triplets, and even quadruplets came later. Then one day in the summer of 1944 the truck from Birkenau brought to block 28 the dwarfs. They all had to undress, and Brosse took the standard shots: one frontal, one from the side, one from the back.

In addition, at Mengele's instructions, he also took close-ups of the dwarfs' hands and feet—of particular interest, as their trunks were nearly normal.

The female dwarfs felt ashamed standing naked in front of Brosse, and it was embarrassing for Brosse as well. He had been ordered not to converse with the petite women with beautiful faces; nonetheless, he tried to make them feel at ease by moving them about gently, and convey by speaking to them softly his regret that he had no choice in the matter. Later on, the SS brought to Brosse's workshop an extraordinarily obese man and a Ukrainian with a giant penis. After Brosse photographed the two men, they were shot outside his studio.

Mengele's research relied primarily on blood tests, X-rays, and anthropomorphic measurements. He had neither the time nor the inclination to personally test his hundreds of specimens, but then he did not need to—not with the abundance of expert professionals among the hundreds of thousands of people passing through the gates of Auschwitz-Birkenau: Countess Dr. Martina Puzyna, for one. A member of the Polish resistance movement, Dr. Puzyna was captured and jailed in March 1943, then sent to Auschwitz five months later. Unlike many of the imprisoned medical doctors who were enlisted as aides by the SS physicians, the forty-two-year-old Puzyna was assigned to hard physical labor. Soon afterward, she contracted typhus and was hospitalized. In Mengele's rounds at the hospital—he checked on patients with bad prognoses; his brief pause at a bed could mean death—he afforded the critically ill prisoner Puzyna one quick look and was about to move on when an accompanying doctor remarked that she was an anthropologist from the University of Lvov. Mengele promptly turned back and asked Puzyna about her training. Her voice feeble, her speech faint, she mentioned her assistantship with the famous professor Jan Czekanowski. Impressed by both her scientific and aristocratic background, Mengele ordered the Countess Puzyna to report to his office.

Too weak to walk on her own, Puzyna had to be carried to Mengele's office by two female prisoners. Mengele greeted her by asking what she had been doing at Auschwitz since her arrival; when she answered that she had been carrying heavy stones, he burst out laughing. They discussed anthropology, his interest in comparative research on twins, and the appropriate techniques for measurement. Mengele ordered that she be rationed additional food, and he had her billeted as a prisoner-physician. "He was interested in seeing my work capacity restored as fast as possible. Compared to my former situation, it was heaven on earth."

Martina Puzyna was assigned a special workroom equipped with all the necessary tools—Swiss-made calipers, protractors, compasses, slide rules—and was furnished with two assistants, a female former anthropology student to help her do the measurements, and a young girl to log the findings. While Mengele's specimens sat naked for long hours in an unheated room, Dr. Puzyna fastidiously measured the length and width and shape of the eyes and nose as well as the various distances from the tip of the eye to the nose, the ear, the other eye, the jaw. "Turn left! Right! Bend over! Stretch up! Don't breathe!" The inmates were bombarded with orders. Tediously and repeatedly, Puzyna measured finger after finger, joint after joint, and the size of every digit was carefully recorded in its proper place on the chart. When the Ovitzes came in for measuring, they seemed to Dr. Puzyna to be consistently cheerful. Mengele never indicated to her the purpose of the Lilliputian measurements, although her impression was that his interest in heredity had prompted him to research the topic more thoroughly through pathology. According to Perla Ovitz, the measuring itself did not hurt, but the process was exhausting and irritating, not to mention degrading. *It was as if my body was being dismantled into its smallest components, and I had no idea why they measured the same limbs again and again. We had stopped growing ages ago, and certainly hadn't expanded or shrunk since the previous week.* As a doctoral student, Mengele had published an article criticizing scientists who lost themselves in details; he had argued that "it is not useful to take as many measurements as possible: one must restrict oneself to the most significant ones." However, with the unlimited time, human resources, and research possibilities available at Auschwitz, Mengele neglected his own golden rule, as he unleashed himself and his team on his subjects in a relentless quest for detail.

A veteran member of the Polish resistance, Martina Puzyna did not abandon her underground activities in Birkenau. She collected incriminating documents regarding Mengele's medical crimes—a sample of her own measurements, a psychiatric test for twins, an X-ray of a female prisoner's lungs—and smuggled them out of the camp in October 1944. Yet she remained ambivalent in her judgment of Mengele's work and insisted long after the war that its results "were of immense value to the science of anthropology. I recognized this fact at the time, and tried to secure these results for myself. I prepared copies and concealed them in containers, and buried them near my office barrack." When the war ended, she hurried to her barrack to retrieve the documents, but she was unable to locate the exact spot where she had hidden them; they had disappeared forever. Documents she smuggled out earlier have survived, including the anthropometric measurements of 296 Jewish girls and women from Hungary, 111 of them twins, on sheets of fading paper partly damaged by weather and time. Long columns in dense handwriting are filled with each prisoner's number, age, and Dr. Puzyna's twenty-four different measurements for each person. But even if the buried documents had been found intact, Puzyna would have found them difficult to use, because the monstrosity of the medical-anthropological activities at Auschwitz, which quickly became evident after the war, made Mengele's name notorious. Dr. Miklos Nyiszli, a Jewish pathologist who was forced to work side by side with Mengele at the camp, himself witnessed to his daily horror how the inmates were "exposed to every medical examination that could be performed on human beings. Blood tests, lumbar punctures, exchanges of blood between twin brothers, numerous other examinations, all fatiguing and depressing."

Kalman Braun was just over thirteen when he arrived at Auschwitz with his twin sister, Judith, and mother, from whom the two children were immediately separated; they would never see her again. When he entered his assigned barrack, Kalman felt completely lost. He stood at the entrance, frozen, when suddenly a bespectacled child came forward and said, "Come, come, boy, you can be with me." After a second or third glance, Kalman noticed that the hands which greeted him, like the smiling face, were wrinkled. This was no child. "Where are you from?" asked the man, and as they exchanged names of towns and people they knew, they were surprised to discover a close family connection. For it turned out that the small, kind, bespectacled man—his name was Ludovit Feld, he was forty years old and a prominent painter in Kosice, Czechoslovakia—had an older brother, who was married to Braun's maternal aunt. "How come I've never heard of you?" asked Kalman. "Because I converted," answered Feld. If his family had already rejected him because of his deformity, when he converted, they ostracized him completely. Nor did Feld's conversion save him from the death camp, though his deformity did save him from death. When the Nazis came, he was sent to Auschwitz with his parents, his three sisters, and their children. All fifteen normal-size members of the family had been exterminated. Only the three-foot-seven-inch-tall Ludovit survived.

"A Jew cannot cut himself from his roots, just as a dwarf cannot alter his size," says Kalman Bar-On, formerly Braun. "From that day onward, I shared the same bench and blanket with my Christian relative, sleeping cuddled together like spoons. He was a source of advice, wisdom, and comfort, and thanks to him, I had someone in the world. In return, I offered him the experience of parental feelings for the child he never had. In matters of daily survival, Ludovit was the child, and I the adult, since he was afraid of being crushed while queuing for food. With the heat of my body I kept him warm at night."

Feld endured the same cycle of medical tests that the Ovitz family did. Although Feld shared the same handicap and fate as the Ovitzes, they resented him because of his conversion, and they refused to exchange a word with him when all of them sat together in the clinic. Once Dr. Puzyna had completed the initial round of anthropometric measurements, Feld was examined by a team of specialists: an internist, a neurologist, a psychiatrist, an ophthalmologist, a dermatologist, a surgeon, a urologist, and an ear, nose, and throat man—all of them prisoners, of different nationalities. While Mengele reviewed all the results, he himself conducted none of the actual examinations.

According to Feld, Mengele behaved properly and politely during his visits; he even offered the dwarfs cigarettes.

The team of prisoner-specialists thus evaluated the dwarfs' entire anatomy by comparing their physical features and physiological characteristics to those of normal humans in search of irregularities that would account for their arrested growth. Feld and the other dwarfs furnished samples of urine, stool, and saliva that were analyzed in the biological, pathological, bacteriological, chemical, and serological laboratories of Auschwitz's Hygiene Institute, all of which had been fitted with the latest scientific equipment and financed by German academic institutions. When it came to the relation between nurture and nature, Mengele's position was clear: he was looking for signs of heredity everywhere—in the hair, skin, and teeth; in the hormones in the blood; in the pigments and blood vessels in the retina of the eye. According to Perla Ovitz, the doctors poured first boiling then freezing water into the dwarf's ears, an experiment that was not only excruciatingly painful but nearly drove them crazy as well. The doctors placed glass eyeballs next to those of the dwarfs, Perla recalled, for purposes of color identification; the drops in the dwarfs' eyes blinded them for hours. Healthy teeth were extracted, hairs and eyelashes were plucked out—all *to see if there was a difference between us small ones and the tall ones.* The married female dwarfs were strapped to a table and subjected to such close gynecological scrutiny that it left them deathly pale and so shaken that they refused to tell Perla what they had endured. She feared they would do the same to her, *but the doctors said, we'll wait with this one, she's too young for it.*

All the medical victims in Auschwitz had their own medical files, which were continually growing with each new diagram, chart, photograph, X-ray, and test result. As Mengele had no access to the medical records in Rozavlea, and since the dwarfs had brought no documents with them, he grilled them endlessly with questions regarding their origins and family history. Again and again, they had to repeat the story of their father and his two wives. Over and over they had to name every aunt, uncle, and cousin, and specify their former occupations and places of residence. Mengele filled his notebooks with scores of names, as each household had ten to twelve members. He pressed the dwarfs to try to recall if there were any other dwarfs in their extended family, no matter how often they told him there were none. Since dwarfs had traditionally been believed to be idiots, Mengele's psychiatrists employed numerous questionnaires to test the Ovitzes' intelligence. Seasoned world travelers locked into Lilliputian bodies, they had Mengele marveling at their wit and incredulous at their knowledge and insight. At one point, he expressed his intention to exhibit them at a prestigious research institute in Berlin. The eight members of the Slomowitz family underwent exactly the same examinations as the twelve Ovitzes. Only the Fischmans, mother and daughter, were exempted, as Bassie had been falsely presented as Micki Ovitz's fiancée. Mengele had other plans for the beautiful twenty-year-old.

Being less than contented with visual representations of his specimens in X-rays, Dina Gottlieb's illustrations, and Wilhelm Brosse's photographs, Mengele ordered Ludovit Feld to also draw his dwarfs and twins. One of the latter was Peter Grünfeld, aged four and separated from his mother and twin sister, who were placed in the women's camp. "Lajos Baci (Uncle Lajos)—that's what we called Ludovit Feld—would place me before a window to catch the light. He would sit on a small stool with a big sketchbook, slowly drawing me in charcoal. Very quickly, I would lose my patience, fidget around, and Feld would rebuke me: 'Sit still on your butt, I can't work when you're moving.' Almost sixty years later, his words still echo inside me." Feld had to deliver all his paintings to Mengele, because any form of creative self-expression by inmates was strictly forbidden and punishable by death. Feld, however, furtively tore small pieces of paper from Mengele's allotment and sketched scenes of camp life that he then hid under the mattress. Under Mengele's instruction, Feld also drew the doctor's own portrait—"He loved so much to be painted, and forced me to constantly draw him."

On June 23, 1944, an International Red Cross delegation had visited the ghetto in Theresienstadt, Czechoslovakia, to investigate reports that the Jews there were being transported to Auschwitz for extermination. The delegation was scheduled to proceed next to Poland in order to inspect the Czechoslovakian Family Camp at Birkenau. But the Red Cross delegates had been so impressed by the showcase Jewish habitat of Theresienstadt, and especially by the camp commandant, who had proudly presented them with postcards written by former residents of Theresienstadt affirming that everyone was alive and well in Auschwitz-Birkenau, that they changed their plans. What the delegates did not know was that the postcards had been written under duress just a few hours before their authors were gassed. Also, the cards were all dated two weeks after the gassing. With the International Red Cross having decided that a trip to Poland was an unnecessary investment of time and energy, the Germans no longer had to fear an inspection of Auschwitz-Birkenau. Further camouflage became unnecessary, and the liquidation of the ten thousand inmates of the "Family Camp" could begin.

It was Dina Gottlieb's second selection, on July 2, 1944. The Seven Dwarfs of the fairy tale had saved her the first time, on

March 8, when she had just finished the fresco that had attracted Mengele's attention and had led her to months of work painting his medical subjects. She and her mother had been among the 27 people selected for life in March; 3,800 others were sent to the ovens. Dina's parents had divorced when she was a baby, and her father had remarried. For years, Dina and her father had not been in contact; then one day in the "Family Camp," she saw him, with his second wife and two children. Very quickly Dina grew very fond of her half-brother, Peter, who was eleven. He was constantly hungry and she smuggled bread to him whenever she could. But she could not save him or anyone else in the family, that awful July. "We all had to march half-naked before the inspecting eyes of Dr. Mengele and his team. I knew them well from my work, and I was friends with one of them, Dr. Koenig, Mengele's assistant. Much to my relief, when my turn arrived, he was looking straight into my eyes, and not at my naked body." Gottlieb and her mother, among the handful selected for life, were moved on to the women's camp. Three thousand other young, relatively healthy men and women were selected for slave labor in Germany. The rest, 7,000 Czech Jews, now faced extinction. Perhaps more than any other of the inmates at Auschwitz, they were well aware of the camp's real purpose, for they had lived for months in the shadow of the crematoria chimneys, and had themselves witnessed firsthand the hundreds of thousands of new arrivals instantly delivered to the gas chambers. On July 10, 1944, a curfew was imposed on the "Family Camp." Three thousand Jewish Czechs were taken out and killed. The day after, the remaining four thousand were shepherded to their death in the ovens.

With the "Family Camp" in the process of liquidation, Mengele could no longer house his dwarfs there, as they might mistakenly be gassed with the others. For the first time in their lives, the Ovitzes were forced to separate. The women, along with little Shimshon, were taken to the infirmary of the women's camp, while their brothers Avram and Micki, as well as Simon Slomowitz and his three sons, were sent to the men's infirmary. Their barracks were too far apart to make mutual sustenance possible any longer. All twenty-two in the Lilliput group worried about the uncertain length of their separation—and the strong possibility that they would never see each other again.

TEN

Auschwitz-Birkenau, August 1944

It was only midday, but Regina Ovitz was so feeble she felt herself slipping into sleep. She picked up a broken brick and put it under her head. Indifferent to the rough earth beneath her and to the shrieks of the guards, she dozed off immediately on her makeshift pillow. From afar, like voices in a dream, she heard shouts: "Look, Lilliputians! Lilliputians!" The joy in the voices evaporated inside her as her reverie continued. Suddenly, a downpour of rain began to fall.

Instinctively she coiled herself up to protect her body from the heavy drops. Only when she'd gotten soaked to the bone did she manage to rouse herself. Shuddering, sleep-drugged, she looked blearily at the barracks, the wet earth, the broken brick. The cry "Lilliputians! Lilliputians!" still echoed inside her head; it prompted her to circle the barrack and enter a forbidden zone. Then she saw them, on the path across from her: five little figures.

Twenty-four-year-old Regina was a relative of the dwarfs. Her grandfather, Israel Meir Ovitz, was the brother of Shimshon Eizik, the Ovitzes' father. The two families came from the same village and had traveled on the same train to Auschwitz-Birkenau, but in different cattle cars. All forty members of Regina's family had been killed, while she had been assigned into slave labor, to harvest grain in the fields near the camp. Bending her back for hours on end had begun to cripple her. Her head shaven, her arms and legs bare, she'd been sunburned in the scorching heat. Abscesses covered her limbs. She could hardly walk. Wracked by pain, she had stopped going to work. She'd have lain listlessly all day on her bunk, had it not been for the block elder.

"If they find you in the barrack, you'll be taken to the clinic," she warned Regina, out of pity and concern. "It's a short stop from there to the gas chambers." She admonished Regina urgently, "Go out! Find somewhere to hide and stay there!" When Regina responded with an apathetic shrug and did not move, the block elder got her to her feet and pushed her out the door. She told Regina to wait until the others came back from the grain fields before she returned. That's when Regina hid behind the barrack and fell asleep.

When the rain awakened her, and she saw the dwarfs, Regina recognized them immediately. For the other prisoners, their parade merely made for a curious scene, but for Regina it was an unbelievable family reunion. She had come to Auschwitz with her grandfather, mother, aunts, uncles, and nieces, and she had lost them all at once upon their arrival; but now here were the five sisters—her five cousins, Rozika, Franziska, Elizabeth, Frieda, and Perla. "They were elegantly dressed, as if for their Sabbath stroll in Rozavlea. I couldn't get near them, so I did all I could to attract their attention, jumping up and down, waving my aching arms, and frantically calling out their names. I was afraid that, being escorted by an SS man, they wouldn't dare respond." But the parade slowed, then halted. All five dwarfs turned their heads, and in their eyes Regina saw only the same puzzled look. "Who are you?" asked Elizabeth Ovitz suspiciously. "I'm Bellush from Rozavlea," Regina cried, calling out her Yiddish nickname. As one, the five women hid their faces in shock. Without her hair, her body clad in a thin, soaking-wet dress, her limbs covered with sores that crumbling paper bandages could not protect, their cousin was unrecognizable. The SS man stepped toward Regina; with the butt of his gun he struck her on the head for interrupting the march. In the excitement of her discovery, she didn't immediately feel the pain, but the blow was heavy enough to knock her backward. She stumbled, and then, as she leapt away, the soldier shouted, "Halt or I'll shoot!" He had mounted his gun; Regina froze. The five Lilliputians were saying something to the soldier. Regina could not hear their words, but he lowered his gun. Then they all withdrew, and continued on their way.

Regina stumbled over to the block elder and begged her to find out where the Lilliputians had been taken. For, incredibly, Regina explained, she had found her family. The block elder agreed, and took advantage of the relative freedom of movement that block elders enjoyed in the camp. She returned for Regina a half hour later. The Ovitzes were about to enter the washroom when the two women approached. The first words of the five sisters were, "Where's your mother?" And they all burst into tears when Regina replied, "You know pretty well where she is." When the Ovitzes met with Mengele two days later, Elizabeth told him that they had discovered a cousin of theirs in the work camp. "How many more relatives are you going to find here?" Mengele teased her. "There's just this one," Elizabeth quickly assured him. Because Mengele wanted to enlarge his research pool, he was ready to be persuaded, and Elizabeth was sent with her block elder to fetch the ailing cousin. For the next sixty years, come any sudden downpour of rain, Regina has shuddered with gratitude for that summer shower in Poland. "If it wasn't for the rain, I would not have woken up to see the Lilliputians, and with my open blisters wouldn't have lasted the week."

Now they were twenty-three. The sixteen women and little Shimshon had a room of their own at the women's camp. The six men shared three wooden bunks in the experimental block for Mengele's male twins and misfits—block 14 of the men's infirmary. Avram and Micki Ovitz needed help for everything. Mordechai Slomowitz's father dressed and undressed them, washed them, and helped them clean up at the toilet. Whenever they had no transportation, and had to walk the long way to the clinic, Mordechai helped his father carry them.

Efraim Reichenberg, who was sixteen when, mistaken for a twin, he was imprisoned with his brother in the experimental block, remembers Avram and Micki: "Alongside the surprise of encountering dwarfs in the real world and not just in fairy tales, came the astonishment of viewing them with a treasure, in the form of prayer shawls and phylacteries. I don't know how they managed to have them, but they were the only ones in the whole block, and we envied them for that. To be able to meditate in prayer and cry to God, retaining such a significant element of your identity, supplied some remedy to the soul in the hell of Auschwitz." The camp authorities strictly prohibited religious practice, and anyone caught engaging in Jewish ritual was severely beaten for subversion. So when either Micki or Avram

Ovitz prayed, the other dwarf stood guard so as to be able to warn his brother. For their part, the female dwarfs similarly placed themselves in peril each week when they plucked threads from their sheets and twisted them into a wick, which, with a small piece of wax, made a Sabbath candle.

The men's infirmary bordered the huge "Kanada" warehouse, which overflowed with personal belongings seized from the masses sent to the ovens. The prisoners who had been assigned to labor at the camp illegally traded in food supplies essential for survival, and the Ovitz men managed to find among them messengers to smuggle whatever scraps they could get their hands on to their sisters in the women's camp. Naturally everyone seized any opportunity to come by an extra morsel of food; the kitchen had a magnetic pull, and groveling before the staff had its rewards. But to the dwarfs, who stood knee-high to the kitchen workers, the boiling pots and sharp carving knives were menacing. On one occasion, the German kitchen supervisor beckoned Elizabeth Ovitz to follow her into her private cubicle. They walked slowly, in silence. When the door slammed behind them, the woman slumped onto her bed. As Elizabeth, fearful, stood and waited, she could only wonder what was in store for her. "Sing me something sad," said the German woman. Elizabeth breathed a sigh of relief, and her mind raced through her repertoire to find one of the songs that had always brought a standing ovation.

"O, yellow rose, if only you could speak, you'd know that life is not worth living." Elizabeth began tentatively, but as she surrendered to the plaintive melody of the song and as tears streamed down the cheeks of her solitary listener, her voice regained its old confidence. Wiping her eyes, the supervisor asked for an encore. "Wherever you are, forget me not. When you left me, you took my soul with you," sang Elizabeth, squeezing from every word the utmost of its melodrama. In the end, both women had been deeply moved by the heartbreaking, forlorn melodies; they took care to dry their faces before returning to the kitchen. Elizabeth was secretly rewarded with nigh-incredible bounty: a potato, a piece of bread, an onion, a bulb of garlic. She would repeat her private concerts, and her grateful audience of one, sobbing on her bed, would always pay handsomely—so much that Elizabeth could feed her brothers, too.

Regina Ovitz was promptly enrolled in the same cycle of medical examinations and subjected to the same painful tests as her Lilliput cousins. Her improved situation quickly revived her, however; her abscesses healed, her hair grew. Perla taught her how to manage sewing with an improvised needle and thread, and when Regina did some mending for the block elder, she was given a sugar cube. "One of the X-ray technicians was a Czech inmate. He ordered me to take my clothes off, and measured my bust, waist, thighs, the inside of my legs, each of my limbs. When it was over, he asked me if I was hungry. I confessed I was and he gave me a sandwich the likes of which I hadn't seen for ages—made with white bread, a piece of cheese inside, a pepper and a tomato, a heavenly flavor. Before leaving, he put four cigarettes in my pocket. In my village it was unheard-of for a Jewish woman to smoke, so after returning to the barrack, I traded them for a piece of pork fat. But since on religious grounds I couldn't use that either, I tried for another exchange. The only thing I managed to get was a small onion. Everyone told me I had been cheated."

By August, the mass extermination of Hungarian Jewry was

over. The camp authorities now turned their attention to the Gypsies. The Nazi regime had been undecided in its policies toward them: should the Gypsies be exterminated as an inferior race, or should they be locked away and sterilized as antisocial elements? By May 16, 1944, the die had been cast. The SS surrounded the Gypsy camp in Birkenau in an attempt to lead all six thousand inmates to the gas chambers. The troopers, however, met with fierce opposition—men and women armed with knives, iron pipes, and any metal object, dull or sharp, that they could find—and were forced to retreat. As a result, the camp administration changed its plan. Able-bodied Gypsy women were sent to slave labor camps, and Gypsy men from Germany were sent to the Wehrmacht to serve as live mine detectors.

Karl Stojka, a fourteen-year-old Gypsy, was transferred to Buchenwald. There he found himself among two hundred Gypsies designated unfit for work and therefore to be sent back to Auschwitz—and certain death. Stojka's brother and uncle appealed to the SS, falsely saying that Karl was not a skinny child, but a tough adult dwarf, fit for any work. In normal times, dwarfs were treated for the most part as outcasts, who were generally denied employment; in extreme times, though, deformity could prove to be a lifeline. So Karl Stojka, a normal-sized boy, exploited the stereotype of dwarfs famous for extraordinary strength. He was allowed to stay in Buchenwald. He survived the war and became a painter.

The liquidation of the Gypsy camp was scheduled for August 2. After the evening *Appell*, a general arrest was ordered for the whole of Birkenau. All the prisoners curled onto their bunks and listened to the roar of the trucks. They could hear the dogs barking savagely and could only guess which part of the camp was next on the SS list for extermination. Mengele had opposed the annihilation of the Gypsies from the outset, and had tried to sway his superiors against it—not out of sympathy for the "*Mischling* (half-breed) Aryans," or, as some have speculated, because of his own dark, "non-Aryan" appearance. Rather, he was simply reluctant to surrender a group of his specimens. From them he had drawn countless blood samples. He had plucked their multicolored eyes, and extracted their skeletons, which were carefully wrapped in large sacks of strong paper— all to be forwarded to the Kaiser Wilhelm Institute in Berlin and marked "Urgent! War Materials!" Mengele had always managed to find ways to move his Gypsies through one selection after another, and thus preserve them for the sake of his research. Annihilation of the Gypsies totally disregarded the needs of his research, and once it had been initiated, Mengele was not allowed to keep his subjects alive in another part of the camp. For the first time in his Auschwitz career, he faced the limits of his influence—and his human guinea pigs faced the loss of privilege and protection.

Throughout his year as chief physician for the Gypsy camp, Mengele had developed cordial relationships with its inmates. He had displayed fondness for the twin children, and often smiled when they called him Uncle Mengele. But when he received the final order to liquidate the remaining 2,897 Gypsies, most of them women and children, he carried it out obediently and diligently. Wholeheartedly embracing the manhunt for his former favorites, he now made use of their blind trust by enticing boys and girls out of their hiding places with the same candies he had offered them after painful experiments. As he led them to their deaths, he ignored their frantic pleas. Listening to the shrieks of the Gypsy women and children that sounded through the night, Dina Gottlieb moaned over the fate that awaited all her painting models. The Gypsy camp was nearly empty when Mengele discovered two more children hiding. He offered them a ride in his car, as had sometimes been his custom. Only this time the trip ended at the gas chambers.

Even at the scene of the gassing, though, Mengele lost no opportunity to advance his research. A large group of children had already stripped naked and was about to enter the gas chambers when Mengele suddenly pulled aside twelve sets of his twins. The children gathered eagerly around him, for they believed he had come to their rescue. With his special blue chalk, he drew the capital letters ZS on their bare chests. Their faulty German led them to assume they were being singled out as *Zwillings*—twins (the proper German plural is *Zwillinge*)—but they were actually being marked for dissection—*Zur Sektion*. They were sent back to the hall, to the gas chambers. The doors slammed shut. As the granules of Zyklon B were released, Mengele turned to the *Sonderkommando* and ordered them to take great care not to burn the ones he had marked with blue letters, but to bring them, instead, straight to the pathology laboratory in the same building.

In this collection of bodies, there were twins of all ages, ranging from newborn infants to sixteen-year-olds, remembered inmate-pathologist Dr. Miklos Nyiszli. "For the moment the twelve pairs of corpses were stretched out on the concrete floor of the 'morgue.' Bodies of black-haired, dark-skinned children. The job of classifying them by pairs was a tiring one. I was careful not to mix them up, for I knew that if I should render these rare and precious specimens unusable for his research, Dr. Mengele would make me pay for it with my life." Nyiszli conducted his pathological studies for several days running, with the greatest possible care. He meticulously prepared every dissection report, which was to stand as the concluding document in each child's personal file. One long afternoon, when he and Mengele became immersed in discussion over a group of unresolved pathological questions, Nyiszli did not hesitate to contradict Mengele—"as if this was a medical conference of which I was a full-fledged member." It appeared that Mengele was willing to tolerate the inmate's firm assertions to the contrary: when it was time to leave, he gave Nyiszli a cigarette.

A week later, Irene Mengele decided to pay her husband a visit. He had not been home for many months—had not even found time to visit after the birth of his first son, Rolf, in March 1944. Leaving the baby with Mengele's parents, Irene took the train to Auschwitz, for what was to be a double celebration: her twenty-seventh birthday and their fifth wedding anniversary. In her diaries, which were never published but were made available to biographers Gerald Posner and John Ware, she described happy days in the SS barracks. They swam together in the nearby Sola River. They picked blackberries, from which she made jam in his kitchenette. Their delight in their "second honeymoon" was further enhanced by a most favorable official report on Mengele by his garrison commander, SS *Standortzarzt* Dr. Eduard Wirths: "During his employment as camp physician at the Auschwitz concentration camp, he has put his knowledge to practical and theoretical use, while fighting serious epidemics. With prudence, perseverance, and energy, he has carried out all tasks given him, often under very difficult conditions, to the complete satisfaction of his superiors, and has shown himself able to cope with every situation. Furthermore, as an anthropologist he has most zealously used his little off-time duty to educate himself further; utilizing the scientific material at his disposal due to his official position, he has made a valuable contribution in his work to the anthropological science." In addition, Wirths praised Mengele for his "tact and reserve," while also noting his "popularity" among his subordinates and the "respect" they accorded him. Following the report, Mengele was awarded the War Cross of Merit, Second Class with Swords, and after the annihilation of the Gypsy camp, he was appointed head physician of the Auschwitz-Birkenau camp. He moved his office to the men's infirmary, where he would not merely continue to orchestrate the myriad medical tests on his 350 Jewish victims, 250 of them twins and dwarfs—but would step them up.

The Ovitzes were never told which tests were going to be performed on them on any particular day, but they learned to guess quite accurately by what route the ambulance would take. They would find themselves lying naked and face-down on the examination tables, and the bustle of medical activity around them only intensified their anxiety, as they wondered where precisely their bodies would be pierced or jabbed or poked, and to what violent and devastating effect. To be forcibly subjected to long series of medical tests and trials that one knew were designed to bring about some remedy would be difficult enough, but the Ovitzes felt they were consistently being violated for apparently needless and endless samplings, puncturings, and probings. They saw their medical files grow steadily thicker, document by document, yet they could see no medically constructive or beneficial purpose whatsoever behind it all. And it seemed that the tests would never end. Still, after their separation, the clinic afforded the family's men and women their only opportunity to meet. The pain and apprehension caused by the medical tests were thus tempered by the hope of seeing their kin from the other camp. On those rare occasions when they did, the guard would turn away and allow them to exchange news, gossip, or a word of comfort.

Solomon Malik was thirteen and a half when he arrived in Birkenau with his parents and five siblings. His father and two of the children were immediately gassed; but Solomon had a twin sister as well as two younger, three-year-old twin brothers, and Mengele's passion spared them and their mother. They had lived in Moisei, a village next to Rozavlea, so Solomon had occasionally snuck into the Ovitzes' performances. Now he was in a barrack with them, and he was often taken to the clinic with them. As their numbers were called, they would silently mount the ambulance that would drive them to the medical block: "We waited outside the door like strangers, and although we went through the same tests, we didn't share or compare our experiences when we returned to the barrack. In Auschwitz, no one moaned about his hardships, as we were all suffering to the same degree. Each minded his own business. You were only interested in your bunk-neighbor if he had a slice of bread you could steal from him. I felt like a slaughtered rooster that keeps on running for a few seconds, oblivious of his slit throat, until he drops dead. We knew we would all end up in the chimney, so there was no point in making friends for the short time we still had."

The last two weeks of August were particularly terrible. The surviving medical records at the Auschwitz State Museum show that starting in the middle of the month, the Lilliput group had to endure an increasing number of tests. On August 16, Simon Slomowitz and his three sons were taken to the clinic with Avram and Micki Ovitz. Blood was drawn for a variety of tests, including syphilis. Two days later, the five dwarf sisters underwent the same tests. On August 21, eight-year-old Batia Ovitz was driven alone to the X-ray lab in Auschwitz. The next day, syphilis tests were administered on two Slomowitz girls, their mother, and Leah and Dora—all of them of normal height. Two days later, it was baby Shimshon's turn, and Batia's, as well as Elizabeth's and Sarah's. On August 29, four of the female dwarfs—Perla was excluded—were summoned again. The Ovitzes feared they were entering a new, far more brutal and agonizing phase in the research. Or worse, that Mengele was terminating his project, and that they too would soon see the inside of the gas chambers.

One day, at the end of August, Mengele brought Dina Gottlieb a huge roll of paper. It was so long that she could not spread it open inside the clinic. She took it outside and stretched it out on the ground; she held the corners down with stones. Then, crawling along it, she enlarged various charts, and mapped out an extremely complex family tree. She filled the square frames with names, years, and genders, as well as symbols—some large, some small—next to each name. She had no idea what it was all about, but Mengele seemed to her to be very tense those days.

ELEVEN

Auschwitz-Birkenau, September 1944

It was almost twilight when Mengele entered the Lilliputs' room at the women's camp. He was holding a small parcel under his arm. "Good evening, *Herr Hauptsturmführer.*" The Lilliputs jumped to their feet at the unexpected visit. He signaled them to sit down, and rested his boot on a chair. Then, clasping his waist, he announced that tomorrow he would be taking them on a special journey to a beautiful place they had never seen. They had to get ready, he said.

The Lilliputs' faces went pale. Mengele smiled, in an attempt, it seemed, to put them at ease. He said that they were to wear their finest clothes and that their hair should be perfectly coiffed and their faces made up—for they were going to be appearing onstage in front of some very important people. Before he left, he laid the parcel on the low wooden table. For a long time, the Ovitz sisters stared at it. Somehow, they were too terrified to move to the table and touch it. Finally, warily, they unwrapped it, and discovered to their delight a face-powder compact, crimson rouge, and brilliant turquoise and green eye shadow.

Shiny red lipstick was tied together with a matching jar of nail varnish. And there was an extra treat—a bottle of eau de cologne.

Thrilled with Mengele's gift, the sisters fiddled with the makeup. They sniffed the scent and rubbed it joyfully on their skin. They already had their own mirror and a small makeup kit—unheard-of in Auschwitz—but the items in Mengele's parcel, they had to admit, were of much higher quality than their own. They went through their few dresses. Each sister selected her most presentable one; then they tried to match each other's colors. Sitting on the low bunk, they reinforced the seams, and with the flats of their hands, smoothed away the wrinkles in the fabric. As they discussed what to sing the next day, they wondered how they would manage with solely feminine voices, without their two brothers. In the past, they had sometimes split the troupe and performed in duos or trios, so they decided to trust their fifteen years of artistic experience and just improvise. They did not sleep a wink that night. They lay awake hoping that tomorrow's performance would transform their destiny.

At dawn Friday, September 1, 1944, Sarah and Leah rushed out to get a bucket of water so they could help their sisters wash up. The Lilliputs dressed each other and combed each other's thick, black hair. In turns, they held up the small mirror for one or another to powder her face. To their lips, eyes, and cheeks they applied a heavy, theatrical layer of makeup. Their glamour restored, they felt jubilant.

Mengele had ordered that the Lilliput Troupe's five female members be accompanied by another contingent, which included their two normal-size sisters, Sarah and Leah; baby Shimshon; sister-in-law Dora and her daughter Batia; and Chaya

Slomowitz along with her three daughters. Regina Ovitz, Bassie Fischman, and her mother, Gitel-Leah, were the only three who had been excluded, and they could not help but wonder why, and what this separation would mean. With a mixture of envy and worry, they watched the preparations. Soon, the group's transportation arrived. A truck stopped near their barrack, and Perla was struck silent with joy: her brothers, dressed in their best clothes, were sitting inside, as were Slomowitz and his sons. Indifferent to the convoy's exultation, the prisoners in the yard simply nodded at the spectacle. In the code of Auschwitz-Birkenau, any special gesture—the promise of a journey, a hearty meal—was a deadly omen.

The truck passed through Birkenau's gate, but instead of driving to the main gate of Auschwitz, it entered a nearby camp they had always bypassed before. It was the SS residential camp and administrative center. Well-guarded and off limits, here there were no shabby barracks; no hairless, emaciated inmates who could barely drag themselves around. Instead, spotless brick buildings faced lush green lawns brightened by colorful beds of flowers. The group of twenty Jewish women and men was escorted to a corner in the shadow of a large, new building. Cars stopped at the entrance and unloaded scores of uniformed SS officers.

The Lilliput group was astounded when china plates and silver cutlery were laid out on the lawn in front of them. For the first time since they had left home five months previously, they were having a proper meal. They balanced their plates, heaped with food, on their laps, and strove not to spill anything on their clothes. Delight and indignation accompanied every morsel. The officers entering the building glanced incredulously at the dwarfs' picnic and chuckled.

After a while a sergeant came to fetch them. They walked in a column; the seven Lilliputs in front, then their family; the Slomowitzes brought up the rear. *We tiptoed into the building, hearing muffled sounds amplified by loudspeakers. It sounded like a speech or something. We were heading backstage, when suddenly two men carrying a stretcher with a body shrouded in black passed us by. We were numb. Where was Dr. Mengele? We hadn't seen him all day. Where had he brought us? Was this going to be our end, too?* Nevertheless, eager to be back in the limelight, they managed to stifle their apprehension. They did wonder, though, why their tall sisters, the Slomowitzes, and the normal-size children, none of whom had any theatrical experience, were being led to the stage with them.

"Off you go," the sergeant whispered. Marching forward in a long line, they mounted the stage. To their relief they saw Mengele at the front of the stage. A solemn master of ceremonies, he waited for them to take their places in a line that stretched from one end of the stage to the other. The auditorium was packed; they had never seen so many medals and decorations. There was a murmur in the hall. The audience stared at the assortment of men, women, and children. The Lilliputs smiled in confusion, for they did not know how to begin. They looked to Mengele for a cue.

He turned to them and snapped, "Undress!"

Aghast, their hands trembling, they fumbled with their buttons. The Lilliputs tried to shrink into themselves, and wished they could disappear altogether. They bent their shoulders forward, they attempted to cover their genitals with their hands. "Straighten up!" barked Mengele. Standing to attention like soldiers on parade, they fixed their eyes at imaginary points at the end of the hall to avoid seeing the naked sibling or relative next to them.

It was not the first time Mengele, like some freak-show impresario, had exhibited the Lilliputs and their group. "This zeal had earned him great praise," recalls Ella Lingens-Reiner. But in the past the show had always taken place in the privacy of their room or in his clinic. *We always had to be prepared for Dr. Mengele and wear makeup, since he had told us, "You're something special, not like the rest of them, and I want my fellow officers and professors to see you." He would bring them to our room, and we would stand to attention until he allowed us to sit down. He used to boast to his visitors, "I have a whole family, they are like dolls, only real." Sometimes we remained dressed, sometimes we were naked. The guests would touch our bodies and measure us and repeatedly inquire about our parents. Once Dr. Mengele asked us to sing—we sang something in German, and they all clapped their hands. Dr. Mengele was so pleased that he then shook hands with each of us.*

Since 1938, Mengele had been engaged in a race against Dr. Hans Grebe. Three years Mengele's junior, Grebe was also an assistant to Professor von Verschuer and specialized in dwarfism. He had enlisted in the SS before Mengele, at the very outbreak of the war. As the war progressed, the rivalry between the two men became increasingly more heated. By 1944, Grebe had already published two papers on dwarfism, in part because he was able to spend his time doing research in Berlin; he was about to become the youngest professor in Germany. In Auschwitz-Birkenau, Mengele had essentially established his own research institute, a modest rival to the Kaiser Wilhelm Institute. To pursue his project, Mengele had recruited several distinguished inmate-doctors and put them to work in his well-equipped laboratories. Occasionally Mengele also organized colloquiums at his Birkenau facilities and chaired discussions of case studies.

But September 1, 1944, was a very special occasion: it was

the inauguration of the new Lazarett in Birkenau's SS camp. Many high-ranking guests from Berlin were in attendance, and Mengele was the main speaker. After Mengele's years in uniform, away from the podium, this was his chance to retrieve his place in the academic limelight. His wife, Irene, sitting proudly in the audience, noted the title of his lecture in her diary: "Examples of the Work in Anthropological and Hereditary Biology in the Concentration Camp." Mengele was, in fact, going public with his work for the first time. Until then, afraid of competition and sabotage, he had been very secretive. His close assistant, the prisoner-anthropologist Dr. Martina Puzyna, testified before the Frankfurt general prosecutor that, even to her, he did not reveal "what he was aiming for in the final analysis and evaluation of the measurements we conducted for him." Mengele kept everything locked in his cabinets. Dr. Lingens-Reiner would not forget her surprise when one day he proudly invited her to glance at some of his files. She leafed through the papers, which were full of charts and measurements of the heads and bodies of twins and dwarfs. "Isn't it interesting? What a pity all this will fall into the hands of the Bolsheviks." Lingens-Reiner would also continue to be struck by this startling moment of indiscretion on Mengele's part.

In the SS Lazarett, Mengele stepped behind the trembling bodies in his human display and stood near the large map of the dwarfs' family tree that Dina Gottlieb had drawn. *Dr. Mengele started lecturing, and I couldn't stop thinking about the long billiard cane he was holding. He was very knowledgeable about our history, including our father's two wives. Whenever he mentioned the name of one of us, he pointed at the map and then touched us with his cane. "This is Rozika, daughter of the first wife; this is her sister; this is Avram, the first son of the second wife; these are his wife and daughter, who are normal-sized." He then moved to the podium, and from his notes described the tests he did on each of us. From time to time he turned to us and touched various of our body organs with his billiard cane. It lasted for ages—we nearly dropped from fatigue. It was hot and we were dripping sweat and shame, but no one offered us a glass of water.*

Since the start of the twentieth century, genetics had been at the forefront of science. Its value for many scientists in the field was the potential it might hold for the promulgation of positive traits and the eradication of negative ones. Some geneticists had tried to develop blood tests by which they could establish the physiological basis for dwarfism. It was also popularly theorized that the condition might be rooted in hormonal deficiencies. Thus, the thyroid gland's functions and stunted growth came under close scrutiny, particularly as some types of dwarfism showed a correlation between the two. Other speculation centered on accidents at birth and lack of vitamins. For their part, the leading German geneticists constructed complex family trees as a means of tracing the progress of the malformation. While still a university student, Mengele had read *Human Heredity,* in which the renowned German scientists Baur, Fischer, and Lenz described and classified various kinds of restricted growth. In his characterization of Ovitz dwarfism, Mengele embraced the authors' term "achondroplasia" for a condition in which "the limbs are dwarfed, whereas the head and the trunk are of approximately normal size."

Recessive inheritance of dwarfism is much more common than dominant inheritance, and the Ovitz family offered an excellent example in which a negative trait was inherited through a dominant gene, not in one instance but in seven, and in seven instances out of ten—a rarity indeed. According to inmate-pathologist Nyiszli, however, Mengele was aiming not only "to discover the biological and pathological causes of the birth of dwarfs and giants" but also to demonstrate that "in the course of its long history, the Jewish race had degenerated into a people of dwarfs and cripples."

Within many cultures and many ideologies, the term "dwarf" has in fact had a pejorative or even degrading connotation. One image of Jews particularly favored by Nazi propaganda was of a bald, fat, hunchbacked dwarf. A caricature published on the front page of *Der Stürmer* in July 1939, for example, shows such a dwarf Jew struggling with a blonde, athletic, half-naked Aryan. The Aryan is drawing a sword, and the caption reads: "He who subordinates himself to the Jews is only a dwarf, never a hero." But despite his deeply held convictions concerning the Jews' racial degeneracy, after three and a half months with the Lilliputs, Mengele actually had very few findings to report.

He knew that the greatest impact he could make upon his peers and his audience that September day was simply the sheer presence of the Ovitz dwarfs onstage. He bombarded his audience with figures and details about the complex family, including the eight Slomowitzes—who of course were no kin to the Ovitzes.

Fifty years later, following Perla Ovitz's recollection that an officer in the front row was filming the proceedings with his movie camera, Hannelore Witkofski, a historian and advocate in Germany for the rights of short people, and Shahar Rosen, an Israeli film director, searched through various archives in Germany and Poland, but could not find the film. *It annoys me to this day that our naked humiliation was preserved for all to see. Maybe Dr. Mengele took the film with him when he fled to South*

America and it's hidden somewhere. Maybe his wife or son has it. I won't feel easy about this until it's found and destroyed. The search has been documented in a film titled *Liebe Perla.*

Colleagues, prisoner-doctors, and historians have expressed varying opinions of Mengele's professional demeanor and scientific ability. "He was the most pleasant companion. I have only the best to say of him," stated SS Dr. Hans Münch, Mengele's colleague at the Waffen-SS's Institute of Hygiene in Auschwitz. Münch also described both Mengele's elegance and his intelligence as outstanding in the "intellectual desert" that was Auschwitz. On the other hand, some of the inmate-doctors have characterized Mengele in less flattering terms, pointing to his plodding diligence, his pedantry, and his fanatical devotion to his concept of genetics. According to anthropologist Martina Puzyna, "It cannot be said that research on twins was a Nazi idea alone. It has always played an important role in anthropology." Mengele's research on heredity in twins and dwarfs, then, was in line with accepted anthropological methods; but what gave him a singular scientific advantage in the field, again in Puzyna's view, was the unlimited human pool at his disposal in Auschwitz. Thus he could conduct his research "on a big scale, to gain results by statistical methods, with acceptable values," Puzyna says. Although "Mengele was clearly capable of killing people to obtain certain research results," he was "at times genuinely interested in serious, factual scientific work. Having myself worked as a scientific assistant, I deemed him capable of doing serious work." Others who worked with Mengele have been far less generous in their assessment: "How we hated this charlatan! He profaned the very word 'science'!" writes Olga Lengyel, who was part of Mengele's medical team. "His experiments lacked scientific value—they were no more than foolish playing." And while pathologist Miklos Nyiszli concurs with Puzyna that medical research was "the most important thing on Mengele's agenda," he also dismisses that research as "nothing more than a pseudoscience. Just as false was his theory regarding the degeneracy of dwarfs and cripples, sent to the butchers in order to demonstrate the inferiority of the Jewish race." Finally, with the sobriety that comes from historical distance, Robert Lifton observes in *The Nazi Doctors* that "Mengele's method was a product of his scientific training and early experience, his Nazi ideology and the peculiarities of the Auschwitz settings."

When Mengele finished his lecture, the audience rose to applaud, and some SS officers left for lunch—but many others darted forward onto the stage. The swarm of uniformed men soon engulfed the Lilliput group. The Ovitzes and the Slomowitzes stood there motionless, naked, waiting for permission to dress. Shimshon Ovitz, only eighteen months old at the time, has no memory of the Lilliputs' humiliation, but he notes that throughout the years his aunts and uncles would constantly allude to or recall "the performance." "The SS officers wanted to see us at close range. They marveled at the doll-like figures and peppered us with invasive questions while staring at the Lilliputs dressing. One of them came close to my mother—she was holding me in her arms—and touched her naked breast. I flung out my hand, so I'm told, and pulled at his swastika with all my might. It fell to the floor, and my mother panicked and started crying, sure he would draw his pistol and shoot us on the spot.

She then stooped to pick up the swastika, but the officer calmed her down, *"Keine Angst, keine Angst"*—never mind, he's just a baby, he doesn't know what he's doing. He picked it up himself, but we only relaxed when he left the room."

Once Mengele's presentation was over, the Lilliput group was actually offered refreshments, but they were too crushed to touch a thing. The truck took them back to the camp, and the men and women in the families were again separated. The women and girls were greeted in their barrack with amazement, as if they had returned from the dead. Back in the SS compound, Mengele could look forward to another week of vacation before the cheerful, easy-going Irene had to return home. On the eve of her departure, however, she contracted diphtheria. She quickly developed an inflamed heart muscle, and had to be hospitalized because of a raging high fever. Her devoted husband visited her three times a day.

In truth, the small empire Mengele was running at Auschwitz was a thorn in the professional side of his fellow SS doctors. They envied his stardom; they resented his theft of the show at the Lazarett inauguration event; they coveted the acclaim and the medal he had won for his research. Mengele had also garnered a recommendation for promotion outside Auschwitz. Some of his SS colleagues tried to emulate him by concocting research topics and employing inmate-doctors to labor on their behalf. Others, like SS Dr. Heinz Thilo, actually tried to sabotage Mengele's research. Thilo—who owes part of his notoriety to his epithet for Auschwitz: "Anus Mundi"—was known to whistle opera arias while performing his selections, just like Mengele. Thilo had been in the camp longer than Mengele, and they were the same age, yet already Mengele was a *Hauptsturmführer*, while Thilo was only an *Obersturmführer*. Thilo was waiting for his moment. It soon came his way.

To take some joy in the last days of summer, the men organized a game of soccer in their camp one afternoon. Judah and Joseph Slomowitz were among the players, all the rest of whom were twin boys. Their father and brother encouraged them from the touchline, while Avram and Micki Ovitz watched the game from their small stools. The crowd was cheering as the two teams kicked the ball across the ground, when suddenly the tall frame of Dr. Thilo shadowed the yard. "Why are you all idling about?" he demanded, and called for an immediate *Appell*. The men and boys stood in line. Then they had to march in front of Thilo.

"Your number!" he barked at those he chose, and the Kapo wrote it down. A curfew was set, the barrack was sealed, and the doors were boarded. As Mordechai Slomowitz recalls things, "Dr. Thilo selected dozens of twin children, as well as Avram and Micki Ovitz and my two young brothers, who were eleven and thirteen. They were all put aside in the barrack. The double portion of food brought in that evening was a sign that they were doomed. The Nazis wanted you to gain weight so you could burn more quickly. My father and I decided that when the truck to the crematorium arrived, we would mount it as well. The SS wouldn't mind killing another two." "Let's pray," said Avram Ovitz, and they all wept and supplicated.

Zvi Spiegel was a twenty-nine-year-old twin whom Mengele had placed in charge of the twin children; thus, he became known as the *Zwillingsvater* of Auschwitz: "Mengele warned me frequently that if anything happened to the twins, I would be hanged. Somehow I managed to open the bolted door of the barrack. I've no idea how I dared, but I ran toward Mengele's office. It was dangerous, because the SS on the watchtowers shot anyone who ran in the camp, but I knew time was of the essence. The SS guards in Mengele's clinic knew me. I told them, 'I need to speak to Dr. Mengele!' Imagine a Jew wanting to speak to Mengele. This was a bit like saying you wanted to speak with God. Only it was easier to have a hearing with God. To this day I don't know why they didn't shoot me for making the request." The guard picked up the phone and dialed. "The *Zwillingsvater* is here, he says Dr. Thilo was in the infirmary this afternoon and selected some of your twins and dwarfs!" If Thilo had counted on Frau Mengele's illness to provide him the opportunity to deplete his rival's human collection, he had got it wrong. Mengele's reaction was swift. Not only did he cancel Thilo's selection, but he also dispatched one of his subordinates to the camp to ensure that no harm befell his research subjects.

Irene Mengele had suffered further complications from the diphtheria, and she badly needed her husband's attention, but he nonetheless continued to fulfill all his duties, including his selections on the ramp. On September 29, he welcomed to Birkenau 2,499 Jews from the Theresienstadt ghetto. He sent 1,900 of them to their deaths. The rest he admitted to the camp. Among them were three pairs of teenage twin boys.

September, season of the Jewish High Holidays, was favored by the Nazis for especially extensive killings. In the arrest warrant and indictment issued in Frankfurt-on-Main in January 1981 by the Twenty-second Criminal Division of the Frankfurt *Landgericht*, Mengele was charged in absentia with having sent 328 children to the gas chambers on Rosh Hashanah, the Jewish New Year festival, in 1944. In addition, the charge read, during the fast of Yom Kippur a week later, "He hung a batten between the goalposts of a football pitch" and "approximately 1,000 children under the required height" were also sent to their deaths.

TWELVE

Auschwitz-Birkenau, October 1944

For some time now, the Lilliput Troupe had been living not only in a house of horror, but also in an environment appallingly unsuited to their size where the simplest object could present a monstrous obstacle. Even short distances seemed vast and arduous to their undersized, bowed legs and tired feet. Their situation was made slightly more bearable by Mengele; he had small wooden stools built for them in the camp carpentry shop, which was located on the first floor of crematorium II. Wherever they went, the dwarfs carried their stools like artificial limbs, so they could rest in the course of a journey that was bound to quickly exhaust them. The Lilliputs had always disliked being lifted like babies, partly out of fear that they'd be dropped, or placed in chairs too high for them to get out of. The stools thus became their makeshift ladders to independence.

When the weather was nice and they were not in the medical clinics, the Ovitz ladies liked to set up their stools in the square in front of their barrack and watch the world go by, just as they had done in Rozavlea. Remarkably, in spite of the horrific events transpiring daily in the camp—or maybe because of them—the magnetic Lilliput Troupe continued to attract public attention. The camp was always abuzz with rumors; tales of dwarfs basking in the sun or strolling about on parade soon spread. Even inmates from distant barracks would find reasons to pass by and gaze. Some of the Lilliputs' former fans were surprised to discover them behind barbed wire, as they had not known the dwarfs were Jewish. Others were amazed and delighted that these star performers had not been changed drastically by the camp. For there they were, still in all their finery—as if the world had not really been turned upside down.

Auschwitz was a Babel of tongues, from Italian and French to Greek and Polish. Having lost their families, inmates naturally gravitated first to any fellow townspeople who may have been spared, and then to anyone who shared their nationality or their language. So it was that even strangers from Maramures County came to chat with the Lilliputs—to inquire who had died, who had survived. Ibby Mann, whose theater-loving father had invited the Lilliput Troupe to dinner in his home after one of their performances in the happy days before the deportations, recalls: "Mother knew they were expert dressmakers, and at the end of the evening she presented them with a colorful fabric to make outfits for their show. Only my twin sister Sarah and I had survived the selection, so when I heard that the Lilliputs were in the camp I rushed over to see them. They not only remembered their visit but had been looking for us in the camp. One of them went back into their barrack, returning with a dress made from the fabric Mother had furnished. I caressed the doll-sized dress and cried. A matching shawl accompanied the dress and they let me have it—the only memento I had left from my mummy."

The Lilliputs enjoyed the other inmates' pilgrimages to their square in the camp. They had always loved being the center of attention, and they welcomed this relief from the bleak anonymity of Auschwitz. They also appreciated their relative luck, so they were always cheerful and patient with their less fortunate visitors. The Lilliputs also made an impression on Auschwitz inmates who had previously never heard of them. When testifying about Mengele's atrocities before the public prosecutor in Frankfurt twenty-five years later, a number of survivors recalled seeing dwarfs in the camp. Nurse Regina Teresa Krzyzanowska remembered the "Lilliputians who were in block 23 and came to the camp from Hungary. They were whole families. They were circus artists, and tried to stage a few shows." And in her memoir *Playing for Time*, Fania Fenelon, a singer in the Auschwitz women's orchestra, speaks of "[dwarfs] jumping, doing acrobatics, shrieking at the top of their voices; there was a banal scene of clowns, their chubby little hands slapping ridiculously: what a pathetic sight." The recurrent mistaken notion that the Ovitzes were circus performers may have arisen from the tradition that stereotypes dwarf artists as clowns and jesters. The Lilliput Troupe's style in performance was, by necessity as well as choice, far removed from clowning—their bowed legs and short, weak arms prevented them from doing any acrobatics whatsoever.

With their brightly colored dresses, painted faces, and coiffured hair, the dwarfs were a surreal, mirage-like presence in Auschwitz. Witness Elzbieth Piekut, for instance, recalls "seeing a sort of a Lilliputian family camp through the barbed wire, the men strolling about in tall hats and frock coats, the women in crinoline dresses." And Fania Fenelon similarly remembers Lilliput men in frock coats and bow ties and women in gala dresses made from magnificent fabrics. "They were all sinking under the burden of jewelry, necklaces hanging down to their bellies, double bracelets on their wrists, their earrings lightly touching their shoulders, framing their painted faces, diamonds shining in their well-coiffured hair. The genuine mixing with the fake, immense wealth, incredible!"

Children, too, were attracted to the Lilliputs' barrack in the camp. Most of them had grown up with fairy tales about dwarfs, and, starved for amusement in Auschwitz, they frequently visited the Lilliputs in their yard. Leah Nishri notes that "someone who was not imprisoned in Auschwitz-Birkenau will find it impossible to understand what it was like seeing dwarfs there. The selection on the ramp was so severe that only the strongest and fittest could pass it, and even then many would not survive the harsh conditions. As an orphaned, desolate girl of fourteen and a half, I gained heart from these small handicapped people surviving intact against all the odds." Nishri recalls simply savoring the presence of the dwarfs for a few hours. She also remembers her astonishment when a tall, robust woman from the group grasped her daughter's hand and said, "Let's go meet Daddy." It was Dora Ovitz with her eight-year-old Batia.

In Nishri's memory, those totally ordinary words still hit her like lightning. As if hypnotized, she followed Dora and Batia to the electrified barbed wire fence, where Avram Ovitz sat on the other side, along with Mordechai Slomowitz, who carried the stool for him. In her mind's eye, Nishri can still see Avram sitting there and Dora pointing for her daughter, saying, "Look, here's Daddy." Nishri recalls: "I watched the reunion from a distance with aching, not believing this glimpse of normality. There were no families in the camp, and if a woman had a young child, both would be automatically sentenced to death. In my curiosity, I followed them back to their barrack, where they had a room for themselves, private and very spacious. Another dwarf lady appeared—decades later I recognized her on TV, and learned that her name was Perla Ovitz. She was wearing a reddish-brown leather coat, padded with fur. A tall woman was walking behind her, carrying a bucket full of potatoes. One potato was an unattainable dream to us, but a full bucket? In the camp I had never seen such a quantity. Perla was walking proudly, like an elegant lady returning with her servant from shopping. No other Jew in the camp walked with so much self-assurance. It seemed these people could get whatever they wished."

Mengele's painter, Dina Gottlieb, gained a similar impression: "They did not look trapped like we did. They seemed hopeful and cheerful and unlike the rest of us, who were frightened and pessimistic. It seemed they did not believe they'd be killed. They had a very good life before the war as VIPs, and continued to see themselves as special and privileged." Sara Nomberg-Przytyk, who lived in the same barrack as the dwarfs, was less than admiring. In her memoir *Auschwitz: True Tales from a Grotesque Land*, she derides them for their endless prattle about Mengele: " 'How beautiful he is, how kind,' they repeated it every minute. 'How fortunate that he became our protector. How good of him to ask if we have everything.' They almost melted in adoration. They were accustomed to exposing themselves in public [sic], and this was like another show for them." One afternoon, continues Nomberg-Przytyk, Mengele entered the barrack, and "we all stood at attention, including the midgets. Next to them, we looked like giants. He looked at them very closely. Then one of them stepped out of the row and fell at his boots. She was just about as tall as his boots. She hugged it [sic] with feeling and started to kiss it. 'You are so kind, so gorgeous. God should reward you,' she whispered, enraptured. He did not move for a minute, then he simply shook her off his boots. She fell. She lay there, tiny, spread out on the floor."

Perla Ovitz firmly denies that such an incident ever occurred. *Dr. Mengele never yelled or swore at us, and, God forbid, never hit us. We all knew he was ruthless and capable of the worst forms of sadistic behavior—that when he was angry he would become hysterical and literally shake from rage. But even if he were in a bad mood to begin with, the moment he stepped into our room he would immediately calm down, becoming a well-behaved boy. When he was in a good mood people would say, "He probably visited the little ones."* And prisoner-doctor Katarzyna Laniewska seemed to confirm this: "Mengele would often come to barrack 23 where the dwarfs were living, to chat with them and even crack jokes."

Sara Nomberg-Przytyk's view of the Ovitzes—their boot-high size and their theatrical sycophantic gestures—may have been distorted by both her envy and her perspective. From her own towering angle, she might easily have perceived every curtsy and nod of the dwarfs as acts of servility—even as boot-licking. Of course, there may have been other cause for envy besides the Ovitzes' being the treasured subjects of Mengele's research. The Ovitzes in fact had many things going for them. For one, unlike most inmates, the Ovitzes were fluent in German. For another, they had remained intact as a family. For a third, as a group, the Lilliputs had managed to maintain some of the glamour attached to their showbiz identity. Wearing their artistic persona enabled the Lilliputs to be detached from the daily misery of the camp, and to put up an appearance. Unlike the other inmates, who had been dehumanized by shaven heads and wasted bodies and ragged clothes, the dwarfs were able to keep up their personal appearances. In their pretty faces and perfumed finery lay much of their appeal for Mengele. He himself was immaculately groomed. His hands were well manicured; his riding crop was polished; his uniform perfectly fit his body, upright and militarily borne; his neatly pressed trousers were inserted into glistening black boots. Mengele found his exquisite dwarfs, with their cheerful natures and theatrical manners, unusually pleasant company. While survivors tend to paint the exceptional relationship between the dwarfs and Mengele in vivid colors, the dwarfs' own testimonies are perhaps more telling—and certainly more ambiguous. *Dr. Mengele was like a movie star, only more good-looking—he could have got prizes for his good looks. Anyone could easily fall in love with him. Nobody who saw him could imagine that behind his beautiful face a beast was hiding. He was a beautiful beast. Among ourselves we always asked how a man like that could become a Nazi.*

In return, Mengele praised the Lilliputs for their appearance. Perla recalls the sorts of compliments he would offer Frieda— the prettiest of them all—and her replies: "How beautiful you look today!" Mengele would say.

"I knew that *Herr Hauptsturmführer* was coming, so I took great care to make myself up in his honor."

"If it was indeed for me, do continue to do so. But tell me, before arriving in Birkenau, did you also put on makeup every day?"

"Of course I did, I'm an actress!"

If Dr. Mengele was not satisfied with Frieda's makeup, he would inquire, "Are you in a bad mood today? Why didn't you apply your beautiful red lipstick?" Once he said to my sister Elizabeth, "You've lost weight. That's not good!" When I heard this I panicked and started to cry, knowing that when he said "it's not good," it had only one meaning: "To the ovens!" "Why are you crying?" he asked me. I said, "Because Herr Hauptsturmführer *said 'it's not good.' " Dr. Mengele lifted his hand. "Don't worry."* Despite the apparently intimate nature of Mengele's conversation with the Lilliputs, they always took care to address him by his full SS rank and medical title, then to grace it all with "Your Excellency." *We approached him the way one addresses a king, because he was king of Birkenau.*

While the main purpose of Auschwitz-Birkenau was to erad-icate its inmates' identity, some professions—mainly the musical and medical professions—did afford their practitioners better survival prospects. Doctors were employed in the camp clinic or the laboratories; musicians played in one of the three camp orchestras—all of them applauded by Mengele, the music lover who whistled arias from Verdi and Wagner as he sent Jews to the ovens. For the Lilliputs, he composed a special couplet that he often sang to them:

> *Auf den sieben Bergen*
> *Habe ich sieben Zwergen.*
> *Over seven hills*
> *I have seven dwarfs.*

In the world of fairy tales, dwarfs always lived behind *sieben Bergen*—seven mountains—but Mengele was also punning here on the proper noun Siebenbürgen, the German name for Tran-sylvania, the region the Ovitzes came from. Because the dwarfs tried hard to please him, Mengele composed another couplet for them:

> *Die ungarischen jüdischen Zwerge*
> *geschützte Häftlinge.*

The Hungarian Jewish dwarfs
Are excellent prisoners.

When Mengele asked them to sing for him, they were reluctant, as they were afraid of what the other inmates might think. "We don't have our full orchestra with us," they protested. "If I can sing a cappella, so can you," Mengele answered, and to prove it he hummed a line from a Hungarian Gypsy song that had been making the rounds of the restaurants: "There's Only One Girl in the World for Me." His joviality somehow injecting confidence into them, for a moment they felt safe in his hands—protected, perhaps truly appreciated; and so they sang him one of their favorites: "Come Make Me Happy."

One day while chatting with the dwarfs, Mengele let slip that ever since childhood he had loved the Grimm brothers' "Snow White and the Seven Dwarfs." Never, though, had he imagined the possibility of a real-life encounter with such a family. The similarities between the Ovitzes and the Grimms' fiction intrigued him: the dwarfs in both instances numbering a symbolic seven; the group of diligent, happy dwarfs all living and working together, never separating. Disney's *Snow White* had been a huge success in Hitler's Germany, as well as the rest of Europe. In Disney's animated film, the dwarfs had their own band, and they played instruments similar to those of the Ovitzes: guitar and accordion, bass and drums. Audiences loved the tale's moral, in which the legendary dwarfs, living apart from society in the thick of the forest, have each—along with Snow White—discovered the benefits of mutual help. Disney's dwarfs protected their princess and secured her future, while she attended to their daily needs.

Historically, in their traditional role as court jesters, dwarfs

were the only subjects who dared speak their minds to the king
without paying with their lives. Likewise, the Ovitzes played
jesters to Mengele's king. He thus became the ace card they
could pull from their sleeves when they faced a serious
problem. Having discovered his soft spot, the Ovitzes dared
voice to Mengele their complaints; occasionally he acceded.
Although Mengele's cruelty remained manifest in the lack of
mercy he showed in conducting his myriad tests, he nonetheless more than once rebuked the Kapos to save their lives. Such
glimpses of a softer Mengele emboldened the Ovitzes, long
exhausted by the endless medical probing, to try and make use of
their special status. They mustered their courage, and, hoping
against hope, elected Frieda to approach Mengele. "Forgive me for
asking, Your Excellency, but when will this all be over so we can
go home?" said Frieda, with all the charm she could conjure up.
"What do you mean, *meine Liebe?* Don't I have a family that I want
to see? I can't go home myself!" Mengele's temper flared, and his
voice rose. "I'm not working here for pleasure but under orders.
You've got nothing to complain about! As long as you're here with
me you're better off!"

Weakened by hunger and suffering the stress of countless
tests, the small and skinny eighteen-month-old Shimshon Ovitz
preferred crawling to walking. Mengele could not decide
whether the child was a late developer or was displaying the
early signs of dwarfism. The blond, long-haired boy never cried,
and he had yet to start speaking. Still, emulating his mother and
aunts, Shimshon tried to stand to attention whenever Mengele
entered the Lilliputs' room. Shimshon had never known his
father, Azriel, who had been taken away for slave labor before he
was born: "My mother told me that whenever I heard the name
'Dr. Mengele' I would say *'tatti,'* and that the word was the only

one I knew. When he came over to see us, I would toddle toward him mumbling '*tatti, tatti.*' Mother apologized to Dr. Mengele: 'He thinks the *Herr Hauptsturmführer* is his father.' But he was actually very pleased, and smiled: 'No I'm not your father, just Uncle Mengele.' He showed affection for me, playing with me and giving me candies and toys that had belonged to children he killed: 'Look what Uncle Mengele has brought you.' I took my first steps on the cursed soil of Auschwitz, and Dr. Mengele was the man I would run to as 'Daddy.' This has spoiled my life."

Officially, the members of Mengele's human zoo were neither recognized as special cases by the camp administration nor accorded special privileges. Only the young twins and their mothers were exempt from work; all the other experimental subjects were assigned to hard labor. Nevertheless, because of their deformity, the seven dwarfs had been allowed to remain in their barrack, and furthermore, so had their entourage. Then, one day in October, they were hit with a new decree: all normal-sized adults in their group were to begin slave labor.

Deeply upset and fearing for the lives of their loved ones, the five female dwarfs again decided to appeal to His Excellency, Dr. Mengele. This time it was Elizabeth whom they sent to try to soften Mengele's heart. At first Mengele dismissed her: "In times like this, everyone has to take part in the war effort. I work, my wife works, and so will your family!" But Elizabeth persisted: "I appeal to Your Excellency like a child in need, pleading to his benevolent father. We depend on Sarah, Leah, and the others for our existence—to mount our beds or get some water. We're lost without them, we won't be able to survive a day. If *Herr Hauptsturmführer* sends them away to work, he'd better send us, too." She was frantic, crying; the words streaming out of her mouth were drowned in sobs. She failed to notice Mengele's smile. "Come to Mengele, Elizabeth. All right, I'll let them stay with you." A few weeks later, however, the dwarfs' efforts to shield the Lilliput group's able-bodied members proved to be futile. The fierce onset of the winter had killed many people in the camp, and with the crematoria no longer working—one of them blown up by rebelling inmates and the others shut down—extra hands were needed to burn the dead in open pits. Sarah Ovitz was among the women forced to load emaciated female corpses into the death carts, and empty them into the gaping pit. Simon Slomowitz and his sons, including eleven-year-old Judah and thirteen-year-old Joseph, had the same task in the men's camp.

For the most part, survivors of the death camp at Auschwitz had the impression that the Lilliput Troupe had no fear of Mengele, but the Ovitz family tells a different story. *In his presence, we shielded ourselves with smiles, but inside we were trembling like fish out of water. We were never fooled by his amiability. When Dr. Mengele said that as long as we were with him, we were not "over there," it didn't make us feel any safer, but rather the contrary. He often said, "I've enough work on you for twenty years," but that was no relief either—it was no guarantee he'd keep us alive all those years. He could finish the tests in a short time, toss us in the flames, and work on the findings for as long as he wished.*

THIRTEEN

Auschwitz-Birkenau, November 1944

Irene Mengele's recovery was proceeding very slowly. After five weeks at the camp hospital, she was finally able to move to her husband's new flat in the doctors' barracks. In another fortnight, she was well enough to travel with her husband to Freiburg, where, for the first time, Mengele met his eight-month-old son, Rolf. Mengele's absence afforded the Ovitzes momentary relief from the endless tests, but it also caused them considerable anxiety. *We were used to seeing Dr. Mengele nearly every day. As much as we dreaded him, we were twice as petrified when he was away. Our hearts stood still then. We were utterly dependent upon him, and were well aware anyone could kill us in our savior's absence.* A week later, Mengele was back in Auschwitz. "Guess where I've been," he teased Dina Gottlieb as, tanned and smiling, he stepped into the workroom by his office. He didn't wait for her answer. "In Argentina," he said. "I had no idea why he picked Argentina," remarks Dina Gottlieb. "He handed me a bag of cookies and two packs of choice English cigarettes. He said, 'I'm having a late celebration of the birth of my son.'"

Two orchestras were operating in Birkenau, one at the men's camp and one at the women's camp. They played twice daily, as the inmates marched to their labor at dawn and as they returned from their labor in the afternoon. Music marked the pace of the laborers' march. It also provided an artistic interlude during the camp commander's speeches. Music was featured at official ceremonies—and at the open-air hangings. On summer Sundays, there were outdoor classical music concerts for the camp staff, but the aloof Mengele, although he was a music lover, did not attend them. The melodic strains of the orchestral presentations traveled to the neighboring barracks; prisoners ventured to the nearest electrified fence to catch a musical phrase from another world.

The living quarters of the orchestra members attracted SS officers and prisoner-functionaries searching for a night's entertainment. The musicians, of course, had no choice but to comply with their whims and wishes. Smaller ensembles were often called upon to play at private staff parties and birthdays. In his book *People and Ashes*, Professor Israel Gutman, an Auschwitz survivor and prominent historian, recalls that "feasts and saturnalias were celebrated at Kapos' and block elders' quarters. The artistic program consisted of obscenities and dirty jokes. Sometimes a prisoner with a sweet voice would sing prewar hits in various languages. The Kapos especially favored melancholy tunes. The 'singers' were mostly Jews, who supplied their service for a ration of bread. The famous stars were very popular among the Kapos, and enjoyed a special income, thanks to their art." Birkenau inmates tried to improve their condition with whatever talents they had. A barber would hope to shave a Kapo for a piece of bread or two cigarettes; a seamstress might mend the block elder's clothing. SS guards often had Dina Gottlieb draw poster-size portraits from photos of their wives, fiancées, and girlfriends, which they then hung by their beds. Once, she was handed a postcard that pictured a naked red-haired nymph sitting by a waterfall and was ordered to paint a life-size copy of it by the following morning. She worked frantically the whole night. "A day later, the SS man brought it back for repairs—there were holes torn into the strategic body parts," she recalls.

When Mengele heard that a champion chess player was among the inmates, he arranged a game for himself. Late one evening, Mengele came to the *Schreibstube,* the clerk's office, where the chess player was already waiting. On the checkered board the black and white armies stood ready for combat. The room was utterly silent. Mengele removed his hat and placed it on a stool. Finger by finger he peeled off his white gloves; he put them inside his hat. He laid his cane across the upturned hat. That first game lasted a few hours, but the match continued over the following weeks. Appropriately for one of Mengele's pets, the prisoner was nicknamed "The Rabbit." Spared death solely to entertain the Nazi doctor, the Rabbit found himself in a tight spot: If he played well and defeated Mengele, he could pay for the victory with his life. On the other hand, if he played badly and allowed Mengele to win, he might be killed for the deceit. The Rabbit played in constant fear.

Eighteen-year-old Abraham Cykiert was among the few permitted to watch the games. Something of a wunderkind in his hometown of Lodz, he had been accepted into the local Yiddish Writers' Association at the age of fourteen, after publishing only three poems. In the ghetto, he had sold his poetry to the ghetto functionaries in order to support his parents and seven siblings. A poem could get him a few potatoes, a pair of shoes, or a shirt.

"Writing poems in Auschwitz was different. It wasn't for an additional slice of bread as much as being vital for existence. To continue doing something so essential to me helped me keep my sanity and preserve my identity. I spread the word that I was a Yiddish poet—not a very practical profession in a death camp. But in Birkenau one never knew."

Cykiert waited one day outside the *Schreibstube* and ambushed one of the clerks. "I'm a poet," he announced, then asked, "can you lend me a pencil and paper?" Startled by the youth's innocent recklessness, the clerk furtively and surprisingly obliged. That night, words rushed from Cykiert's mind onto paper, and in the morning he searched out his benefactor, the *Schreiber*. The clerk's face was mask-like as he read the poem; Cykiert could not tell if he understood a word. "Can you also write left-handed poetry?" asked the *Schreiber*, to the young man's incomprehension. The *Schreiber* then pulled out a sheet of paper filled with jottings and scribbles. He handed it to Cykiert. The young poet from Lodz blushed as he read gutter rhymes, obscenities, abominations. "Try it," said the *Schreiber*.

The next day, Cykiert showed his latest creation to the *Schreiber*, who was so pleased that he paid the teenager with a hot bowl of soup. "Can you recite as well as you write?" he asked. Cykiert nodded. "The following night, he took me to the weekly binge of all the inmate-VIPs in the camp: veteran prisoners who assisted the SS in running the place. They were sitting around a table laden with delicacies: cheese, sardines, sausage, fruit. The alcohol flowed freely. There were other inmate-performers with me: singers, actors, musicians. We performed from the back of the room as they devoured the food. We were not allowed to touch anything, but when the party was over we could share the leftovers. I read my pornographic lines and they rolled with laughter. I was consequently accepted as the group's permanent jester. Every week, each of us had to come with new material—to this day I'm ashamed of the poems I was forced into writing. Decades passed before I could start to write again."

Perla Ovitz insists that she and her family never took part in the "nightlife" of the death camp: they never performed in the bacchanalias, they never sang in public, they never privately entertained parties of Kapos and SS men. Yet nearly all the Ovitzes' former fans, acquaintances, and neighbors from Roza-vlea who also survived Auschwitz, as well as the inmates who shared their barrack, vividly recall the dwarfs performing for the SS. One such witness was Eta Tessler: "I knew the Ovitzes from Maramures, as I was from Visheu, a nearby village. In Auschwitz I was part of the *Scheisskommando*. We had to collect the daily excrement of thirty-two thousand women from the latrines, sift it into barrels, and carry it outside the camp. All day long, we were crisscrossing the camp, filthy and smelly, pushing the heavy cart with overloaded shit barrels. One day I came across two of the dwarf ladies. It was extremely cold, and I envied them for being able to have coats and warm pockets. I asked them where they were going and they answered, 'Singing.' I would run into them a few more times, walking in the same direction, but I couldn't tell if it was always the same duo or if they took turns."

Sunday, July 30, was the fast of *Tishah B'Av*, commemorating the destruction of the temple in Jerusalem, first in the year 586 BC and again in 70 AD. Before the war, on this day, pious Jews in towns and villages all over Europe would stop work and gather in synagogues to lament the catastrophe, which inaugurated a bitter exile. A man familiar with the Jewish calendar, Mengele perversely ordered the leader of the women's orchestra to prepare a special concert, for which he himself selected the program—military marches, circus music, waltzes, the fox-trot. The forthcoming concert caused much excitement. The orchestra arranged extra rehearsals, not just to master the exceptional program but to master it brilliantly enough to please the unusual guest of honor. Rows of wooden benches stretched out over the clinic yard. Opposite the dignitary box, a special platform was erected to hold the SS staff and their inmate assistants, doctors, nurses, and camp functionaries. In the center of the dignitary box sat Mengele himself, the arena's emperor.

As the orchestra struck its first notes, Fania Fenelon, one of the performers that day, noticed a group of dwarfs crossing the stage in a straight line. "It's a very famous dwarf circus from Hungary," whispered one of her friends. As Fenelon describes the proceedings in her book, "We start with a fox-trot, Mengele waving his hand, the dwarfs filling the stage, some couples dancing, other participants only managing a kind of grotesque, depressing twist. The men bow with a touch of servility; the women follow. Their jewelry, silk, ornaments, glitter in the sun, igniting thousands of sparkles, dancing, swinging, intermingling. These creatures emit joyful sounds, trying to sing along with Clara, Lotte, and me. They have high shrieking voices. The orchestra plays a march, and they accompany with clapping and stamping. There is something unreal and awful about the fifty tiny hands covered with rings, the bracelets clicking on their little arms, the little legs stamping. . . . The circus is at the foot of our stage, a circle with distorted creatures moving about, clapping like children, some of them fifty years old. The SS men burst out laughing. The young girls present at the scene start to tremble with fright at the uproar, the music, the dwarfs, the masquerade."

Despite the negative tone, and although Fenelon repeats the cliché that links the Ovitzes to the circus and errs somewhat with the ages (Rozika Ovitz was then fifty-eight, her sister Franziska fifty-five), she appears to offer a fairly realistic account here of what the Lilliputs would endure to ensure their survival. For her part, Perla Ovitz remembers that she and her family were taken by Mengele to an open-air concert, but she maintains adamantly that they did not appear or perform onstage. Rather, she insists, they watched the performance from their tiny stools in the audience. Also, the musical program that Perla recalls was entirely different: romantic, melancholy German songs that moved her and her sisters to tears. In any event, against the bleak backdrop of Auschwitz-Birkenau, the evening was so sensorially vivid that it became deeply etched in the memory of many survivors.

Isaac Taub was present that evening. He was part of the group of twin boys enlisted to carry chairs and benches and arrange them in rows. They were allowed to stand at the back during the performance; afterward, they dismantled the seats and carried them back to the depot. "There were about two hundred spectators," as Taub remembers it, "and it was a full, professional show, with stage lights and music. I remember that the female and male dwarfs stood onstage. If I'm not mistaken, this concert was repeated once more. We all knew that the dwarfs were performing for the Nazis, but it was nothing to be ashamed of." After two hours, Mengele lifted his hand and declared the concert over. "Mengele stood in the midst of the smartly dressed dwarfs, in their grotesque outfits and jewelry.

He turned to us and said, in his ironic manner, *'Sie haben ein gutes Publikum,'* (You have a good audience)" recalls Fania Fenelon.

The deportation, everyone in the ghetto had been told, would be the start of a new life; thus, the craftsmen and professionals had carried their tools with them. But in the havoc on the ramp upon their arrival at Auschwitz-Birkenau, everybody was ordered to leave their belongings on the trains. The Ovitzes were no exception; they had to abandon their portable instruments. "You'll get them later," they had been promised. "They were always grumping about their little musical instruments, which had been taken from them," recalls Dina Gottlieb. "They asked me if I could help get them back, as they were entertainers, and needed their tools."

Auschwitz-Birkenau was another planet. Daily, its inmates were exposed to murder, torture, and hunger. So it is not surprising that only the weirdest incidents retain a strong hold in survivors' memories. Numerous survivors recount a surrealistic scene in which a dwarf is playing the violin in a yard between the barracks. Gitta Drattler, who had lived next door to the Ovitz family on the main street of Rozavlea, remembers being "happy to see them once again in the camp. The Nazis forced them to play in the SS barracks, and I could hear the music from outside. They had their tiny musical instruments, and when I met them after the war in Romania and went to hear them play, they said, 'These are the instruments we had in Auschwitz.' " Likewise, Maria Halina Zombirt, who had worked in the infirmary as a clerk, testified to the Frankfurt general prosecutor that she had heard the family of ten Hungarian dwarfs "playing on musical instruments—a very peculiar piece." Kalman Bar-On, who lived in the same barrack as Avram and Micki Ovitz, recalls that "I would call them 'the two Toulouse-Lautrecs.' They always boasted, 'We are an artistic troupe!' They told us they arrived with all their equipment, stressing that it had been important for them to bring their musical instruments, even at the expense of clothes and household utensils, since their whole future depended on it." And Regina Teresa Krzyzanowska, who worked as a nurse at Auschwitz, testified that the "Lilliputians tried to please Mengele" by putting on "a few shows"—which naturally would have been impossible without musical instruments.

Since so many survivors have commented on the Lilliput ladies' tiny, glamorous stage dresses, it would appear that at least part of the luggage they had brought with them on the death train was located and delivered to them. It is not clear whether the instruments were eventually restored to them as well; it would have been easy enough to replace their equipment with child-size violins and guitars. For the "Kanada" warehouse held the plunder from hundreds of thousands of murdered children, many of them musically gifted.

From the moment the Lilliput Troupe set foot on the ramp back in May, and Micki Ovitz began handing out fan cards to anyone who would take them, the dwarfs had not stopped spreading the word promoting their artistic talents. The news was enthusiastically received by the German criminals who had been transferred from jails in Germany to serve in Auschwitz as heads of barracks or supervisors of labor groups. Having been locked away for years and hungry for amusement, they seized every opportunity to exploit inmates with talents to entertain, and they did it with utter ruthlessness. Even if the Lilliputs had been willing to make do with Auschwitz's starvation diet rather than deliver a song for bread, in reality, they would have had no choice once they'd been ordered to perform.

Still, the case remains that Perla Ovitz insisted throughout her life that neither she nor her sisters and brothers ever performed in Auschwitz. *We only sang among ourselves in our room, to remind ourselves of the good old days, have a good cry, and try and forget for a moment where we were. Everyone in the camp knew that we were artists, and we could not escape from it completely. So there were occasions when one of us, from fear of being killed or from no choice, succumbed to the demand of a kitchen supervisor or SS officer and sang for a candy or a bit of margarine. But we never put on a performance, and in any case did not have our musical instruments.* Why, despite considerable eyewitness testimony to the contrary, such stubborn and persistent denial?

The Ovitzes had always had a strong sense of their own artistic standards. Before the war, they carefully weighed each invitation to perform, and accepted only those they considered appropriate showcases for their talent. As pious, God-fearing Jews, they would have deemed public performance in Auschwitz to be an abomination, like partaking of festivities in a graveyard. Nor would performance under coercion have lessened their shame—not with the painful awareness that while they were entertaining Nazis at the camp's notorious SS parties, the chimneys outside never stopped smoking. All told, it would be no wonder if the Ovitzes strove to erase their experience from the records. And from their minds.

FOURTEEN

Auschwitz-Birkenau, December 1944

I n the middle of December, without warning, the trucks stopped taking the Lilliput Troupe to the clinics. Energetic as ever, Mengele was still running busily about, but he seemed to have lost interest in his family of dwarfs. The camp was covered in snow, and the Lilliputs shut themselves up in their barrack. Over and over, again and again, they discussed the sudden change in Mengele's behavior toward them, but they could come to no conclusions as to why he no longer seemed to need them. However much they dreaded new applications of Mengele's evil instruments, however much they trembled at the screech of a truck slowing down outside their barrack or at the snap from a piece of paper handed to the Kapo, Mengele's absence from them was the greater terror.

"Is he going to try and stretch us?" Perla broke their tense silence one afternoon. That was not the worst scenario that haunted them; there were other horrors they imagined but did not speak of. "Dirty whores" is how Mengele referred to Jewish women, according to Dr. Gisella Perl, a Jewish gynecologist forced to work with him. In her book *Five Chimneys*, Olga Lengyel, another prisoner-physician, recounts how Mengele "never missed a chance to ask the women indiscreet and improper questions. He made no secret of his amusement when he learned that one of the pregnant deportees had not seen her soldier husband for many months; another time, he hunted out a fifteen-year-old girl whose pregnancy was clearly dated from her arrival in the camp. He questioned her at length, and insisted on the most intimate details. When his curiosity was fully satisfied, he sent her off with the next herd of selectionees. The camp was no maternity ward, it was only the antechamber to hell."

"Now tell me, how did you live with your midget?" In her memoir of Auschwitz, Sara Nomberg-Przytyk recalls Mengele posing this question to Dora, the tall, full-bodied wife of Avram Ovitz. Mengele hinted at the stereotypical notion of the male dwarf as a subhuman characterized by an unusually potent sex drive and wild, unnatural desires. Dora Ovitz blushed, dumbfounded, her blood pounding in her ears. "Speak!" screamed Mengele, and then proceeded to interrogate Dora, vulgarly, in front of her young daughter and the rest of the barrack. Had she conceived her child with her dwarf husband, he demanded, or was the father someone else? Dora tried to respond by praising her husband's intelligence and industry, and meanwhile, writes Nomberg-Przytyk, "we all stood there like blocks of stones.

" 'Don't tell me about that, only about how you slept with him.'

"Mengele was salivating. The sweat poured down her face in big drops, on her clothes. She spoke and he asked questions. I cannot repeat the conversation. It was grotesque, inhuman torture."

At times, Mengele's sexual curiosity took him beyond interrogation. Two pairs of identical teenage twins testified for the Frankfurt prosecution that he forced them to have sex with other twins in order to determine if the women would bear twins in turn. The Lilliput group feared the same fate. "We were three young women in the Lilliput group," recounts Regina Ovitz: "Fanny Slomowitz, who was seventeen, Bassie Fischman, who was twenty, and myself, twenty-four years old. We had all been brought up in strictly Orthodox homes and had never been out alone with a man. Since childhood we had known that our marriages would be arranged by our parents, and that our husbands would be the only men in our lives. We all knew that Mengele had bizarre ideas—we were terrified he intended to couple us with dwarfs for the sake of the outcome. We were sure this was his next move, the only reason he was keeping us alive."

Whenever Mengele came into their room, the girls wished they were invisible, but they could only stand in the corner, shrink into their bodies, and avoid his gaze. Raised in a community that expected girls to be virgins until their wedding night, the young women faced an abyss. They feared that their wombs would become laboratories, and that they'd be forced to produce offspring which, full-size or otherwise, would themselves be doomed to serve as human guinea pigs; thus would the nightmare repeat itself year after year at Mengele's discretion. Regina and Fanny and Bassie had long since abandoned any hope of leaving Auschwitz alive, but the wretched prospect that they now faced—insemination by a pair of older dwarfs, one forty-one years old and married, the other a bachelor of thirty-five—deepened their hopelessness into utter despair.

"Among us in the experimental barrack for male twins and dwarfs was a misshapen, hunchbacked gnome, a little less than four feet tall," recalls Efraim Reichenberg. "He was forty years old, had a fissure in his skull, and could only walk with the aid of two crutches. He had been a watchmaker in Budapest, and we came together on the same transport. Each of us was enduring his own private hell, but when he let us know what he was going through, there was still room for pity. Nearly every day, he was put in a room and stripped naked. The SS brought him Gypsy women infected with syphilis, and forced him to have sexual intercourse with them. The SS doctors stood watching. Every morning when he arrived, and at the end of the day before he left, they checked him thoroughly, to see if he had already caught the disease. When he first told me I didn't want to believe him, but one day I saw him through a crack in the door. A male nurse was holding him, forcing him down on a woman, because he was no longer able. The unfortunate man didn't last long—he died some time later, not of syphilis but of exhaustion."

With the test results piling up over the summer, Mengele's clerks had no respite. Hour after hour, day after day, they filled out forms headed *Klinische Diagnose—Zwerge*, to which they appended lists of names. Ludovit Feld appears on one such list, along with the Ovitz brothers and the Budapest watchmaker. Pointing up the hideous irony of their status in the camp, Feld notes that "although our living conditions had been markedly better than those of other inmates, we suffered terribly from an awareness that sooner or later we would be killed, our skeletons displayed in biological museums. We heard it from the prisoner-doctors and from other prisoners. Word got out that near the crematoria ovens Dr. Mengele had a *Sezierraum*," or autopsy room.

Pathologist Miklos Nyiszli provides a description of the *Sezier-raum*. It was located in crematorium II, to the left of the entrance. The walls were painted pale green, the floor red. "In the center of the room, mounted on a concrete base, stood a dissecting

table of polished marble, equipped with several drainage chan-
nels. At the edge of the table, a basin with nickel taps had been
installed." Like other SS doctors in the camp, Mengele routinely
sent his pathologist the bodies of prisoners who had died of disease or hardship—or who had been killed expressly to be autop-
sied. The autopsy report was the essential conclusion to the
research on each subject. A copy of it accompanied the skeletons
and organs that were regularly exported to the Kaiser Wilhelm
Institute in Berlin and to medical schools throughout the *Reich*.
In June 1943, for example, 115 prisoners were transported from
Auschwitz to the Natzweiler-Struthof concentration camp near
Strassburg. There they were killed and their bodies, still warm,
were sent to SS *Hauptsturmführer* Professor Dr. August Hirt, who
was building up a collection of skulls at the Anatomy Institute of
the Reich University in Strassburg. In particular, he was looking
for "Jewish-Bolshevik commissar types" as examples of "a repul-
sive but typical species of sub-humanity."

In Leeuwarden, northern Holland, Alexander and Julia Katan
had been nicknamed "the Lilliputians." "In a small town, people
are straightforward when someone is different," explains their
only son, Alphons. "Father's legs were badly malformed due to
a childhood illness, and Mother was also very small." Katan—
the Hebrew word for "small"—was the only dwarf among eight
siblings; in 1930, he and Julia rejoiced when Alphons arrived
and grew to be normal-sized and healthy.

An extremely energetic and active man, Alexander Katan was
an economist, accountant, and interpreter who spoke seven
languages. He was not a practicing Jew, and in 1940, when Germany occupied Holland, he and his wife refused to stitch the
yellow star to their clothes. Katan, who could move outside his
home only with the aid of a special cart, was summoned to the

headquarters of the *Sicherheitsdienst*, or security service. "As Father had difficulties climbing the high staircase to their office, I had to accompany him. The Nazis called him in again and again, simply wishing to toy with him and laugh at his deformity." In July 1942, Alexander was imprisoned in the *Strafgevangenis* (prison for serious crimes) in his hometown. At the beginning of September, he was brought to the concentration camp of Amersfoort, and in October was deported to the Austrian concentration camp of Mauthausen. In August, Julia was taken to the town prison, and in October was deported to the German concentration camp of Ravensbrück. On November 29 she was sent to Auschwitz, where she was killed on arrival. Because of her short stature, she had no chance of being selected for work; Mengele was not yet stationed at the camp, and thus there was no dwarf research yet. "I was twelve years old," recalls Alphons, "and my aunt managed to convince the German authorities I was not my father's son, but rather the illegitimate child of a Catholic friend of the family. This saved my life. I found shelter with one of my aunt's non-Jewish friends."

Mauthausen was smaller than Auschwitz—but no less brutal. Block 27 now houses a pathological museum that exhibits 286 specimens of human organs harvested by the camp doctors: faces, skulls, skeletons, hearts, lungs, kidneys. Prisoners with spectacular tattoos evidently had been put to death, and then had their skin stripped from them; an album of tattooed skins in the museum displays the most outstanding designs. Physicians from the camp's Race and Hygiene Institute were continually combing the barracks in their search for prisoners with abnormalities whom they could add to their pathological collection. With his distorted limbs, Alexander Katan—Mauthausen prisoner 13992—caught their eye. For several months, he endured the same sorts of tests that the Lilliput Troupe was subjected to at Auschwitz.

Hans Marsalek, then a prisoner working in the camp's administrative department, recalls an occasion when a group of distinguished civilians, led by Commander Franz Ziereis, visited the specimen collection at Mauthausen. One of the tour's high points was a display featuring The Tall and The Short: the former, the strapping, six-foot-two-inch Paul Liese, a delinquent from Hamburg; the latter, Alexander Katan. "One is a Jew, the other a German, a criminal. Observe the difference between the two," Commander Ziereis instructed his visitors. "After this comparison between Jew and Aryan," Marsalek remarks, "Liese took Katan in his arms and carried him out of the barrack. They were using Katan as an example of the degeneration of the Jewish race." The presentation was repeated at every official camp visit.

Joseph Herzler, a prisoner who survived the experiments, was familiar with the pathological unit at Gusen, a sub-camp of Mauthausen: "I particularly remember a Dutch professor. Regrettably, I don't know his name. He was a unique individual. If I were asked to describe his looks, I must say he had a typical midget form. That is, his height was less than one meter. His exterior: a normal head of enlarged form, a full beard, and a child-sized body. He was extremely intelligent, had broad knowledge, was a university professor, and spoke seven languages fluently. He was kept tied in a corner of the room all day long, and was examined by various SS physicians, doctors, and visitors from other camps. Of course, he was not spared malicious remarks—'this is the size of a Jewish existence' and so forth. Once someone said in mock sympathy, 'Well at least he'll soon be dead since now his fate's been sealed.' "

On January 27, 1943, SS *Sturmbannführer* Dr. Karl-Joseph Gross ordered that forty-three-year-old Katan be given a lethal injection of phenol. It was injected directly into Katan's heart; he died instantly. Katan's body was then skeletonized, with every step of the process documented by a photographer. A special ambulance drove 180 miles to deliver Katan's bones to the SS Medical Academy near the University of Graz.

After the war, Alphons Katan knew only that his father had died in Mauthausen. It took him fifty years to muster the courage to go there. What greeted him at the museum in block 27 were four poster-sized photographs of his father; one in which he was wearing the striped prisoner's uniform; nude photos, front and back, taken just before the deadly injection; and one of Katan's skeleton.

After a long, humiliating battle waged by Alphons Katan, and intervention on his behalf by the Dutch government, the Austrian interior minister instructed the museum authorities at Mauthausen to remove the Katan photographs. Alphons Katan's struggle to restore his father's dignity, however, continues. The photographs of his father are still in circulation at various Holocaust museums for all to see and purchase. They are printed in books and displayed at medical conventions; they can be downloaded from the Internet. Historians argue that such photographs need to be displayed, because they document Nazi atrocities, and thus serve as vital tools in the dispute with those who would deny the historical fact of the Holocaust as well as of anti-Semitism in general. "But it's a never-ending humiliation of my father," says Alphons Katan, who argues that the claim of historical truth does not outweigh the dignity of an individual or a family. Katan has demanded, too, that the medical school at the University of Graz return his father's skeleton to him for a proper burial. The university alleges that it is unable to locate the skeleton, and cannot provide any information regarding its whereabouts.

The SS doctors were so certain of the scientific necessity of their activities that they did not bother to hide them, and the information about the medical atrocities quickly spread among the prisoners. Mordechai Slomowitz recalls that "we lived under constant fear of our fate being the same as the two male dwarfs who arrived in Auschwitz and were killed, their bodies put in boiling water to be cooked until the flesh separated from their bones."

This happened in August 1944. During a selection of Jews transported from the Lodz ghetto, Mengele noticed a hunch-backed man of around fifty. Beside him stood his son, a hand-some boy of fifteen with a deformed right foot, for which he wore an apparatus made of metal plates. Mengele waved the two of them aside. When the newcomers had passed beyond the crematoria gates and the ramp was empty, he signaled the father and son to approach. He inspected them briefly, asked a few questions, and then took out his notebook and wrote a mes-sage to Dr. Nyiszli: "These two men to be examined from a clin-ical point of view, exact measurements taken and clinical records set up, including all interesting details, and most espe-cially those relative to the causes provoking the bodily defor-mations." Mengele tore out the page and folded it. He then handed it to one of the SS guards, with the instructions that he deliver the two men to Dr. Nyiszli.

The Hungarian Jewish pathologist examined the hunchback and his son at some length. Chatting with them to ease the ten-sion, Nyiszli learned that the devoted father, a prosperous wholesale-clothing merchant, had taken advantage of business trips to Vienna to visit specialists there and have his son's foot examined and treated. The mother had died in the ghetto. Nyiszli tried to console the two men with the possibility that they would be sent to a labor camp. As they were famished from the transport, he also saw to it that they were fed.

The father and son had just finished eating when SS *Oberscharführer* Muhsfeld, accompanied by four members of the *Sonderkommando*, arrived and took the two of them to a nearby room. Muhsfeld ordered them to strip naked. Then two revolver shots were fired. The bodies were immediately returned to Nyiszli, who was so sickened by the sight that he could not perform the autopsy. He entrusted the dissection to one of the other inmate-doctors. It is not clear why Mengele did not add the short man from Lodz and his crippled son to his collection of dwarfs. Perhaps he realized that the father's deformity stemmed from rachitis, which was not hereditary, and therefore of no interest for his genetic research.

Later that day Mengele arrived at Nyiszli's workroom. He read the pathology report with growing excitement and declared that "these bodies must not be cremated," as Nyiszli recounts in his memoir, *Auschwitz: A Doctor's Eyewitness Account.* "They must be prepared, and the skeletons sent to the Anthropological Museum in Berlin. What methods do you know for the preservation of skeletons?" Mengele asked Dr. Nyiszli. Mengele and Dr. Nyiszli then proceeded to discuss the pros and cons of the various methods. Mengele chose the quickest: cooking. Bricks were laid in the courtyard, a fire was kindled, and "two casks, containing the bodies, placed upon it. Two *Sonderkommando* men were given the job of gathering wood and keeping the fire hot. After five hours, I tested the bodies, and found that the soft parts were now easily separable from the bones." When the water had cooled, the skeletons were cleaned and polished in a gasoline bath. After they were dried, Nyiszli's assistant arranged the skeletons for display. Mengele, who had come with several other officers, was highly pleased. He ordered the skeletons to be wrapped and taken by two soldiers to Berlin.

That was the first time Dr. Nyiszli was ordered to perform this gruesome task, but it would not be the last. One of the sights that haunted *Zwillingsvater* Zvi Spiegel to his dying day was that of a dwarf being tortured to his death by Mengele. Afterward, the miserable victim was placed in an acid bath until the flesh was stripped from his bones. *We had reconciled ourselves to the thought that we wouldn't walk out from the camp and would have no grave, just like all the others murdered in Auschwitz. But the notion that our bare skeletons would be exhibited in Berlin, even a hundred years later, people arriving to gawk and stare, was ghastly beyond words. We had never taken part in a freak show or lived in a Lilliputstadt, and had not publicly displayed our bodies, considering it degrading. We were professional musicians, and that's how the world had regarded us. If there was some relief in the idea of death, there was torment in the idea of being displayed in a museum.*

To paraphrase a famous line by the poet Paul Celan, death was indeed a master of Auschwitz. It could strike at any moment, select any inmate as its prey. Its toll each night was piled outside for all to see, like so much garbage waiting to be collected. A space suddenly empty in a bunk did not shake heaven and earth. No, the survivors of another night simply walked about, as if wrapped in an invisible shell; perhaps they'd live another day. The Lilliput Troupe, however, received special attention from their fellow prisoners, who viewed the dwarfs with concern and wonder, and cared about their fate.

The Lilliputs drew the eyes of the inmates beyond their shells. The whereabouts of the Lilliputs were noticed.

"One day, the dwarfs from block 23 were taken away," recalls Dr. Katarzyna Laniewska. "I don't know what was done with them." Her colleague Ella Lingens-Reiner confirms that "after about three weeks, the family disappeared suddenly. We were convinced they had been gassed." Another doctor, Sigmond Hirsch, a French-Jewish roentgenologist and a Resistance fighter, recalls that the experiments had ended, and the dwarfs had been delivered to the ovens. Complete strangers to the dwarfs, inmates who saw them only briefly, like Maria Gasiorowska, a block elder at the women's camp at Birkenau, noticed that they had "disappeared after a relatively short period of time, about two months. Following their disappearance, which attracted attention, there was news around the camp that they had been gassed. The news came from the crematorium workers."

One of these was *Sonderkommando* Philip Müller: "The only thing I saw regarding the midgets was how they executed them. He [Mengele] killed most of them, or had them killed, in order to perform autopsies on their bodies." Maria Halina Zombirt, who had been a clerk in charge of the sick registry, testified for the Frankfurt prosecution that she "met a group of ten Hungarian dwarfs, and was told that they were a family who performed in a restaurant. When one of them died, he was prepared and skeletonized and sent to the museum in Berlin." Two survivors have gone so far as to describe the death of the dwarfs in great, appalling detail. Sara Nomberg-Przytyk remembers Mengele ordering that little Shimshon be brought to his office. When Mengele had finished with Shimshon, he locked the door behind him and left. Later, as Nomberg-Przytyk tells it,

Leah Ovitz arrived, and discovered a terrible scene: she "grabbed the half-dead child and ran into a mad frenzy of pain [*sic*]. Not one drop of blood was left in his little face. 'He will die. He has to die,' she said, choked with tears. At night, the little one died. He never regained consciousness. In the small room, on the little table, lay the little boy. Around him, like pillars of stone, stood a large woman, along with the child's mother, slim and frail; the three midgets sat in miniature chairs. They did not cry. They were all frightened of the torturous death awaiting them." In the evening, supposedly, the dead child was placed outside the block with the other corpses to be taken to the crematoria. Nomberg-Przytyk also claims that she witnessed the death of Avram Ovitz: "The old midget wanted his wife," and he tried to slip through the wire; a guard spotted him, and, when Avram got close enough, shot him. "He never made it to his wife."

But little Shimshon did not die on Mengele's operating table; he survived Birkenau, and eventually settled in Israel. Likewise, his uncle Avram was not shot; he lived to see liberation day, and immigrated to Israel with his wife and daughter. What, then, caused Nomberg-Przytyk to make such basic mistakes? Most likely, she was compressing a number of events, and attributed to the dwarfs two common occurrences in the daily life of the camp: the death of a child in a mother's arms and the shooting of inmates who approached the electrified fence.

In a similar manner, the singer Fania Fenelon maintains in *Playing for Time* that immediately afterward "the handsome doctor was seen crossing the camp, followed by his merry, squeaking army of dwarfs." She describes Mengele as a Pied Piper from Hamlin proudly marching in front, with the dwarfs—joyful, self-assured, apparently unworried—behind him. "Who could dream of exterminating such tiny creatures, always joyful and happy! Mengele laughs with them, he seems quite amused, he so enormous ruling over such small ones." Fenelon then reports that later Mengele returned alone, his hands in his pockets. He has proved himself capable of the unimaginable and Fenelon concludes *"La Comedia e Finita!"*

Memory is similarly processed in an account by Renee Firestone, an Auschwitz-Birkenau survivor: "The Germans found a community of midgets, transported them to Auschwitz, shot them en masse, and then were forced to let them sit in a pile for three days until the crematoria could take them." A mass killing of dwarfs was not registered only in the memory of camp survivors, however. Documents in the Auschwitz archives have led some researchers to conclude that Mengele killed eleven female dwarfs on December 7, 1944.

In fact, early in December, Mengele did come to the female dwarfs' room and order them to pack in preparation for a brief journey. They were terrified; any change, in their minds, could only be for the worse. When the truck arrived, they could barely mount it for their trembling. To their relief, it did not turn toward the crematoria. Their new location was much closer to the men's infirmary, where their loved ones were located. In the "Labor Deployment List" of December 5, 1944, under the heading "sick and unable to work," a new category appears for the first time: *Zwerge*. It indicates that sixteen female dwarfs were transferred to the women's camp in BIIe, which had previously been the Gypsy camp but had stood empty since the extermination of all its inhabitants in August. The transfer was part of a rearrangement of Birkenau. The prisoners were being moved into fewer barracks, as the women's camp had been liquidated. Healthy women prisoners were transferred to BIIb, while the ill, as well as female twins and dwarfs, were transferred to BIIe. Three days later, the number of female dwarfs in the roster dropped from sixteen to five; the roster does not indicate the fate of the missing eleven.

Many researchers have tried to guess at what happened to the eleven missing female dwarfs. "They probably died the previous day as a result of the experiments conducted on them by SS Dr. Mengele," concludes Danuta Czech in her Auschwitz research. Still, despite the constant fact of death by intent or by experiment in the macabre world of Auschwitz-Birkenau, it is most unlikely that Mengele would have arbitrarily eliminated eleven of his carefully maintained dwarfs at one go, before he had finished his work on them. Furthermore, he considered the autopsy vital to his research, and would have been well aware that Dr. Nyiszli could not possibly have dealt with eleven corpses in any exacting, productive way.

There were of course sixteen females in the Lilliput group: the five Ovitz dwarf sisters; their two normal-sized siblings; Avram's wife and her eight-year-old daughter; cousin Regina Ovitz; Chaya Slomowitz and her three daughters; Bassie Fischman and her mother. Since Mengele regarded them as an extended family, he moved all sixteen of them together to the new accommodations in Birkenau. Elizabeth and Perla Ovitz both confirmed that all sixteen were transferred. And clearly, contrary to the conclusion of Danuta Czech and many other researchers, eleven of them did not die. All sixteen lived to see the end of the war, and then immigrated to either Israel or America; five were still alive at the time of this writing, nearly six decades later. It would seem, in fact, that the disappearance of the eleven was simply a bureaucratic error. When the sixteen females of the Lilliput group arrived at their new barrack, they

were duly recorded in the camp registry as dwarfs, in confor-
mance with Mengele's note of transfer. In the accounting three
days later, however, the officers in BIIe noticed that only five of
the women were in fact dwarfs, and the eleven other normal-
sized women and young girls were thus excised from the category of *Zwerge*. While they no longer appeared in the same slot
on the list, they nonetheless continued to live in the same room
as the dwarfs.

This being the case, why so much testimony concerning their
brutal collective murder? One plausible answer might be that
Birkenau survivors, who regarded their own deliverance as
miraculous, nevertheless found the chances slim that someone
as helpless as a dwarf could survive. In addition, the fact that
the Lilliputs were transferred several times from one side of the
camp to the other caused their fellow inmates to lose touch with
them, and in Auschwitz, when you stopped seeing someone, it
could mean only one thing.

Though Jewish holidays were set aside for extensive killing in
the camp, Christmas Eve 1944 in Auschwitz-Birkenau was relatively peaceful—a momentary respite from horror. Elizabeth
Ovitz, escorted by her tall sister Sarah, went to wish a merry
Christmas to the kitchen staff. On her way back, two SS officers
stopped them, and took Elizabeth into a back room while
Sarah, frantic, waited outside. The officers mounted Elizabeth
on a chair and demanded entertainment. Elizabeth's songs won
her a shower of cellophane-wrapped candies, a piece of salami,
and some margarine, all of which she took back to her family.
Christmas festivities were taking place in various parts of the

camp. Dr. Lucy Adelsberger remembers watching a party in the men's infirmary from behind the fence: "Physicians and nurses were allowed to strike up dance tunes with a jazz group. It was an open-air performance on the grassy area close to the wire. The women crowded around on the other side of the fence, shouting 'Bravo!' and clapping their hands. The program was good, nothing was forbidden, no sentry shot into the crowd." The experience of Solomon Malik, then a fourteen-year-old twin, was even more extravagant: "I went to a Christmas party in a large hall in the 'Kanada' camp, near the crematoria. It was open only for camp functionaries, but our Kapo, Frau Schmidt, took me along with her. There was lavish food, drink, music, and dance. It was a complete show: someone lifted a table with his teeth, clowns amused the crowd with their tricks. I remember that one of them rode a broomstick and laid eggs, to the cheers of the spectators. The Lilliputs were part of the artistic program. I don't remember exactly how many of them were there, but they sang and played their tiny instruments."

For the revellers, all of them "Aryans," the future was bleak. The Russians were closing in; the German army was engaged in desperate battles. But at the camp the orchestra played on.

FIFTEEN

Auschwitz-Birkenau, January 1945

By the summer of 1944, the Red Army had already advanced as far as the Sandomierz region, only 120 miles from Auschwitz. But the Russians did not become a real threat to the SS at the death camp until four months—and tens of thousands more victims—later. As the thundering of the cannons grew audible, the inmates grew even more uneasy. "We always feared that as the front approached Auschwitz-Birkenau, the Nazis would kill each and every one of us," comments Erich Kulka, a survivor and historian, in his book *Auschwitz—Death Factory.*

The steady advance of the Allied forces in Europe prompted the Third Reich to begin liquidating the concentration camps and centers of mass extermination in its conquered territories. One by one, they were demolished. Auschwitz-Birkenau, the biggest death factory of them all, was the last in line. To cover up unimaginable crimes, the crematoria were blown up. The pits, in which countless corpses had been burnt, were filled and covered with earth. Buildings and offices were razed, wooden barracks were dismantled; the construction materials and the furniture were shipped into the heart of Germany.

In January, all the able-bodied members of the Lilliput group were recruited for the demolition. Sarah Ovitz, who had been hauling the dead to the pits with the *Leichenkommando*, was now assigned to help dismantle the barracks. If her former job had been emotionally straining—she kept visualizing her own body swinging lifelessly from the death cart she was pulling— at least, at her new task, she could fantasize about living to see the hell end. Slomowitz and his three sons had meanwhile been transferred to the "Kanada" warehouse, where they frantically packed shoes, spectacles, clothes, toys, and innumerable family treasures to be sent to Germany.

The Nazi war machine was reluctant to lose the enormous force of slave labor it had gathered at Auschwitz. In order to keep exploiting it, the SS implemented a massive evacuation. In a period of five days, fifty-eight thousand prisoners were marched on foot in heavy snow about fifteen miles, to the train station. From there, they were transported in open wagons to concentration camps in Upper and Lower Silesia.

Twice in the past, Mengele had saved Dina Gottlieb from selections, for he required her skills as an illustrator. With his experiments now coming to an end, he needed her less, and left her to her fate. Dina and her mother were among those consigned to what was aptly dubbed "the death march," for its destination was uncertain, and those who could not keep up were simply shot by the SS on the spot. Quenching their thirst by sucking on pieces of snow, mother and daughter made it to Ravensbrück.

Mordechai Slomowitz recalls the death march: "We all stood for *Appell* and an officer shouted, 'All those who can march fifty kilometers, step forward!' Several men and boys did, forming a group. 'Who can march forty? Thirty? Twenty?' One by one, the barrack, including the frail and ailing, was split into groups, which started to walk toward the unknown. Physically our family could make the journey, but Father did not want to desert the dwarfs."

"Can you march five kilometers?" demanded the officer. Simon Slomowitz looked at the two Ovitz dwarfs. The brothers exchanged glances, and Avram, the elder, nodded. "We can make it," said Slomowitz. It was obvious that the dwarfs could not walk even a hundred yards, especially in the heavy snow; equally obvious was their urgent desire to get away from Birkenau as quickly as possible. Three miles was the distance from Birkenau to the main camp of Auschwitz. The Ovitz and Slomowitz men surmised that if the entire Birkenau camp was being liquidated, at Auschwitz they would be able to rejoin the women of the group.

Simon and his son wandered around the camp yard looking for some means of transporting the dwarfs. Next to the kitchen barrack they found a cart that had been used both to distribute bread and to dispose of the dead. Slomowitz lifted Avram and Micki into the cart and wrapped them in blankets. Then they left the camp, with Slomowitz and his three sons pulling the two dwarfs in the cart behind them. The roads were buried in snow, and in the thick wall of fog they could see no farther than the tips of their fingers. They had only the footprints of the droves of inmates who had ventured out before them, along with some scattered corpses, to mark their way. They had gone no more than a few hundred meters when the heavy wooden cart tipped over. They could go no farther. "There's no point— we'll freeze to death here," said Simon Slomowitz. "If we're going to die let's die in our bunks, not like dogs in the fields." They wrenched the cart from the snow and retreated. In the prevailing disorder at Birkenau, where the discipline among the SS guards had gone lax, the six of them managed to steal back into their barrack. As they settled quietly in, they wondered where Mengele was, and if he could help them. Unlike the other SS doctors, he had continued his research up to the last possible moment, but it had been days since they had seen him.

Until the evacuation, Martina Puzyna had worked mainly in a special barrack in the former Gypsy camp. "Written measurement data was kept there. I well remember that Dr. Mengele showed up in January 1945, several days before the evacuation, and silently packed his records, preparing them for transport like a wild man." She had stood aside and watched, since he allowed no one to help him. Flushed from exertion, he stuffed two trunks with instruments, slides, and specimens. Leafing frantically through the files in a huge cabinet, he pulled out the essential documents. Then he slammed everything into his car and drove away. It was January 17, 1945.

At midnight, SS officers ordered all the inmate-doctors who had worked with Mengele to collect his remaining medical documents. "In less than an hour, the documents were gathered in front of the bureau quarters. They were heaped upon the earth and made quite a mound of papers. An SS guard promptly set them on fire," recalls Olga Lengyel in her memoir. Perla supplements that account with her memory of those January days: *No one knew that Dr. Mengele had left for good—it took several days for us to realize we were not going to see him again. Throughout the months that we'd known him, he had always promised, "when I move to another place I'll take you with me." When the camp was torn down, we waited in our room for him to come, but he didn't keep his* word. When he ran away, the only thing he took was our papers, which were more important to him than we were. Mengele had in fact traveled to Berlin for a brief meeting with Professor von Verschuer at the Kaiser Wilhelm Institute. Most likely, Mengele wanted to discuss the possibility of returning to the institute so that he could continue to work on the material he'd collected in Auschwitz. Meanwhile, he had to report to the Gross-Rosen concentration camp in Silesia.

On January 18, 1945, the SS marched 5,300 women and children out of Auschwitz-Birkenau, among them dozens of twins led by Zvi Spiegel. The Lilliputs, however, stayed behind, along with a few thousand inmates who, too sick to move, remained in the now nearly empty barracks. "A number of sources indicate that the SS planned to liquidate them, not only as witnesses to their crimes, but also as an unwanted burden," concludes Polish researcher Andrzej Strzelecki. In essence, the camp had ceased functioning. No food whatsoever was being distributed. Order of any kind was no longer enforced. Instead, the prisoners were now left to the mercy and whims of a small, nervous SS force that spent most of its time looting the warehouses and shooting prisoners for pleasure. Seven hundred inmates were murdered in the camp's final days. In one instance, more than two hundred of them were locked in a barrack and burned alive.

Pandemonium was general in both camps, and one night in the commotion Avram and Micki, along with Simon and his three sons, sneaked out of the men's infirmary and stole into the women's camp, where they found their families. Over the following days, whenever one of the remaining SS guards approached the women's barrack, the six men quickly hid themselves. Together, the Lilliput group spent most of the time praying, whispering psalms, and imploring God for deliverance. Like other prisoners in the now virtually deserted camp, they raided the kitchen and storerooms, and for the first time in many months they satisfied their hunger with a warm meal cooked by the Lilliput women. The "uncanny atmosphere" of Auschwitz's closing days is etched into the memory of Kalman Bar-On: "The busy, densely populated camp became desolate, suspiciously silent. Great fires consumed the remaining goods at the 'Kanada' warehouse. Explosions could be heard, as well as collapsing buildings. We were in a no man's land—no SS guards at most of the watchtowers, but the barbed wire of the outer fence was still electrified and we could not get away. From time to time, out of nowhere, soldiers would burst into a barrack, order everyone out, and shoot them. One day they called an *Appell*, announcing they would lead us out of the camp the following morning at ten. I sensed a trap, that they were going to shoot us the moment we passed the gates. Even if they let us march, it would be very hard to survive. I stood by my uncle Ludovit Feld, knowing that with his tiny legs and weak body he wouldn't be able to make it. I didn't want to leave him and didn't know what to do."

"Son, we're not going anywhere," said Feld, convincing not only Kalman but also fourteen other teenage twin boys who had remained in the barrack to stay put. They covered themselves with blankets, and for ten days they lay motionless, on the frozen ground, beneath the lowest wooden bunk. They had nothing to eat but crumbs. They could not go outside to relieve themselves for fear of the SS.

"For the first time in my life, I dared to disobey an SS order," notes Kalman Bar-On. "It was a strange feeling. I feared their revenge if they found us, but I was happy to be taking my fate into my own hands. Those who walked out of the camp thought they were saving themselves. But for many of them, including my poor mother, the walk meant death. Those of us who followed the advice of a wise and resourceful dwarf who could not move and didn't want to be left alone were saved." In the last days of January at Auschwitz, Russian cannons were thundering at close range, American airplanes were buzzing overhead, and the German guards were in a panic. But freedom was in the air. Fervently, the Lilliputs prayed that they would not die by friendly or enemy fire in these last days. At night they slept in their clothes; one of them always stood guard.

On Saturday, January 27, at around 3 P.M., the first Red Army reconnaissance troops entered Birkenau. The 5,800 remaining prisoners were too exhausted to greet them. According to the Jewish calendar it was Shabbath Shira, the day for the annual reading of the "Song of the Sea" from the book of Exodus—the eulogy in which Moses and the Children of Israel praise God for drowning Pharaoh and his army in the Red Sea. *We all felt God's hand was at work, redeeming us on the Saturday commemorating the miracle of our forefathers' deliverance from certain death. But we were not so lucky as to be delivered by the Americans. We got the Russians instead.*

The Lilliput Troupe had performed for Hungarian soldiers and for German soldiers; they now had a new audience, again in military uniform, as jubilant Russian soldiers crowded into the barrack to gape at the seven dwarfs. The Russians brought vodka with them, and asked the Lilliputs to perform. The Ovitzes were happy to oblige. For drums, they used some metal pots from the kitchen, on which Micki and Elizabeth hammered out their rhythms with wooden spoons. The party lasted through the night, with the Lilliputs again and again singing the few Russian songs in their repertoire. "In the midst of the celebrating I was full of fear," recalls Regina Ovitz. "The Russian soldiers frequently entered our room, always tipsy, and I didn't like the way they stared at us. Whenever their footsteps grew louder, we three girls hurriedly climbed to the upper bunk. We lay there quiet as mice until they left. I didn't trust them—they made me feel threatened."

All twenty-three members of the Lilliput group were examined in Birkenau by Russian doctors, who found them to be in better health than most of the survivors; none of them required hospitalization. "How many dwarfs like you were in the camp?" Ludovit Feld was asked by a Lieutenant Misivrov from the military prosecution office of the Red Army, who was sent to Auschwitz to gather evidence. "In Birkenau where I was, we were ten Lilliputians. Five men, five women." "How did the doctors and the SS treat you?" "The doctors treated us fairly, but the SS laughed at us, although they never hit us. Whenever they made selections, we were kept alive."

This testimony from March 1945 is the earliest evidence on record relating to Mengele's research on dwarfs. It also establishes their precise number: ten. However, this is not a figure on which researchers and survivors agree. Gisella Perl, for example, indicates in her book that "one of these barracks housed Dr. Mengele's pets, Polish and Hungarian Jewish midgets, about forty of them, some alone, some with their entire family." The singer Fania Fenelon recalls an even larger number: "Mengele surrounded by around fifty dwarfs who informed us he had removed them from the convoys being sent to the crematorium." Some research places the figure as high as one hundred or more. Nevertheless, there were only seven dwarfs in the Lilliput group, and the Ovitzes insist there were only three other dwarfs besides them.

That the dwarfs involved in Mengele's research at the camp

totaled no more than ten is in any case corroborated by many survivors, such as Maria Halina Zombirt, the inmate-clerk in Mengele's clinic. She stated for the Frankfurt prosecution that the only dwarfs she saw in the camp were the Lilliputs—testimony that, with small variations as to the precise number, is borne out by a range of witnesses: inmate-doctors Halina Cetnarowicz, Katarzyna Laniewska, and Ella Lingens-Reiner; Auschwitz twin Otto Klein; the Czech dwarf Ludovit Feld; inmate Stanislawa Rachwalowa. Furthermore, the figure cited by Misivrov, as well as by Ludovit Feld in his Frankfurt testimony ("108 pairs of twins, and approximately ten people of small size. . . . These persons always returned to our barrack. None of us were murdered—people only died from starvation") is backed up by the surviving Auschwitz archives. Between May 1944 and January 1945, listed under the category *Zwerge*, are the names and camp numbers of the seven Ovitzes, Ludovit Feld, Arthur Seligsohn, and the Budapest watchmaker. There are fourteen additional numbers and names; they identify the normal-sized members of the Ovitz and Slomowitz families.

Arthur Seligsohn, from Breslau, was transported first to Theresienstadt, and then, in May 1944, to Auschwitz-Birkenau—he was prisoner number A-1199. Because of his handicap, the fifty-six-year-old dwarf was transferred by Mengele from the "Family Camp" to the men's clinic, where he lived with the male dwarfs. He was thus spared the fate that awaited the other Czech Jews when the "Family Camp" was liquidated. (According to the Red Cross, Arthur Seligsohn was alive and well, living in Grussau in July 1948.) No one knows the number of dwarfs who, like Lya Graf and Julia Katan, arrived at Auschwitz-Birkenau before Mengele's tenure there and were sent instantly to their deaths. It is likewise difficult to determine how many dwarfs arrived at the camp but failed to gain Mengele's attention and were systematically exterminated.

Close scrutiny of 159 photographs taken by SS men Ernst Hofmann and Bernhard Walter during selections of Hungarian Jews in May and June 1944—a collection known as the "Auschwitz Album"—discloses at least three more dwarfs on the ramp: two of them old men, one a teenager. The teenager, evidently too deformed and weak to stand on his feet, reclines in a wicker chair that he'd probably brought with him from home. These three nameless dwarfs were killed a few hours after being photographed; no doubt Mengele did not find them sufficiently interesting for his research.

When anti-Jewish decrees were imposed on Hungary in 1940, famed fifty-nine-year-old dwarf Zoltan Hirsch was expelled from the circus. Soon thereafter he was arrested for wearing a yellow star that did not meet Nazi requirements: it was too small. His defense—that the badge was proportionate to his size—failed to sway the authorities. He was imprisoned, and later sent to Auschwitz with the Jews of Budapest. According to Gjorgi Szilagyi, who had run a Lilliputian town in Budapest, the celebrated Zoli was made a doorman in the camp. This remarkable dwarf, who had traveled the world as a favorite of statesmen and kings, was reduced to being a laughingstock for the SS. Day after day, dressed in spectacular uniforms, he stood by the camp gates and saluted the Nazis as they came and went. This service did not save him from the gas chambers. Strangely and poignantly, Zoltan Hirsch has nonetheless been immortalized as a collector's item: the Roli-Zoli, a tin wind-up toy of a clown riding a red scooter.

Mengele wanted fame. Never willing to settle for the lot of just another anonymous scientist, he was determined to go down in history as a pioneer, an innovator. Mengele did not look upon his research on dwarfs as a marginal item of scientific curiosity. Instead, he made the Lilliput group the focus of his lecture at the official inauguration of the SS Lazarett. In the last months of the war, when the camps were forced to close down their offices and laboratories, Mengele still found himself standing in the shadow of his old Nazi rival, Hans Grebe. The inmate-doctors who worked under Mengele surmised that he aspired to unlock something resembling a "genetic code" for dwarfism, but not for another fifty years would science have acquired the knowledge to realize Mengele's dream.

By the 1950s, scientists had begun to taxonomize the various types of dwarfism. In 1952, an honored and distinguished Hans Grebe published his papers on a rare form of short-limb dwarfism, to which he would lend his name: the diagnostic term Grebe Syndrome is used to this day. Grebe identified the syndrome after studying a pair of Brazilian sisters, aged seven and eleven. Had Mengele had the time to continue his research on the Ovitzes at Birkenau, he, too, might have defined a particular type of dwarfism that would in honor bear his name. But he did not, and in 1959 it was Pierre Maroteaux and Maurice Emile Joseph Lamy, two French physicians, who defined the Ovitz type of dwarfism. They named it Pseudoachondroplasia.

In light of such taxonomization, though, one can only speculate how Mengele, who was said to manipulate results to meet his aims, would have explained away the robustly built bodies of the Slomowitzes, who had managed, throughout their internment in Auschwitz, to masquerade as members of the Ovitz family.

SIXTEEN

On the Road, 1945

The day after liberation, a Russian army film crew arrived at the camp. As the crew had missed the actual historical moment, they decided to stage it. Children always heighten the poignancy of a war story, so when Captain Alexander Voronstov, a cameraman, chanced upon a group of Mengele's twins leaving the camp, he detained them. Dissatisfied with their randomly improvised clothing, he had them change back into striped prisoners' uniforms.

In his search for a dramatic location, Voronstov had found a narrow path that ran between two fences of barbed wire. He had another cameraman climb up a watchtower to get a bird's-eye view. Along the path, accompanied by nuns and nurses, the children in striped uniforms were paraded again and again. At the director's cue, they would stop and roll up their sleeves; then they'd point at the numbers tattooed on their arms. The scene eloquently captures at the same time both the significance of the liberation and the scope of the atrocities. Extracts from the film are screened every half hour at the Auschwitz State

Museum. At first glance, the bespectacled face and tiny form of forty-year-old Ludovit Feld is bearly discernible among the marching children.

Feld's helplessness had left him no choice but to stick with Mengele's twins, with whom he had been imprisoned for the past eight months. "When the Russians came," recalls Kalman Bar-On, "I gave Uncle Ludovit my hand and we walked over to Auschwitz through the deep snow. I left him alone in one of the buildings and began searching for food. There was a huge store-room with noodles and sugar. I found an empty tin, made a fire, and cooked our first meal in freedom." Moments like this were unfolding throughout the camp, but the commanders of the 60th Army of the First Ukrainian Front were anticipating a Wehrmacht offensive, and they advised those who could get away not to linger. Too weak to undertake a long journey, Feld had to remain in Auschwitz. His nephew headed for Palestine.

All twenty-three members of the Lilliput group were now reunited. They found strength and safety in their number as they prepared for the journey back to Rozavlea. There they hoped to meet up with Frieda's, Elizabeth's, and Leah's hus-bands, who had been taken to Hungarian labor camps two years earlier. They would move back into their houses; they would find their hidden money; they would resume their lives.

Simon and Mordechai Slomowitz rushed back to the camp kitchen; the bread cart still stood where they had left it when the weather forced them to return to Birkenau. The dwarfs and the small children, along with the group's few belongings, were lifted onto the carts. Simon and his son tore blankets into strips, knotted them together, and tied one end to the four-wheeled cart. Slinging the makeshift rope over their backs, holding the other end they slowly pulled the cart out of the camp. Sarah and

Leah took turns helping at the front, while the other women pushed the cart from behind. To ease the load, the children struggled alongside in the slippery snow. "I was sitting between my aunts and uncles, watching my poor mother hitched to the cart like a human horse," recalls Shimshon Ovitz. After a few miles of pushing and pulling, they stopped by the ruin of a bridge. It had been blown up by the Wehrmacht to slow down the Russian offensive. "There was no way we could slide the cart with the dwarfs across the frozen river," explains Regina Ovitz. "We unloaded them, and Simon Slomowitz picked up Avram, the heaviest of them all. Simon walked warily, and we anxiously watched every hesitant step until he succeeded in setting Avram on the opposite bank. He returned for another one. Sarah carried one of her sisters, and since Micki was the lightest, I cradled him in my arms, carrying him like a baby to the other side. I was twenty-four, he a thirty-five-year-old man less then a meter tall, but at the time, I didn't feel embarrassed. It was the least I could do to reciprocate for the dwarfs having saved my life." This incident would take on an ambivalent quality for her months later, when the Ovitzes voiced the hope that she would become Micki's wife.

When everyone was safe on the opposite bank, Slomowitz and his son went back across the river to retrieve the cart. The group then continued the journey. Proceeding at a snail's pace, they struggled both with muddy roads and their own disorientation. For they had no idea whether they were still traveling in a zone liberated by the Russians, or had in fact wandered back behind German lines. At every crossroad they stopped, to rest and to determine in long, animated debates where to turn next. Each passing Red Army vehicle presented the threat of robbery or the humiliation of abuse and ridicule—but the human horses pulling the dwarf-laden cart amused the Russians. The drivers would hoot joyfully, and the soldiers, springing to their feet, would wave and toss them bread and vodka.

Touched by the refugees' plight, one officer gave them a horse to draw the cart. He also directed them southeast, toward Kraków, the largest town in the area, where they hoped to find a train and start the long journey home to Romania. When the cart began zigzagging erratically, they discovered that one of the gift horse's eyes was blind. And as they passed through the ruins of demolished Polish villages, they realized that they could not expect their own houses, or Rozavlea, to be intact.

It was dark when they reached the desolate village of Zator, and they spent their first night of freedom in a place that was far from a haven. Every shadow seemed menacing, for they were strangers to the area and the people. They feared that the peasants, out of sheer hostility toward returning Jews, might decide to kill them; or that the villagers might murder them in their sleep and then rob them of their scant belongings. Deciding not to enter Zator at all, they settled instead for a deserted farm on the outskirts of the village. The next day, they chanced upon a Russian soldier who advised them not to continue eastward, but rather to head north to the village of Babice and proceed from there to Kraków. In Regina Ovitz's memory, it took them a whole day to travel the six miles to Babice: "The Russian soldiers outnumbered the Polish peasants. They invited us to their camp and promised food. Considering what I'd been through in Auschwitz, I was fairly good-looking, and they were notorious for their behavior toward women. I evaded their offers and pleading, and Bassie and Elizabeth went to get the food for all of us. For the first time in my life I ate from a plastic plate." The news that a company of dwarfs had arrived in Babice traveled fast. They were summoned to the local Russian army headquarters, where what seemed like mountains of food were laid out before them. After months of near starvation, they had to resist devouring the food so as not to overload their shrunken stomachs and risk their lives.

In the morning, the Lilliput refugees said good-bye to their half-blind horse and clambered onto a military truck. On their arrival in Kraków, the Russians put them up in a hotel that previously had been confiscated by the SS, near the central square, Rynek Glowny. *The Russians treated us well, attending to all our needs. They threw a victory ball and we were invited to sing and perform. It was nearly a year since our last concert, but we hadn't lost our touch and they applauded fervently. From then on we performed for them at every birthday or holiday. One of the officers tried to tempt us with an offer for a Russian tour from an impresario friend in Moscow. We declined politely, as our hearts were longing for home.* Relaxing the rigorous survival instincts that had sustained them in Auschwitz, the Lilliputs surrendered to the joys and splendors of Kraków, which had somehow managed to escape destruction. They welcomed the attention and hospitality of the Russians; they felt flattered to be in demand again. Kraków restored their spirits and sanity, and so they delayed their departure. Weeks slipped by during which they were unconscious of the loss of independence and freedom of movement that was increasingly accompanying the Russian army's tightening hold on the region.

And then, stranded at the hotel for days on end with nothing to do, they finally broke down. The horrors they had survived and suppressed over the past endless months invaded their consciousness. "The horrifying suppressed memories began to float out and hit us," says Mordechai Slomowitz. "We now talked ceaselessly about the hell that was Auschwitz. While there you got used to seeing people burning and sealed yourself off from your surroundings. We hadn't shared our shock and fear—we had never cried, as it would have made us weak. Now, in the safety of Kraków, we talked obsessively, not omitting any of the ghastly details. We cried very often and it left us feeling drained."

When the group was finally ready to move on, they realized that their considerable number, an advantage in the camp, had now become a burden. Finding transportation for twenty-three people, not to mention food and shelter, complicated every move they planned. Nor could they travel easily as a group on roads already jammed with refugees, some of them lost and wandering aimlessly, others trying to find their way home. The Ovitzes' difficulties in continuing their journey out of Kraków were compounded by bad advice: they were told to return west and try to find a train to Romania from there.

It was Easter, April 1945, when Solomon Malik, the four-teen-year-old twin who had lived with the Lilliput men in the same Birkenau barrack, saw the dwarfs again. At liberation, he had been ill with typhus, and for two more months had remained hospitalized in Auschwitz. Once he'd recovered, he had walked and hitchhiked the twenty-five miles to the refugee camp at Kattowitz, where he was overjoyed to discover his twin sister and two four-year-old twin brothers. The Ovitzes were with them. Soon, however, the Maliks and the Ovitzes, indeed the entire camp was on the move again, because the Russians suspected that German soldiers were getting rid of their uni-forms, adopting Jewish identities, and hiding among the refugees. "It was difficult to determine on the spot who was kosher, who a murderer. So they decided to take us all to Russia and do the sorting out there," recalls Solomon Malik. They were taken to the railway station. The Lilliputs were aghast to find cattle cars awaiting them once more. This time, though, the doors were left open so the refugees could look out at the countryside and breathe fresh air during the long journey. There were frequent stops for food, as well as for relief in the woods.

They were traveling east, and as the hours passed, the Ovitzes began to find the landscape more and more familiar. Then the train pulled into the station at Czernowitz, and they could barely contain their joy. Just a few hours' drive by car from their beloved village, Czernowitz had always been one of their favorite stops when they were on tour. They had frequently appeared in the splendid Fekete Sas (Black Eagle) concert hall there. Only now their destination was the city's secondary school, which was to be their new temporary dwelling. They could walk around the town as they chose, but under no circumstances could they leave for home. It was the end of the war, May 9, 1945. The refugees found themselves in an odd situation: in Russian hands, they were neither captive, nor free.

"We know you're looking for SS soldiers. You don't suspect us of being them, so why don't you let us go?" The dwarfs pleaded with every officer who would listen. In reply, they received only sympathetic shrugs. "The Russians provided us with food and all the necessities," recalls Mordechai Slomowitz. "But after all, we were living in town and needed money. Micki and Elizabeth suggested going to the city center and giving an outdoor performance. I took a small hand cart, mounted them on it, and pushed it through the streets like a pram." Using the cart as their stage, the two smartly dressed dwarfs immediately attracted an audience. They knew the tastes of the local people well, and Micki and

Elizabeth sang for them the same favorites the Lilliput Troupe had performed there just a year or two earlier. A half hour later, coins had piled up around their legs. Mordechai pulled the cart to another spot, and another audience.

After a fortnight, the refugees were marched to the railway station. "You're going home," they were told. Avram Ovitz was skeptical: "Trust me, I know the place like the palm of my hand. If the train stands on the right platform, we'll see Rozavlea soon. But if it's on the left, we're going to Russia." The train was on the left platform. Four days later, they were in Slutsk, Belarus.

The camp in Belarus, much larger than the last one, was divided by nationality. According to Solomon Malik, "There were Jews and non-Jews, Romanians, Hungarians, Poles, and people from France. Even an entire Italian football team that had come to entertain the Italian soldiers on the front, and found themselves prisoners of war. I was put in charge of the kitchen storeroom and would steal bottles of spirit, diluting it heavily with water and making a fortune by selling it to the Italians. Our county, Maramures, had changed hands so often, from Hungary to Romania and back again, that we no longer knew to whom we belonged. But then Stalin made a goodwill gesture toward King Michael of Romania and allowed all captured Romanian soldiers to return home. We rushed to the camp commander and said, 'We're Romanian, too.' He was kind and let us join the soldiers."

As the train approached Sighet, the Lilliput group collected its belongings and hurried to the doors. The train came to a halt. But no one was permitted to deboard—an order had been issued that all passengers were to continue to the last station, Arad. It was two hundred and fifty miles farther on, at the far ends of Romania. But even in the border town of Arad, because the Russians still suspected the presence of SS men among the SS's victims, they refused to allow the passengers off the train. That night, all the suspected were assembled and ordered to raise their left arms, as the SS had tattooed the blood group of their troupers into their left armpits. Several men were arrested and sent back to Russia. So it was not until the end of August 1945, seven months after the liberation of Auschwitz, that the Lilliput group was finally, truly, free.

When all twenty-three members of the Lilliput group arrived in Rozavlea, the Slomowitzes returned to their home, as did Bassie Fischman and her mother. Regina Ovitz, who had lost her entire family in Auschwitz, had nowhere to go; she continued on with her dwarf cousins. The Ovitzes were profoundly happy to be home—even if weeds now covered their flower and vegetable beds, even if the chickens and geese no longer ran around the yard, even if the cows had disappeared from the shed. At least the house looked to be intact. Soon enough, however, they discovered that the door had been broken open. Inside, only the childlike furniture, not useful to anyone but the dwarfs, remained. The thick carpets, the filmy curtains, the hand-embroidered tapestries, all were gone. Other objects had been slashed or shattered. The floor planks had been torn up, probably in the course of someone's search for gold and other valuables. Avram and Micki rushed outside to inspect the car. It still stood dust-covered in the yard. Some parts had been damaged, and its paint had been scratched by the village children, who, it seemed, had played in it during the war. Apparently, though, no one had attempted to move it from its place. Avram and Micki waited anxiously until midnight to investigate the ground beneath it. They crawled under the chassis and groped around until they felt a small hollow. Silently, like moles, they clawed the earth away. The jar was there, just as they had left it, filled to the brim with their jewelry and gold coins.

Bad news soon followed. From Jewish refugees returning from the camps, the Ovitzes learned that their brother Arie, with eight of his friends, had managed to escape the Hungarian labor camp to which he had been sent, only to be betrayed in Bihorpnspoki, where they were hiding on a deserted farm. A peasant woman informed on them; all nine were summarily shot. Already devastated, the Ovitzes then learned the terrible fate of his wife, twenty-four-year-old Magda, who had arrived at Auschwitz with her parents and a four-month-old baby just four days after her in-laws. The four of them were immediately sentenced to death. More bad news came from a group of men who had been in a slave labor camp in the Urals: Izo Edenburg, Frieda's husband, had died of hunger.

For the traditional seven days of mourning the dead—the *Shiva*—the Ovitz women wore black, and the men did not shave. Each day they assembled in one room to cry and to pray. They watched the candles they'd lit for the souls of their loved ones flicker. Worried, they watched. For they had still no news of the husbands of Elizabeth and Leah.

SEVENTEEN

Sighet-Antwerp, 1945–1949

Six hundred and fifty Jews had been driven out of Rozavlea in the spring of 1944. A year later, only fifty had survived to return to the village of their birth.

In their year's absence, some of their houses had been occupied by Romanian squatters, and the authorities showed no inclination to evacuate them in favor of the lawful owners. Their neighbors, meanwhile, viewed them with eyes full of envy as they retrieved furnishings from the homes of dead family members in order to make their own looted dwellings once more habitable. The Ovitzes strove to restore a sense of normalcy. Simon Slomowitz nailed their floor planks back down where they belonged; Sarah gathered a collection of essential pots and pans. They all agreed that for the time being they could live without curtains. The nights were getting chilly, so they were thankful that at least the fireplace had not been damaged. In their backyard they lit a bonfire, and around it each of them waited with a little pile of the clothes they had worn in Auschwitz. First, Avram threw in his coat, and they all watched as the flames scorched and devoured it. Next it was Rozika's turn, and once her dresses had dissolved completely, Franziska threw hers into the blaze. As if they were participating in an ancient ritual, the Ovitzes stood silently in their circle until every trace—every ruffle, feather, button, and patch—had turned to ash.

Soon after arriving back in Rozavlea, Bassie Fischman found a new love, Abe Glazer, who had himself just returned from Auschwitz. Along with her mother, they applied for immigration visas to America, where Bassie's brother was already living. The Ovitzes, meanwhile, had enlarged their household. They had seen their neighbors' orphaned daughter, Gitta, crying on the stairway of her deserted house, and taken her in. "There were not enough beds, so I shared one, sometimes with Perla, sometimes with Sarah," recalls Gitta Drattler-Budimsky. "They did everything they could to cheer me up and taught me some songs. I was a shy, fourteen-year-old Orthodox girl, and didn't know any dances. So the dwarf women played some tangos and waltzes, and Micki led me through the living room and taught me the steps. He was such a skillful teacher that I hardly noticed he was half my size. I wanted to do my share of housework, but they wouldn't hear of it."

The Lilliputs viewed their seventeen-month absence from the stage as an intermission forced upon them by the war, but with the war now over and liberation secure, they were ready to resume their lives and their careers. Rozavlea would once again be home port, and from there they would travel to perform. But Rozavlea had changed. *When we asked for our belongings, the neighbors refused to return them. They said, "You suffered in Poland, but we suffered here." They did not hide their hostility: "We had it so good without you, why have you returned?" I fired back, "It was God's*

Baby Shimshon, in Sighet, just after liberation from Auschwitz.

The Slomowitz Family: The photo was taken in Sighet in 1946. **From left to right:** father Simon, his sons Judah and Josef, in the middle daughter Helene (Hannah), and in the bottom row—youngest daughter Serene (Sarah), and mother Chaya. (Courtesy of the Slomowitz family)

Avram (right), wife Dora, and daughter, Batia, in Sighet, 1946.

Left: Dina Gottlieb and her mother Johannah, Nice, 1946. (Courtesy of Dina Gottlieb-Babbitt)
Above: Regina Ovitz, Sighet, 1946. (Courtesy of Regina Ovitz-Preisler)

Antwerp, 1949: Rehearsing for a Hanukah skit. **Left to right:** Elizabeth, Micki, Shimshon, Perla.

Rehearsing the skit "In the Tailor's Shop," in Antwerp, 1949. **From right to left:** tall man, Perla, Micki, Elizabeth.

Program for the musical and comedy revue of the Lilliput Troupe. Antwerp, 1949.

P R O G R A M M E

P R O G R A M M E

I.

1). Marsch
2). Hofmans erzehlung
3). Honsredil
4). Hitz
5). Je suis seul ce soir
6). Cu dona soapte dulci
7). Dus pintele jid
8). Fun in Fkarel
9). No
10). Hikewini
11). Di veiber

II.

Komedie in 1 act
DI FALSE LIEBE

Anteil nemmer :

Ovici Dolly
in rol van gii benitzer Kalman Klaps
Ovici Greta
in rol van di almune Madam Flamensip
Ovici Elizabet
in rol van di cardi dame Lara
Ovici Perla
in rol van di dinst moid Fania
Ovici Markus
in rol van kutscher Don

Eine bearbeiting in Regie von Jakob Cyterman

Micki on the deck of the Atzmaut ship on the way to Israel, May 1949.

Immigrant camp: Two photos taken at the Bat Galim immigration camp in 1949, where they lived until 1955.

Top photo, left to right: Avram, Frieda, Elizabeth, Micki, Perla.

Bottom photo, left to right: Elizabeth, Perla, Rozika, Frieda, Franziska, Micki.

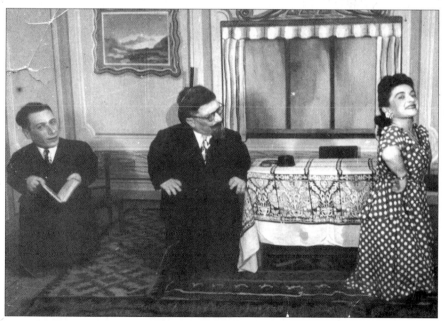

Micki, Avram, and Perla onstage, Israel, early 1950s.

Perla, Frieda, and Elizabeth onstage and backstage, in Israel, early 1950s.
Clockwise from top left: Perla (right) and Elizabeth, Elizabeth, Frieda, and Elizabeth.

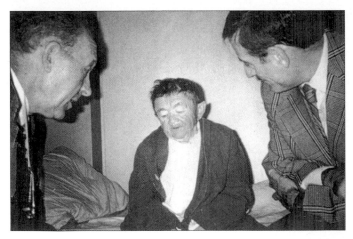

Top: Ludovit Feld (in the middle), with Kalman Bar On (left) and Peter Grunfeld (right), in Slovakia, October 1989. (Courtesy of *Yedioth Achronot*, Tel Aviv).

Above: Perla on the Haifa promenade in May 2000, with Yehuda Koren. (Courtesy of the authors)

Left: Perla celebrating her 80th birthday (January 10, 2001), with Eilat Negev. (Courtesy of the authors)

Frieda and Micki, backstage, in Israel, early 1950s.

Reading the Megila scroll on Purim: Haifa, Israel,
late 1950s. **Left to right:** Frieda, Perla, Franziska, Sarah,
Avram (reading), Elizabeth, Moshe Moskowitz, Micki.

will that we survive." But I was frightened by this homecoming. Rozavlea had become a graveyard. The stillness of the empty houses, the lost synagogue, the faces missing from the street—Rozavlea was increasingly unbearable.

They decided to move to the town of Sighet, now a haven for Jewish refugees who had been uprooted from their villages. At 40 Bogdan Voda—on the main street, and just a short walk from the only synagogue still standing—the Ovitzes found an apartment: the entire first floor of a grand house that had been the property of a wealthy Jewish family exterminated in Auschwitz. The Slomowitz family followed suit, and occupied a flat near the Ovitzes.

Once again, the Lilliputs assembled their orchestra. They replaced the missing instruments; they rehearsed their repertoire. On weekends, they converted their spacious living room into a ballroom. The entrance fee was affordable. "Only the young had come back from the camps. We were on our own, youth with no authority or responsibility, no longer as pious as before the war," observes Shoshana Glazer, who lost her parents, grandparents, and six brothers and sisters in Auschwitz. "Just a year and a half before, Jewish teenagers like myself had not been allowed to mix and never thought of really dancing together. Now, the floor was always packed with dancing couples." Nevertheless, patrons were limited in Sighet—and everywhere else in northern Transylvania. The region's community of 154,000 Jews on the eve of the war, had, after all, been reduced to only a few thousand, and they were trying desperately to rebuild their lives. The Lilliputs had lost their core of Jewish fans. Not only were the survivors too poor and too few to provide an audience, but Romanian towns and villages had also been rendered destitute. The Lilliputs soon realized they could not possibly earn a living in the area, but neither could they leave. For Leah and Elizabeth had still heard no word from their husbands.

Just ten days after her wedding in November 1942, Elizabeth Moskowitz's husband had been torn from her. In spring 1945, freed from labor-camp slavery, Moshe Moskowitz rushed home to find her. What he found was a house looted and empty, with no sign at all that the Ovitzes had returned to Rozavlea after liberation. Neighbors were no help, and answered his anxious inquiries with blank stares. The Lilliputs were in fact still in Russian captivity. Moskowitz lost hope of ever seeing his beloved Elizabeth again. He left Rozavlea with a last memento: a photograph he found in a drawer. In the photo, as elsewhere, Elizabeth is safely embraced by her family.

Taken in 1927, the oval-shaped photo constitutes one of the few remnants of the Ovitz clan's prewar life. It shows Batia Ovitz surrounded by her children. Twenty-four-year-old Avram is sitting authoritatively next to her, his legs dangling above the ground; Elizabeth, only thirteen, is lying on the carpet, with her head resting against her six-year-old sister, Perla. All the dwarf children are leaning back, as if they are trying not to strain their weak spines while the photographer fusses with the focus and adjusts his camera. The boys are wearing top hats and bow ties; they have snow-white handkerchiefs folded neatly in the upper pocket of their jackets. Apparently, Avram already needs a cane, while Micki, at eighteen still shy about his handicap, uses an umbrella as a crutch—although it was a warm day. Batia's dark dress has long sleeves and a high neck; a modest scarf hides her hair. Her daughter Frieda, though, is wearing a low décolletage, and long earrings peep out from her thick black curls. Not long after the camera captured a blissful Ovitz family in this photograph, Batia would fall ill and be bedridden until death.

Moskowitz put the photo in his suitcase and headed southward for the Romanian capital, Bucharest, where he hoped to collect some information about the fate of the Ovitz family. He was lucky. At the office of the Jewish community, quite by chance, he ran into his brother-in-law Azriel Ovitz, Leah's cousin and husband, who had also recently visited Rozavlea. Like Moskowitz, he had found no evidence to indicate that their loved ones had survived Auschwitz. For days the two men carefully pored over survivor lists, but they found nothing. Then, Moskowitz learned from another survivor that his sister was alive and well in Rome. So with limited options, and in a state of desperation, he took the train to Rome, while Azriel decided to try his luck again in Transylvania. In Sighet, the beadle at the synagogue directed Azriel to the Ovitzes' new apartment. There, for the first time, he saw his three-year-old son, Shimshon. A year later, Leah bore a daughter they named Batia.

In January 1946, Moskowitz, still in Rome, accidentally bumped into a relative of the Ovitzes who was on his way back to Sighet. On a piece of paper, Moskowitz scribbled some words of love and hope, along with his address; to the note he attached the photograph. He had no idea whether Elizabeth and her family were still alive, but he used every opportunity to look for them. Through the Jewish community in Sighet, the messenger traced the Ovitzes, and Elizabeth cabled her husband immediately. Once he arrived at Sighet, the Ovitzes were finally able to leave.

The only country that agreed to provide the Ovitzes with entry visas was Belgium. Although they had never performed there, and had no knowledge of the country's languages, they were encouraged to learn that many of their compatriots had already begun a new life among the diamond merchants in

Antwerp's Yiddish-speaking community. In Belgium, too, they thought they would be closer to America.

Cousin Regina, reluctant to join the family on its new odyssey, chose to remain in Romania. The Ovitzes allowed her the use of their devastated house in Rozavlea, which she made as livable as she could. She would always appreciate the parcels of food that they later sent her from Antwerp. As for Simon Slomowitz, who had stood by the Lilliputs' side for the past three decades, he would follow the troupe wherever they decided to go. His wife was not happy with the prospect of Antwerp, especially since their grown children were not joining them; Mordechai and Fanny had decided to stay in Romania, less because they were emotionally exhausted than because they no longer wanted their destiny to be bound with the dwarfs'. Years later, Mordechai and Fanny would immigrate to Israel.

We took a taxi, to see our village for the last time. In the cemetery we bid farewell to our parents. We wept by their tombstones, asking for forgiveness at having to leave them behind forever. We knew we would never set foot in that country again.

In the spring of 1947, there were a quarter of a million displaced Jews in Europe. Most of them were living in tents and barracks at refugee camps, under the administration of relief organizations. The Ovitzes, their family intact, had escaped that sad fate. In Antwerp, where half of the Jewish community had perished, the Ovitzes easily found a vacant and furnished apartment on Maria Magdalena Street. The Slomowitzes rented a flat just opposite.

The death camps had left the survivors exhausted. After the horrors they had witnessed, and the cries they had heard, they wished only for peace and quiet. Placid Belgium afforded the Ovitzes simple pleasures. They enjoyed the life of Antwerp's Orthodox community, which, while decimated, had retained remarkable prosperity. As they became more familiar with the country and its customs, they began considering how they might revamp their performances to suit new audiences. Meanwhile, each of the men found work—in the diamond market, the furrier workshops, or the American army warehouses.

The Ovitzes were embraced by their next-door neighbors, a childless Catholic couple who owned a fruit and vegetable shop. Perla in particular was the apple of their eye. Whenever she passed by, the greengrocer would lift her up like a doll and plead with her to take whatever she liked: "You've suffered enough," he'd say. Perla was twenty-eight at the time but was happy to be babied. The grocer always diverted his eyes from her arm. Begging her to cover her tattooed number, he'd say, "I can't be reminded of what they did to you."

At this time, Dina Gottlieb and her mother were in Paris. They had survived the wintry death march out of Auschwitz, and the liberation had found them in the Neustadt-Glewe concentration camp. Once freed, Dina and her mother had headed immediately for their hometown of Brno, where Dina was anxious to rejoin her boyfriend, Karel Klinger. She had not seen Karel in two years. In Brno, a mutual friend who had been imprisoned with him at Dachau handed Dina a note. "I declare Dina Gottliebova to be my lawful wedded wife," she read. It was dated a few days before Karel died, on the eve of liberation. He would remain the great love of her life. With her only reason for staying in Brno gone, Dina and her mother moved to Paris, where Dina had an uncle. There, she resumed her artistic studies and met an American, Arthur Babbitt. It seemed like destiny when she learned that he had been a senior animator on Disney's *Snow White and the Seven Dwarfs*. Babbitt introduced Dina to the world of film animation. Eventually, they married and settled in Hollywood, where Dina became a housewife and raised two daughters. She returned to the art of animation after her divorce, which followed fourteen years of marriage. Despite her longtime fascination with Disney's classic, she could not ever bring herself to paint dwarfs again.

"One day," Dina recounts, "I met a man who offered to take off my tattooed Birkenau number for fifty dollars. I didn't think much and let him do it. Now whenever I look at the thin white scar on my forearm I regret it. I realize it was my lucky number and I shouldn't run away from my past. When I play the lottery, I use my camp number, 61016, and I've also made it my e-mail address." In 1973 Dina learned that seven of the Gypsy portraits she had executed for Mengele, including the one of Celine, had miraculously survived and were being exhibited at the Auschwitz State Museum. Since then, Dina Gottlieb-Babbitt has been battling the museum authorities to retrieve them.

Dina's case embodies a clash between two opposing principles. On the one hand is the American faith in the paramount value of individual rights; on the other, a strong conviction— one solidly grounded in Poland's communist era—of the paramount value of the collective good. The result is a tangle of conflicting moral and legal rights that King Solomon would have found difficult to sort out. The museum claims that everything found and made in the death camp should remain at Auschwitz unto perpetuity, as evidence of the Nazi atrocities and as a memorial to the victims. As the portraits were not undertaken at Dina's initiative but commissioned by Mengele, the museum contends, they are not one individual's expressive works of art; rather, they are medical illustrations that constitute the documentation of a crime. "My paintings saved my life, and thanks to them I lived to raise a family," argues Gottlieb-Babbitt. "They are a part of my soul, and I won't be complete without them. As long as they are there, I'll still be a prisoner in Auschwitz."

After the liberation, Ludovit Feld, one of the ten dwarfs in Mengele's collection, returned to his Czechoslovakian hometown of Kosice, where he resumed his artistic career and became one of his country's renowned painters and art teachers. Although his long-standing conversion to Christianity had not prevented his deportation, the experience of Auschwitz did not immediately propel him back to the old faith. On his return he sought refuge first in the Christian church, but he found no real peace of mind. He then turned to various Marxist and Leninist models of secular religion, which likewise failed him. Disappointed and disillusioned, he began attending synagogue services regularly. It took Kalman Bar-On and Peter Grünfeld forty-four years to track down Feld. In the autumn of 1989 they traveled from Israel to Czechoslovakia to meet him again. Then eighty-five, Feld had never married and continued to live on his own, almost blind, bedridden. At his bedside, he kept an album of his drawings, entitled "Children Are Also Led to Death."

"Throughout the years, I've been waiting for you," Feld said to his visitors. "I can hardly see, but each of the twin's faces I painted in Birkenau is etched deep inside me. I remember the pretty face of one child with special sharpness—Pepicheck, who couldn't sit still when I painted him. What happened to him? Did he survive?" Peter Grünfeld knelt by Feld's bed and let the blind man feel Pepicheck's wet cheeks. Ludovit Feld died in May 1991. A black marble tombstone in the Jewish cemetery of Kosice bears his full Hebrew name in Hebrew letters.

🖋

Liberation and the war's end did not, for the most part, bring harsh justice to Josef Mengele and his associates. SS *Obersturm-führer* Dr. Heinz Thilo, Mengele's Auschwitz rival, was transferred to Gross-Rosen concentration camp at the end of 1944. His fate remains unknown; he is thought to have been killed either in Hohenelbe in May 1945 or in Berlin in October 1947. Professor Otmar von Verschuer, Mengele's professional sponsor and head of the genetic and hereditary research program at the Kaiser Wilhelm Institute, was declared a Nazi sympathizer by a Frankfurt denazification court in 1946; he was fined six hundred marks. In 1951, he became professor of human genetics at the University of Munster; three years later, he was promoted to the position of dean of the medical faculty. On his sixtieth birthday, in 1956, he was commended as a "master and teacher" by the distinguished Italian eugenecist Luigi Gedda in the Italian magazine of eugenics, *Acta Genet*—a citation that stands among similar honors bestowed on him by the American, Italian, Austrian, and Japanese societies for human genetics. Von Verschuer died in 1969. His wicked deeds went ignored to the end.

Mengele's academic rival, Professor Hans Grebe, obtained a teaching position in the Department of Human Genetics at the University of Marburg in 1953; in 1957 he became president of the German Association of Sport Doctors. Grebe, like von Verschuer, vigorously denied any collaboration with Mengele at Auschwitz. He also destroyed all incriminating documents. The medical records kept by von Verschuer at the Kaiser Wilhelm Institute are not available to researchers: in a bizarre irony, sixty years after their extermination, the Nazi doctors' Jewish victims have been transformed by German officials into esteemed patients whose right to privacy must be steadfastly safeguarded.

In 1948, the Kaiser Wilhelm Institute was renamed the Max Planck Institute. A half century later, in June 2001, the society's president, Professor Hubert Markl, issued the following statement: "There is scientific evidence proving beyond the shadow of a doubt that directors and employees at the Kaiser Wilhelm Gesellschaft were together intellectually responsible for, and sometimes even actively collaborated in, the crimes of the Nazi regime." This came as no news to Efraim Reichenberg, a survivor of Mengele's experiments. "Over all these years, I've been aware that Mengele was simply a little cog in the machinery of mass murder. The biggest crime in history was carried out under the direction of leading scientists and distinguished institutions." Reichenberg and six other victims were flown to Berlin to hear Markl express his formal "apology and deep regret . . . personally and on behalf of the Max Planck Institute . . . [that] crimes of this sort were committed, promoted, and not prevented within the ranks of German scientists."

On January 17, 1945, Mengele left Auschwitz. He traveled first to Gross-Rosen, where he shed his SS uniform. Then, dressed in a Wehrmacht uniform, he continued on to Saaz in the Sudetenland to work in a field hospital. He carried with him two suitcases filled with his research data. It is highly likely that the data included reports on the Lilliput group experiments. It is also likely that Mengele viewed the data as a potential noose—as the proof of his crimes—at the same time that he saw it as a potential springboard to a new academic career. On the night of May 8,

1945, the date of Germany's unconditional surrender, Mengele deposited the two suitcases with a nurse who had worked with him in Saaz. He then fled to Saxony, where he was captured by the Americans in late June 1945. He was registered under his real name in an American POW camp. The United Nations War Crimes Commission had already declared him a major war criminal, but the "wanted" list never reached the camp. Josef Mengele was released two months later.

Mengele did not go straight home to his wife and child; nor did he visit his parents. Instead, risking capture by the Russians, he set out on a long journey to the Thuringian town of Gera. There he visited the nurse with whom he had entrusted the two suitcases. Upon his return, he sped south from central Germany to Bavaria, and took shelter on an isolated farm near the village of Mangolding. His wife, Irene, afraid that she'd be followed by the American military, hazarded only one visit, in the summer of 1946. Posner and Ware suggest that around that time Mengele's marriage was coming to an end; the fugitive doctor no longer held the promise Irene had pinned her hopes on.

Mengele must have followed the Nuremberg trial of his former Nazi medical friends and colleagues in December 1946 with some degree of apprehension. Seven of them would be hanged; five would receive life sentences. On the other hand, the apparent social and professional rehabilitation of his superiors—the onset of their embrace by postwar Germany's academic community—must have stirred in him considerable envy. They had accomplished what to him was now unattainable. For Mengele had decided to stay away from Europe until it tired of pursuing Nazi war criminals. He arrived in Buenos Aires in late August 1949 and passed through customs with a suitcase containing his data on the Auschwitz medical experiments. A month later, the special German academic commission that had already rehabilitated von Verschuer threw Mengele a lifeline as well: "From the available evidence, it is not clear how much Dr. Mengele himself knew of the atrocities and killings in Auschwitz during the times in question," it announced. Evidently, Mengele did not consider the lifeline reliable enough. He decided to remain in South America.

In 1949, the Lilliputs were themselves trying to decide whether to stay on in Europe or leave for good. After two admittedly tranquil years in Belgium, they still felt rootless. *We were expelled from our parents' house, from a country where we were famous. We managed to survive one Hitler, but who can promise us another miracle?* Perla Ovitz would say to her siblings in their family debates. The memory of Auschwitz clung to all of them, and none of them believed the virulent European anti-Semitism had ended with the war. America seemed a safer place. Their career still on hold, they gladly accepted the occasional invitation to sing at a benefit for the newly established state of Israel. And on every Passover they enunciated the traditional "next year in Jerusalem." Never, though, had they seriously considered turning the prayer into actuality.

Before the war, immigration to Palestine had been controlled by its British rulers, who issued a limited number of entry visas for distribution by the Jewish Agency. The Zionist vision then favored the young and able-bodied. The image of the New Jew— a broad-shouldered, hard-working, suntanned pioneer—conflicted rather starkly with the Ovitzes' deformity. In any case, only a handful of their normal-sized neighbors in prewar

Rozavlea had immigrated to Palestine. As Orthodox Jews, the Ovitzes were not eager to follow them, as they were not keen on the Zionist society taking shape there and turning its back on religion. For the Lilliput Troupe, a new life in a land where Yiddish was frowned upon, where the old culture was scorned and the folk traditions banished, would have been artistic suicide.

Following the Second World War, Palestine had become a haven for the refugees who had survived the "final solution." Still, the obstacles placed in the path to the Promised Land seemed insurmountable to the Lilliputs. The British Mandate authorities were issuing only 1,500 visas a month, so their chances of obtaining even one were virtually nil. Nor were the Ovitzes capable of smuggling themselves illegally, boarding an ancient, overloaded cargo boat that might land them in Palestine furtively, at nightfall, off one of its deserted beaches. Tens of thousands of Jews had already resorted to just such a strategy, some of them making their way into the arms of Jewish underground members who would guide them through the water to the shore—and then living in hiding, with the constant fear of being arrested by the British police. Those were the lucky ones. The majority would in fact be caught and sent to internment camps. It was obvious that the Ovitzes were not fit for such an ordeal. And the War of Independence, which started on November 30, 1947, marked the onset of an even worse time for them to immigrate. Israel was thus relegated to last on a list of possibilities.

The Lilliputs missed the stage. The offer to perform in Russia was still on the table. And there was a Lilliputian village in Budapest, but they were too independent—some found them superciliously so—for such an enterprise, and they deplored any vulgar exploitation of their handicap. They had reconciled themselves to the idea of a final, if early, retirement from show business when suddenly they received a dream invitation: the impresario Irving Jacobson was offering them a long-term contract to perform in one of New York's Yiddish theaters. The financial arrangements were especially tempting. And then, equally out of the blue, came a second option. Israeli immigration emissaries, dispatched throughout Europe, had been channeling Holocaust survivors toward the new Jewish state, and when the Belgian branch learned that the Lilliputs were planning to leave for New York, they knocked on the Ovitzes' door. The War of Independence was over, the Israelis told them, and proceeded to promise financial benefits that matched the American offer.

By 1949, the Israeli option had also become culturally more appealing to the Lilliputs. While Hebrew had been the dominant language of art and culture in Jewish Palestine, the tens of thousands of European refugees now expanding the population of the new Israeli state meant that Yiddish had gained a new audience. And the Lilliput Troupe had gained a new chance. *When our next-door neighbors in Antwerp heard that we planned to leave, they begged us to stay, promising they would designate us as sole heirs. But while we were divided between America and Israel, we did agree on one thing—not to stay in Europe any longer. In the family discussions I favored America. I said Israel is like a young chick that has just emerged from its egg, let's go to America, make money, and then settle comfortably in Israel with full pockets. Those who preferred going to Israel right away pointed out that our previous fans had been immigrating there by the day, while in America nobody knew us. We were frightened by what people said about America being a competitive, cruel society, about us not being able to live up to its tempo. When we were too weak to perform, we'd be thrown to the dogs.*

The head of the family, Avram Ovitz, cast the final vote:

"Enough wandering. It's time we settle down and live among our kin." So they changed the forwarding labels on their packed crates from "New York" to "Haifa." On May 4, 1949, the *Atzmaut* (Independence) set sail from the port of Marseille. The Lilliputs and 2,150 other passengers celebrated Israel's first Independence Day in the middle of the Mediterranean.

EIGHTEEN

Haifa, 1949–1954

On Monday, May 9, 1949, Leah Ginzburg-Fried, the correspondent in Haifa for the newspaper *Ma'ariv*, took the bus to the port downtown. It was a routine stop on her morning rounds, since thousands of immigrants were disembarking daily. Standing by the gangway, chatting with her colleagues, she threw an occasional glance at the descending passengers. A middle-aged, elegantly clad man walked nonchalantly down a gangplank. The press people instantly recognized the face of Sidney Stanley and besieged him with questions about his involvement in a British government financial scandal. He answered them with the arrogance of a man who had, after all, escaped from London in the middle of his trial. He seemed to feel safe in his new haven.

Stanley commanded attention, certainly, but out of a corner of her eye, Ginzburg-Fried caught a peculiar sight. Seven dwarfs were carefully negotiating the gangway. They each held the rail with one hand to balance themselves as they stretched out a leg to reach the step below; their strange parade moved slowly forward.

Ginzburg-Fried wavered between the two attractions. She hastily scribbled down the fugitive Stanley's statements while keeping an eye on her other newsworthy catch. She lost sight of them for brief moments when the dwarfs got hidden in the general commotion on the dock, but at her first opportunity she dashed over to them.

"The unusual phenomenon of seven dwarfs caused much attention, and the passersby gaped at them," she later reported in *Maariv*. "Someone tried to drive the intruders away. Someone else lowered his voice and reproached the onlookers: 'They're human beings like us, only small. Of all people, Jews should not be prejudiced and offend handicapped people with an intrusive gaze.' " When the crowd began to disperse, Perla Ovitz, in a long black dress and with a red flower tucked into her hair, stepped forward with a buoyant smile. "We're not intimidated by inquisitive eyes," she is quoted as saying. "Millions of people have been watching us throughout our entire lives. Naturally we'd like to be no different than you, but if this is the shape God destined for us, we have no complaints against him."

Leah Ginzburg-Fried stooped down. Her pleated skirt touching the ground, her pad resting on her knee, she began to take down the Lilliputs' story, from the limelight of prewar Romania to the cesspool of Auschwitz. They spared no details and candidly discussed one event in particular—their humiliating presentation at the SS medical convention, when Mengele ordered them to strip naked. In this respect, the dwarfs were unusually frank, for it is now well known that a great many Holocaust survivors, guilt-ridden by their own chance deliverance, have been extremely reluctant to explore their traumatic memories, let alone to disclose the horrors they experienced.

The Lilliput Troupe had planned their grand entrance. The

dwarfs refused any assistance offered them in their difficult but not undramatic march down the gangway. They handled the interview skillfully. They knew what to withhold and what to reveal; they knew how to make their opinions and disclosures quotable. They showed themselves to be in good shape and in good spirits, for to solicit pity or display weakness, they knew, would harm the chances of a comeback. The sixty-three-year-old Rozika Ovitz said she was forty-five; twenty-eight-year-old Perla demurely declared she was nineteen. Six-year-old Shimshon, heedless of the shock he was causing, ran around proudly showing off his tattoo. They would ask for no special favors from the state, Ginzburg-Fried jotted down in her notebook. Indeed, they had a message to the contrary: "Our only wish is to bring some laughter and joy to our brethren in our new homeland."

Exactly five years earlier, the Hungarian press had documented the dwarfs' expulsion to Auschwitz. On that hot May day in the Dragomiresti ghetto, they had been dressed in layers of winter garments, as they were traveling into an unknown future. For their arrival in Haifa they had appropriately chosen more summery clothes. Franziska and Rozika were wearing identical long, flower-printed cotton dresses; Elizabeth wore an elegant two-piece summer suit.

One photographer asked a uniformed policeman to stand beside one of the lady dwarfs; as before, the contrast between big man and small woman made for an eye-catching image. The UPI photographer set up the seven dwarfs in a semicircle. In his photo, Micki and Avram have taken off their summer jackets and rolled up their white shirtsleeves; their engraved, silver-handled canes cast aside, they're standing energetically erect. With their neat and fashionable garments, their makeup and styled hair, the dwarfs made everyone around them look shabby. They are smiling at the camera, as if they are about to bow to an applauding crowd. To this day, the UPI photograph is reprinted in a university genetics textbook to illustrate the "human pseudoachondroplasia phenotype determined by a dominant allele that interferes with bone growth during the development."

Ginzburg-Fried followed the Lilliput Troupe to the immigrant camp of Bat Galim. In the first year of Israel's independence, the nation of 650,000 had to absorb 200,000 new immigrants. As accommodation for the influx of newcomers was next to nonexistent, vacated British army camps, abandoned Arab houses, and makeshift tent cities became their temporary homes. The Ovitzes had barely unpacked their suitcases when agents and producers came courting. While the Lilliputs basked in their renewed celebrity, they nonetheless remained cautious, and diplomatically postponed a decision. "First, we want to see the country, then we'll find a place to live. Only after performing for the Israeli soldiers and making them happy will we talk about business."

The Ovitzes' new start would incidentally end their thirty years of friendship with the Slomowitzes. The two families had jointly struggled in a daily battle with the harshest conditions of human survival imaginable. Only two of all the extended Jewish families that had entered Auschwitz emerged intact: the Ovitz and Slomowitz families from Rozavlea. If it had not been for the Lilliputs' willingness, at a risk to their own lives, to falsely present to Mengele their neighbors as family, the Slomowitzes would certainly have perished. But with the danger over, the dynamic of debits and credits that had strengthened their relationship in the death camp no longer served as a bond; instead, it strained the relationship.

"Mother demanded that we not see them anymore once we set foot in Israel," recalls Judah Slomowitz. "She was always scolding Father: 'You have a wife and children, whom you neglect all the time to serve those dwarfs hand and foot.' Father was torn: 'They saved our lives! We owe them everything.' But Mother had the last word: 'You're turning us into their slaves and I've had enough of it.' So we sailed on separate boats, and while they settled in Haifa we went south to Ramla."

The fate that the Ovitzes and the Slomowitzes had shared had bred in the two families a mutual sense of resentment over each other's lack of appreciation. Indebted to the Lilliputs for their lives, the Slomowitzes felt that they could do nothing, ultimately, to sufficiently gratify their saviors. Regina, as well as Bassie Fischman and her mother, felt the same way.

"No doubt I owe my life to them, but at the same time they wouldn't have survived Birkenau if we hadn't been there to care for them," says Bassie Fischman, now Glazer, living in New York. "We carried them in our arms, stood in line to bring them food, helped them dress and wash up. We were their human horses, and without us they couldn't have made the journey back home. We're equal parties—they saved us and we saved them."

The break was also favored by the Ovitzes, who felt that they had been exploited by their debtors. Only Simon Slomowitz truly regretted the rupture between the two families, and he couldn't keep away. To his dying day, in 1977, he would travel discreetly up to Haifa in order to spend some cheerful hours with the dwarfs and provide a helping hand around the house; he would continue, too, as always, to bask in the presence of his Frieda.

All fifteen members of the Ovitz family settled in a long wooden barrack near the sea. Each received an iron bed, a straw

mattress, a woolen blanket, two sheets, and the maximum set-
tlement allowance of forty dollars. Hanging blankets divided the
barrack into small family units and allowed for some intimacy.
*Part of the outer wall was missing, and the blanket we hung in its
place did not help much to keep away the wind and chill. There was
no escape from the constant noise of the waves, especially at night,
and I lay awake for hours. We became bitter: was this the "villa" they
promised when they convinced us not to accept the American con-
tract? Dr. Mengele had at least provided us with a room with a toilet;
here in our new homeland they didn't want to waste proper accommodations on us because we were dwarfs.*

Still, the family of dwarfs soon became magnets for the press.
One Israeli weekly offered its readers five photos of the Lilliputs
engaged in various pursuits: in one, the dwarfs are being interviewed by kneeling journalists; in another, Micki and Avram are
wrapped in their prayer shawls; a third shows Rozika and
Franziska with their small violins; in the fourth, Frieda is hug-
ging her nephew and niece, little Shimshon and Batia. The
fifth—a photo of the elderly sisters powdering their noses—carries the caption "A woman is a woman, and makeup is essential,
regardless of age and size." The Lilliputs also attracted Kalman
Ginzburg, the Israeli impresario, who persuaded them to join
his list of such celebrity clients as Jascha Heifetz, Isaac Stern,
Yehudi Menuhin, and Leonard Bernstein. Ginzburg bombarded
municipal and governmental offices with letters demanding that
the Lilliput Troupe be exempted from the high entertainment
taxes. To reinforce the letters, he had all seven dwarfs storm the
offices.

The Israeli bureaucracy did not act promptly upon
Ginzburg's petitions, so, adding more pressure, he organized a
press conference at the distinguished Tel Aviv Commercial

Club. The invitation promised lunch—one way to ensure a full journalistic presence in a time of austerity; the tables were indeed lavishly laid. Ginzburg opened the occasion by describing the Lilliput Troupe's European career and widespread popularity. He pointed out that the dwarfs had received alluring offers from both Moscow and New York, yet they had chosen to settle instead in Israel, despite the financial sacrifice. He lauded the unique style of their performances, which preserved a Jewish heritage that the past decade had greatly endangered and nearly destroyed. And he declared the Lilliputs' intention to establish their own theater in Israel.

Then, Avram Ovitz rose, and not a single eye missed the tattooed number on his arm. He briefly described the troupe's Auschwitz experiences before taking questions from the floor. To one reporter he explained, "Our first performances will be in Yiddish, but we are already making an effort to acquire Hebrew as quickly as possible and use it onstage." He was vague about the repertoire: "First of all, we'll show the Israelis what a dwarf family can do." Soon after the press conference—and before the troupe had publicly performed even one song—the Ministry of Finance had granted Ginzburg's demands on their behalf. They would receive the same tax-exempt status accorded such celebrated institutions as the Israeli Philharmonic Orchestra and the Habima Theater. While the ministry did not mention the Lilliputs' dwarfdom, it most certainly influenced the decision; for if the troupe found itself unable to perform and make a living from music, then the fifteen Ovitzes would add a far from negligible burden to the state's already sorely overstretched social services.

Some publicists disapproved. "A short stature is not a guarantee of high standards," Alexander Tauber wrote in one tabloid. "The only grounds for judgment is artistic excellence, and this even holds true for dwarfs. Let them first perform, and if the critics declare that they have raised artistic standards in Israel, then they have grounds to apply for a tax exemption."

Even before the ministry's decision, the Lilliputs, certain that they would be granted the exemption, had booked the most prestigious halls in Israel for the entire month of August. Their publicity campaign was intense and expensive. Huge advertisements in ten newspapers and billboards all over the country announced: "The Lilliput Troupe: first performances ever in Israel, in songs and music, folklore, comedy and drama." Racing against the clock so as not to lose the summer season, they had to hire carpenters to work day and night to build the set and props. The chairs and tables were built in miniature, as they had been in the old country; assisted by a professional, Egyptian-born seamstress, Elizabeth and Perla made glittering new costumes for the entire cast.

The Lilliputs' career was launched anew on August 4, 1949—exactly five years, by the Jewish calendar, after the performance perversely commanded by Mengele at Auschwitz on the day of the Tishah B'Av fast. Observing tradition, the Lilliputs ate nothing the whole day; they prayed and lamented the temple's destruction. But three hours after the fast had ended, they were onstage in Armon (Palace Hall) in their hometown of Haifa. They had fierce competition for audiences that month. The Israel Opera was staging *La Bohème* and *The Barber of Seville;* mime Marcel Marceau was bringing his show from Paris; the Habima Theater was presenting its big hit *In the Negev Prairies,* a controversial play about the sacrifice of young men in the War of Independence. But the competition did not diminish the Lilliput Troupe's success. Their show proved to be a tour de force; it ran for more than six weeks, and all forty-one performances were sold out.

The Lilliputs did two shows daily; the matinee was designed for children on school vacation. A favorite part of the Lilliputs' act was the presentation of six tall men from the audience onstage, to offer a comic contrast with the stars.

The theaters that the Lilliputs played were often packed with immigrants who hadn't seen them perform for years. Yet the show was not merely a trip down memory lane, bathed in nostalgia for a world utterly devastated by war and for loved ones abruptly lost. It was also a jubilant reunion of the dwarfs with their audience, and frequently of friends in the audience. In the foyer, families and neighbors would suddenly recognize relatives or acquaintances long thought dead, and they would fall into one another's arms. A feeling of triumph charged the theaters' atmosphere: five years after Auschwitz, the show was again going on. The audience roundly applauded the Lilliputs, of course, but they were also celebrating their own resurrection.

Surviving Rozavleans were admitted to the show for free. One day, the newly married Gitta Drattler-Budimsky spotted a notice of the Lilliput Troupe's performance. The last time she had seen the Ovitzes was in the summer of 1945, when they had given her shelter in their house in Rozavlea. A year later, the fifteen-year-old orphan had immigrated with a group of other children and teenagers to Israel, and this advertisement was the first sign of life for Gitta that her former benefactors were still alive. "Throughout the show I was crying and laughing and couldn't wait for the last curtain to fall so I could see them. I rushed backstage then and joined the queue of people who were already waiting. When I entered their dressing room, I was delighted that they immediately recognized me. We hugged and they gave me their souvenir photo, which I cherish to this day."

After the Lilliputs had wrapped up their first season, they began considering how to revise their show, for they realized that they could not win over the larger Hebrew-speaking public with their material as it stood. In the past, the Lilliputs had always played to homogenous audiences; thus they had specially tailored their shows for each group, be it Romanian, Hungarian, or Czechoslovakian. In Israel, with its Babel of languages and numerous cultures, that strategy would no longer suffice. They needed to put together a repertoire with a wider and more general appeal.

It was not entirely the Lilliputs' choice. A governmental regulation forbade resident artists from performing solely in a foreign language, Yiddish included. The Ovitzes, then, had to add content in Hebrew to their show. They had observed that Israelis responded more enthusiastically to tragicomic material than they did to songs, so Avram sat down to write some. Domestic relationships provided an inexhaustible source of ideas for marital scenes, which had a hidden advantage for the dwarfs: they could sit on a chair or sofa onstage—a welcome relief when doing their second performance of the day. To conserve their stage energy—and to avoid rivalry between the siblings—they made a point of sharing the stardom by evenly splitting the solo parts and leading roles among all the members of the troupe. For the first time in their performing careers, the Lilliputs hired a professional director, Jacob Ziterman, and incorporated themselves as a company, "Lilliput Entertainment Ltd." After nine months of rehearsals in their flimsy wooden barrack by the sea, they were ready to hit the road again with a new show. Its program was divided into two acts: "Import-Export," in Hebrew;

and, after the intermission, "An Angel Among Men," in Yiddish. In the latter, Perla played the peace-making angel who shot cupid's arrows from her miniature bow at a quarrelsome wife and husband. Throughout her life, Perla kept her cherished white-winged dress in her bedroom's overflowing wardrobe.

As time went on, the Lilliputs enriched their repertoire. *In one of our most popular plays, "The Double Wedding," my brother Micki was my fiancé and Elizabeth was Avram's fiancée. We never got to the marriage ceremony, because in the Jewish religion when a man says, "With this ring I thee wed," it's legally binding even if said in jest or onstage. After the show, men would come to my dressing room and timidly inquire, "Are you really engaged to that man?" I would laugh and reassure them, "No, I'm only his sister."* Perla in fact had a whole range of new roles. Her schoolday experience with the pointer and the geography map inspired her brother to write a skit in which she, as a pupil, impresses the school supervisor with her knowledge. In another piece she played an awkward secretary at a job interview. Perla, the youngest in the troupe, proved to be perfect in the role of an old lady. With deep wrinkles painted on her face, talcum powder dusting her hair (the Lilliputs never used wigs) and a quiver in her voice, she was so convincing that fans who came backstage to compliment the granny were incredulous when Perla's sisters pointed at her. Elizabeth, too, captivated audiences, not as an angel or a granny, but as an unfaithful sweetheart who dances a sensuous tango until she's discovered by her jealous lover, Micki, who stabs her with his knife. Her melodramatically prolonged dying scene in "Death Tango" never failed to get a standing ovation.

That summer of 1950 again brought a box office sellout, and the Lilliput Troupe extended the season until winter. Every night, after the applause and the curtain calls, the Lilliputs folded up their extravagant costumes and took a taxi back to their drafty barrack at the immigrant camp. Despite the uncomfortable conditions and lack of privacy, the Lilliputs were reluctant to move. They had not yet found a house that could accommodate all of them, and more than anything they feared separation. Besides, their barrack had become a contact point for people who had known them in their various circumstances. "After I had brought my jewelry workshop tools to Israel, they kindly agreed to keep them for me, since I was still a soldier and had no home," recalls Herman Szabo, the next-door neighbors' son from Rozavlea. Zvi Klein—the thirteen-year-old twin who had lived with them in their Auschwitz barrack—recalls that the experience "made us kin. I had no one left in the world, so I took to the sea. For fifteen years, whenever I returned to the port of Haifa, I prayed with concern that they were alive and well, and would only breathe a sigh of relief when I saw them in their doll-like prettiness. With each year that passed I viewed their presence as a small victory over the Nazis." And Arie Tessler remarks that "they were very cheerful and welcoming and time flew by when we visited. When it was late I would feel uncomfortable and want to leave, but my brother always wanted to stay. He seems to have been fascinated by the contrast between Avram and his huge wife—he was interested in peeping into their makeshift bedroom. Once the partition stirred slightly and he saw Avram lying cuddled up to his wife's legs."

Shimshon Ovitz had turned out to be a late developer, and his parents feared that he was manifesting the Ovitz genetic propensity. Thinking of the future, the family decided to prepare him for a role in the Lilliput Troupe. They bought a second-hand piano and hired a music teacher. To help Shimshon overcome stage fright, Avram tailored a small part for him in the show.

Over the school vacation, he performed onstage with his uncles and aunts, but Shimshon could not muster much enthusiasm. The family's plans for him soon faded.

In 1951, the troupe was preparing for its third season and toying with the idea of performing abroad. In the midst of their preparations, though, the Lilliputs suffered an unexpected blow. They discovered that their new impresario, Isidor Gruenberg, had embezzled their earnings. Gruenberg falsely claimed he had spent it on hiring performance halls and on visas to Germany, and the dwarfs sued. On May 6, 1953, the day that all seven of the Ovitz dwarfs appeared in court, the media came running.

While Avram Ovitz was head of the family and manager of Lilliput Entertainment Ltd., Elizabeth Ovitz-Moskowitz was the troupe's ambassador. She assumed the responsibility of presenting the Ovitzes' case. When she walked into the courtroom, of course, her lawyers realized that if she spoke from the witness stand she would be hidden from the magistrate. She was thus allowed to testify from the counsel's bench; still, she needed an additional small stool. "For two hours, she was questioned in Yiddish by the prosecutor, and her confident, self-assured answers proved that she was well-versed in the ways of the world," reported the influential daily *Ha'aretz*. "The dwarfs' appearance in court attracted much attention. Their heads are like those of normal people; only their body and legs are short. They were beautifully dressed, the lady adorned with diamond-studded rings, gold bracelets and other expensive jewelry." Gruenberg was found guilty and sent to jail.

The Ovitzes' disappointment with Gruenberg was something of a last straw. They had been performing for five years in Israel, and felt they had exhausted the country's small market: the gimmick of seven dwarfs was no longer working. Israel was now flooded with Yiddish shows, and competition was tough. In any event, life had left its mark on them. They had endured the ordeal of Auschwitz and its aftermath, and they had been performing for more than twenty-five years. Rozika was sixty-eight; Franziska, sixty-five; Avram, fifty-one. Perla excepted, the others were not far behind. All in all, the demands of theatrical life had become too rigorous for them: leaving the barrack at noon without lunch (so as not to overload their bodies); traveling two hours to the theater, then performing two hours onstage; a short break after the matinee, then another show, and then the long return journey home; arriving at the barrack well after midnight. The routine was exhausting, and in a family council they discussed their options and decided to change course: they would retire from the stage and search for another occupation, one that would provide a livelihood without forcing them to separate.

They had never given up on the financial promises they had received from the Israeli authorities in Antwerp, and now they presented the bill to be paid. The Jewish Agency responded by offering them leases for a cinema and laundry in the beach resort of Natania, less than an hour's drive from Haifa. But the Ovitzes did not find the terms adequate. In November 1954, after months of fruitless correspondence, their patience ran out. They traveled to Jerusalem and alerted the press that they were planning to stage a protest in the Jewish Agency's head office. To avoid bad publicity, the security guards were instructed not to forcibly evict the dwarfs. Instead, the corridor where the Ovitzes were squatting was sealed off from the outside world.

On the third day of the sit-in, Elizabeth felt faint; she was taken to the hospital. That afternoon, a spokesman announced that a special committee had been formed to consider the Ovitzes' demands. At that point the dwarfs agreed to return to their barrack in Haifa.

NINETEEN

Haifa, 1955–1979

On October 30, 1868, Christoph Hoffmann and Georg David Hardegg of Würtemberg's Temple Society arrived in the Holy Land. Hoffmann, a theologian who had drifted away from the organized Lutheran church, established a new religious movement based on the centrality of a spiritual temple. He preached for the creation of a new nation, the People of God, who would gather in the Land of God—the Land of Israel—and prepare it for the second coming of Christ. At the foot of Mount Carmel they laid a cornerstone for the first residential house in Haifa.

By the end of the 1930s, 650 Templers had settled in Haifa's flourishing German Colony; an additional thousand were living in six other settlements around the country. The Templers made their living from agriculture, light industry, and hostelry. They had their own sports club, a bicycle association, a football team, cafés, and restaurants. Of the seven cinemas in prewar Haifa, two were located in the German Colony. One of them, the Stadt-garten—an open-air, eight hundred-seat cinema at the corner of

Jaffa Road and Carmel Boulevard—was built in the early 1930s on a site owned by Herman Keller. In time, a second, roofed cinema, the Carmel, was added at the same location.

After the outbreak of World War II, all eligible Templer men were called back to Germany to join the Wehrmacht. As the war progressed, any men still living in the Templer settlements were at first detained by the British authorities as enemy residents of Palestine, and later deported with their families to Australia. Dozens of Templer women with children, as well as the elderly, were thus left on their own in Haifa; the Templers' Arab partners and employees meanwhile ran the businesses on their behalf. When the war ended, those Templers who had been left behind gradually returned to Germany. The last of them departed when the state of Israel was established, whereupon their houses were confiscated as enemy property for the use of Holocaust survivors. So it was that the Carmel—and the Stadtgarten, which was translated into Hebrew as Ganim (gardens)—had become available, and were now, in 1955, being offered on lease to the Lilliput Troupe. The vast plot also included a car-repair shop, a locksmith's, a carpentry shop, an upholstery shop, and a small waffle bakery; the Ovitzes would collect the rent from these businesses as part of the deal. More attractive to them, though, were the residential apartments in the compound, and they did not hesitate to sign the contract.

After six years in the crumbling barrack at the immigrant camp, the Lilliput Troupe finally moved into proper quarters in the German Colony. Each family had its own space in the cinema compound. Avram and his wife lived on the top floor at one apartment (having married young, their daughter, Batia, was living elsewhere with her husband). Elizabeth and Moshe Moskowitz had a smaller flat for themselves in the same building, as did Sarah and her husband, Erno Deutsch. So did Frieda, who had gotten married a second time, to Sami Melamed. Next door Leah lived with Azriel and their two children. Another apartment housed Rozika and Franziska in one room, Perla and Micki in another room (when she changed clothes, he turned his back). For the first time, each of the Ovitz families now had the chance to run its own affairs; however, they all continued to share Sabbath and holiday meals around the long table in the communal flat.

In 1955, the Lilliput Troupe marked its retirement from the stage with a week of farewell performances that ended with a lavish ball. Thereafter, Lilliput Entertainment Ltd. devoted itself not to offering theatrical presentations, but to promoting films on the silver screen. *It was very convenient, to live on the premises, just a few steps from work—I had moved from stage lights to a narrow box office cubicle. It was in no way humiliating, since I was still in show business. As a cashier, I needed to know what the film was about, to present the story to the customers in an attractive way. I was always carefully dressed and made up like in the old days when I was the show.* Perla was in fact no ordinary cashier. She was herself an attraction, and the cinema's best publicist. Customers enjoyed chatting with her, and to show their appreciation, they often brought her small gifts.

As they always had, the Ovitzes continued to divide the work between them, with Avram maintaining his role as manager. Elizabeth chose the films, and Micki operated the translation roll. Tall sisters Leah and Sarah worked in the cinema buffet and café. When things got hectic, everyone pitched in, except Rozika and Franziska, now nearly in their seventies, and Frieda, who had developed a kidney disease. The porters and ushers were local Arabs.

As in the Lilliputs' theater days, summer continued to be their busy season, because then they were operating both cinemas and offering 1,200 seats for each of the three daily shows. Since they could not afford to rent the expensive Hollywood films, and as their neighborhood consisted mostly of Arabs and newly arrived Jews from Arab countries, the repertoire for the most part consisted of films in Hindu, Arabic, Turkish, and Greek—languages the Ovitzes did not understand. *I liked the films all the same. They were so sentimental, love stories in different languages. The actors were so handsome and the serenades stirred my heart.*

At the age of thirty-five, Perla was still hoping to find her storybook prince and don the bridal veil. *There was a butcher who wanted me, quite a handsome guy. But he had a beard and I didn't like it. I always wear makeup, so bearded men are not for me.* One day a suitor from her past showed up, although she had already rejected him back in Transylvania, as she had not wished to leave her family. *He now said, I am single, you are single, we both survived the camps, let's get together. But I didn't want him, because he was a Communist and I would have none of that. I'd suffered enough from the Russians and didn't want one of them in my house.* Yet another suitor, a waiter named Jonel, did manage to break down Perla's wall of resistance. She came to terms with her fears, set the date, sent out invitations, and prepared the menu for the celebration. But then, just twelve days before the wedding, she learned that the future groom had been boasting that all the Lilliput's immense property would soon be his. The marriage was called off; the wedding dress was quietly stored away.

Unlike most dwarfs, who depend upon the mercy of others for any sort of livelihood, before and after Auschwitz the Lilliput Troupe had always been able to manage its own destiny. In their theatrical careers, the dwarfs held center stage, while the other, normal-sized family members supported them from the back. The same pattern came into play in their new career. The Ovitz dwarfs were the employers, and they bossed the tall relations around—the minds versus the hands and feet. To bystanders the Lilliputs may well have appeared to be the proverbial jolly dwarfs, playing out a utopian fairy tale of mutual assistance and camaraderie in a bustling commune. In reality, they were a bit more autocratic than that.

Despite the pleasure that all the Ovitzes were taking in their newly gained privacy, working and living under one roof was gradually taking its toll. The desires, actions, plans, and habits of each of them were continually subject to comment and criticism from any—or—every other member of the family. Individual deeds or dreams prompted heated family debate and inevitably split the clan into camps. The Ovitzes functioned rather like a miniature parliament, with coalitions and opposition, pacts and deals. Still, the dwarfs' needs and opinions always held sway, and sibling ties prevailed over the bonds of marriage.

"I didn't grow up in a normal house," says Shimshon Ovitz. "The place was actually a hellish mixture of hospital, geriatric home, and institution for invalids. The tall sisters, Sarah and my mother Leah, sacrificed themselves for the sake of the dwarfs. They were so physically helpless that if you forgot to pour them a glass of water they would dehydrate. Sarah's husband left her because he couldn't cope with it, and she gave up on having a family of her own. My parents had no married life whatsoever. When I needed something Mother would say, 'Do it yourself, you have hands and feet, they don't.' So from the age of ten I washed my own clothes, made my own meals. I was never cross with her, because I understood her obligations. In any case, Mother couldn't raise me to her liking because all her childless sisters meddled and treated me as their own. I had seven mothers, was flooded with attention, but lacked a single intimate moment with my own mom."

From childhood onward, Shimshon had to carry his uncles down the stairs to the waiting wheelchair, which he would then push through the streets. The neighborhood kids mocked the dwarfs' wobbly gait and short, spade-shaped hands. They harassed Shimshon by shouting "Midget! Midget!" at him, since he was the shortest in the class. Sometimes he tried to respond in kind: "As tall as you are, you'll be as short as my uncles, just wait until a car runs over you and cuts off your legs." That tactic failing, he would get involved in street fights. He soon gained a reputation as a local menace.

Shimshon was so short that throughout his childhood he was himself convinced he was a dwarf. He was relieved when, at the age of thirteen, he started growing again. "I began to overeat—stuffed myself with food and became a human mountain. If I had remained a dwarf I would have killed myself. It's horrible suffering. With no hands and legs you are totally dependent on others for all your needs." After his army service Shimshon became a sailor, in order to escape the family—and himself. He wanted to decorate his body with tattoos like every seaman, but in her letters his mother begged him not to: "The Nazis have already tattooed us," she wrote. Several times, with drunken resolve, his money paid and the design selected, he'd sat ready in the tattoo parlor, his shirt off. Then he'd seen his mother's face in the shadows on the wall or window, and fled.

When he finally gave up the sea, Shimshon drifted between jobs, got into brawls, and had a few run-ins with the law. "I was the terror of Haifa. These fists sent many people to hospitals," he asserts with some pride, and repeatedly. Still, he was all in all an appealing young man, albeit one reluctant to marry, for he feared that genetics would smite his offspring, too. The fact that his cousin Batia, Avram's daughter, had borne healthy children did not ease his mind. He made it a practice to introduce his girlfriends to his dwarf family in order to see their reaction; the visit ended many a relationship. Miriam Shoshani stuck with Shimshon, however, and in 1970 they got married. "When I was in school I told the children that the tattoo on my arm was my ID number from Germany," says Shimshon Ovitz. "Miriam is from Morocco, where the Jews escaped the Holocaust, and she had no idea what the number meant. Once she took some steel wool and tried to scrape it off my skin."

There were other changes in the Ovitz family. Frieda and Sarah divorced their husbands; Dora died; Avram married again, divorced, married for the third time—to another Holocaust survivor—and was widowed some years later. The clan celebrated the birth of Shimshon and Miriam's first child, a daughter, Ariella—named after dead Arie. To the great relief of the parents, her growth was normal. "With every pregnancy Miriam and I were terrified," explains Shimshon Ovitz. "In two or three cases, when the doctor said, 'There's an extra test I want you to have,' we quickly arranged an abortion, not wanting to take even the smallest chance."

Pseudoachondroplasia, the Ovitzes' type of dwarfism, is a rare syndrome. Inherited through an autosomal dominant, it occurs approximately once in every sixty thousand live births. It produces a normal-sized head and face, as well as internal organs, but the arms and the legs are short. The total height of an adult with Pseudoachondroplasia ranges between two and a half and a little over four feet.

The problematic gene was finally identified in 1995 by Dr. Jacqueline Hecht of the University of Texas's Houston Health Science Center. Located on chromosome 19, the gene is called "the cartilage oligomeric matrix protein" (COMP). In cases of Pseudoachondroplasia, the gene mutates, and the protein that produces cartilage restricts the growth of the spine and bones. Researchers are currently looking for a substance capable of weakening the harmful effects of the flawed gene.

In 80 percent of cases, the affliction is a result of spontaneous genetic mutation, not heredity. However, a person with Pseudoachondroplasia and an average-sized partner have a 50 percent chance of giving birth to a dwarf. The dwarfism of Shimshon Eizik Ovitz, the family patriarch, was a spontaneous occurrence, as he had been born to normal-sized parents. His abnormal gene, however, was dominant, and he passed it on to seven of his ten children. Leah, like her two normal-sized siblings, had not inherited the abnormal gene. Her son, Shimshon, and daughter, Batia, could thus expect their children and grandchildren to have the same chance for normal-sized offspring as the rest of the population.

"Logic and statistics cannot pacify the heart," says Shimshon Ovitz. "We have no peace, and fear we will not be spared. Fortunately our three additional children were all healthy, but every pregnancy in the family—and now the grandchildren are coming—is followed by tension. Right now we have five grandchildren and they are developing normally."

In August 1972 the Ovitz clan was shaken when Micki died of a heart attack at the age of sixty-three. The obituaries described him as "an actor and owner of two cinemas." His body was placed for a formal viewing in front of the Ovitz cinema so that his many fans and clients could pay their last respects. He was buried in the newly purchased family plot in the main Haifa cemetery. Four months later came another blow, when Avram Ovitz, head of the family, died at sixty-nine. That same year Leah suffered a major stroke that left her speechless and paralyzed in a wheelchair for the next fourteen years. Frieda died in 1975. *It was horrible, agony upon agony, the pain and mourning accumulating and multiplying.* It became increasingly difficult for the remaining siblings—Perla, Elizabeth, Rozika, Franziska, tall Sarah, and Leah, now helpless in a wheelchair—to continue managing the cinemas. In 1979 they sold the entire compound and bought a large flat for the six of them.

When they retired from the stage in 1955, the Lilliput Troupe stored away its miniature musical instruments; the dwarfs never touched them again. When the surviving Ovitzes vacated the cinema compound, Shimshon sold the instruments cheaply to a local antiques dealer. The collection then disappeared. What were claimed to be the Lilliput Troupe's instruments resurfaced in late 1997 as the property of a dealer who began negotiations for their sale to the Jewish Museum in Berlin. News of the prospective deal reached Yad Vashem, the Israeli national Holocaust museum and research center in Jerusalem, which immediately expressed interest in purchasing the collection. Unable to meet the asking price of $80,000, Yad Vashem made an appeal for donors, and ultimately purchased, at a reduced sum, two violins with missing strings, a bowless cello, a flawed cymbal, and a set of drums. Missing from the collection were both an accordion and a pink guitar of the sort used by Perla. The sale was executed without an expert's appraisal and with no proof of provenance.

Amnon Weinstein, a violin maker and a world-renowned expert on ancient string instruments, has had considerable experience identifying musical instruments that survived World War II. He carried out his inspection on the alleged Ovitz collection in the presence of this book's authors, Yehuda Koren and Eilat Negev, as well as Haviva Peled-Carmely of Yad Vashem, who is charge of purchasing articles for the museum's collection.

The delicate string instruments in the collection sold to Yad Vashem had come stripped of their cases, and were not even wrapped in cloth, as professional artists like the Ovitzes would have taken care to do, as Weinstein points out. Nonetheless, he immediately recognizes some of the instruments as those in a collection offered to him in Haifa in the 1970s. "The story said to be behind the instruments was very moving," he recalls, "but there was something fishy about the whole sale, the instruments and the dealer, so I backed off and never regretted it. In any case I have an excellent memory and some of the instruments now in Yad Vashem are not the ones I saw at the time."

Examination of the cello's size and design reveals that it is clearly not the same cello that appears in the Lilliput Troupe's publicity photos. The cello in Yad Vashem, although beautifully carved, is old and badly damaged; Weinstein estimates that a crack in its soundboard dates back at least a century. It could not therefore, have been used by the Lilliput Troupe as recently as 1955 or even as early as 1930. "And on top of that," adds Weinstein, "the cello is too big for a dwarf to play."

Wearing special soft white cotton gloves, Weinstein lifts up one of the violins, turns it from side to side, and sniffs at it with the care of a detective. "It is a child's quarter-size violin and has the smell and heavy traces of a woman's face powder. Children usually play such an instrument for two or three years, moving on to a larger one as they grow older. The violin is passed on from one child to another so it never becomes worn in the same places. But this worn-down violin was used by the same musician for many years—the chin and fingers repeatedly rubbed it in the same spots." The violin thus may well have belonged to Rozika or Franziska.

Of much poorer quality is the second violin, which comes from a different manufacturer; it bears no distinctive marks or identifiable traces of makeup. There is nothing to connect it to the Ovitzes. On the other hand, the cymbal, a folk instrument built by a village craftsman, and the intricate set of drums, both probably belonged to the Lilliput Troupe. One of the sticks accompanying the drums, however, is a wooden mallet of the sort used to flatten steaks and schnitzel; it is unlikely it was ever used onstage, although the crack in the mallet attests to a long life in someone's kitchen. The differences in the quality of the various instruments—some finely made, like the drums; others bric-a-brac, like the nondescript violin—makes it doubtful they were used by the same group of musicians.

To determine whether or not the instruments were played in Auschwitz, Weinstein gently inserts a thin, flexible tube into the sound box of the violins and moves it around, while peering through the periscope's eye. "If these are really the instruments that were with them there, there might be traces of human ashes inside, since the black smoke filled the air. But the absence of ash here might only mean that the violins were not played in the open air; they could still have been used indoors."

The general impression is that the original collection was deliberately split up: the particularly valuable instruments may have been sold separately, and replaced with items picked up by the dealer in some flea market to complete the ensemble. The fate of the Lilliput collection thus perpetuates the exploitation of Holocaust victims, with objects belonging to them, whether real or forged, being sold to willing buyers at exorbitant prices.

TWENTY

Haifa, 1980–1992

ina Gottlieb-Babbitt's intimate encounter with Mengele in Auschwitz, when he was her "painting model," has haunted her ever since. Years after the liberation, on another continent, in a bus station on Hollywood Boulevard, she panicked at the sight of a man who resembled him. "I thought, oh my God, he's after me. I was sure he knew I was the only person in the world who could clearly identify him, and he or his messengers would come to silence me." Six decades later, her telephone number remains unlisted, and she never discloses her address. Yet her attitude toward the Nazi doctor is unsettlingly ambivalent: "The entire world was after him, but I decided that if he were ever captured, I would not come forward to testify. Not that I feel any gratitude, he didn't care if I lived or died, and did nothing to save me. But for a fleeting moment he spared me, letting me hang on for a little while and come through."

Early in December 1968, a police officer called at the Carmel-Ganim cinema. Perla had just opened the box office. He introduced himself as Inspector Kolar, and had barely mentioned that he was collecting evidence against Josef Mengele when she interrupted him: "Have you caught him?" she asked. "We will, we will," he assured her apologetically, "but meanwhile we're helping the German prosecutors to prepare a dossier against him." *I was not looking for revenge, but it was clear to all of us that when an inspector came to investigate Nazi crimes we would cooperate. Although I must admit I never hated Dr. Mengele. I should have hated him, I know, because he was a murderer, but he let us live. Not that he liked us, he only used us to further his ambition of becoming a famous scientist. But thanks to him we had some human freedom in the camp.*

In the family assembly that evening, the Ovitzes decided that Elizabeth should be the one to tell the story of their ordeal in the death camp. Elizabeth's memory did not fail her, and Kolar quickly filled four pages with her testimony. "I don't know what concrete experiments Mengele performed on me. He was interested in everything; they thus often dripped a liquid into our eyes that left us nearly blind the entire day. They gave us shots in our ears and as said in nearly all our organs. We often felt sick and miserable and still had to deliver ourselves into his hands."

It was the first time in twenty years that the Ovitzes had been asked to tell their story. Upon their arrival in Israel, they had spoken openly about the torments the unrelenting Mengele had inflicted on them at Auschwitz. Like most survivors, though, they very quickly realized that their painful accounts fell on deaf ears. So they stopped talking.

The Israelis after all, had had troubles of their own. In 1939, and for the duration of Hitler's war, the Jews in Palestine were effectively cut off from family and friends who had been trapped in Nazi-occupied Europe. A decade later, successive waves of new immigrants brought with them dreadful confirmations that the Israelis' parents, brothers, sisters, cousins, uncles, and aunts had perished in the Nazi camps. Horror and guilt—the incomprehensible horror of the Holocaust; guilt at not having done enough to save their European brothers and sisters—closed the Israelis' hearts to the survivors' endless tales of suffering. At the same time, Israel was mourning its own tremendous losses in the War of Independence: a grief so immense and immediate left little emotional space to mourn those killed in a different time and place or to pity the survivors. In a clash of catastrophes, pain at the death of six million Jews in Europe came second, at the time, to the loss of six thousand young soldiers in Israel.

"The kids at school echoed the general mood of the country—'Why did you go like sheep to the slaughter? Why didn't you fight back?' " recounts Shimshon Ovitz with some bitterness. "I was so angry at them. I had only been a year-old toddler then, but even if I could have thrown a rock, what harm could I have done them? We were so weak and hungry; the Nazis, well-armed sadists. Anyone would have responded like we did." Burdened with agonizing and exhausting memories, the survivors withdrew into themselves. Gradually, they learned to put the past aside as they built new lives in a harsh land. But the Ovitzes, who had together borne the Nazi torments and survived intact, seemed to be able—indeed, found it natural—to live simultaneously in the present and the past.

"Having invaded our veins, Mengele was one of our household names," says Shimshon Ovitz. "Dr. Mengele wanted this, did that. I ate Mengele for breakfast, he was my bedtime story, and I couldn't sleep at night hearing my aunts and uncles scream at their dreams. We breathed Auschwitz the whole day through, as if we were still there. Every tiny daily event reminded them of something in the camp. I grew up on these stories and passed them on to my children. We are all broken vessels who, even if glued together, cannot be whole again. You can't expect people like us to be normal."

Sixty years later, Shimshon Ovitz's refrigerator is always stuffed with food, as if he is expecting a siege or a war. His wife, Miriam, cannot close the doors of the kitchen cupboards, which are bursting with food in packets, bottles, cans, bags, jars. Obese to the extent that it threatens his life, Shimshon finds his hunger insatiable. He cannot stop eating.

From the moment the trial of Adolf Eichmann opened in Jerusalem on April 11, 1961, the Israeli attitude toward the Holocaust changed dramatically. The public trial, held in the newly opened city theater, was broadcast live on the radio daily. People gathered in the streets; riveted to the loudspeakers, they followed the proceedings. The testimony of 110 witnesses, each one representing an obliterated community, revealed for the first time to the Israeli public, and established for history, the full scope of the "final solution." The Holocaust now stood horrifically on the Israelis' list of national calamities. For the first time, survivors could openly cry their hearts out, and the country cried with them.

On his isolated farm near Sao Paulo, Brazil, Mengele must have followed the news accounts of Eichmann's kidnapping by the Israeli Mossad in nearby Argentina, and then his much-publicized trial and execution, with considerable trepidation. After arriving in Argentina in 1949 with forged documents, Mengele had worked for his family's agricultural-equipment firm as its South American agent. To protect his true identity, he had not practiced medicine, and it appears that even in the privacy of his own quarters he had refrained from working on the experimental data from Auschwitz. In all probability, he stashed away the incriminating files. Their whereabouts remain unknown.

In March 1954, Mengele divorced his first wife, Irene. Two years later he married his brother's widow, Martha, who had flown with her son from Germany to Argentina to be with him. By 1956 he apparently felt secure enough to officially change his false name, Helmut Gregor, back to his real one at the West German Embassy in Buenos Aires. In 1959, though, he moved on to Paraguay—a safer place for a war criminal to hide from the American, German, and Israeli intelligence services, as well as the scores of journalists and private Nazi hunters who were now trying to track him down. That same year he moved again, when a court in Freiburg issued the first warrant for his arrest and summoned witnesses to testify against him. This time he moved back to Brazil, and using false identities hid out on isolated farms, and later in a one-bedroom bungalow in a Sao Paulo slum. Life on the run did not seem to suit Martha Mengele; the couple soon separated.

In 1964, the Administrative Court of Hesse and the universities of Frankfurt and Munich annulled Mengele's medical and anthropological degrees, in the face of his earlier honors, "because of the crimes he had committed as a doctor in the concentration camp of Auschwitz." Nonetheless, his early research continued to be cited in medical books and articles all over the world well into the 1970s. In the investigative arena, meanwhile, none of the secret services were really making an effort to find him. In 1959, the public prosecutor Freiherr von Schowingen in Freiburg assembled testimonies that led to nothing. A decade later, Mengele's case was transferred to the Frankfurt criminal-judicial system, where the investigating judge, Horst von Glasenapp, had interviewed three hundred more witnesses around the world. Although he had no authority to look for Mengele, von Glasenapp made several failed attempts to trace him.

Years, then decades, passed, and the survivors of Mengele's experiments grew only more indignant at the lack of any sustained effort to catch him. Hoping to take their outrage at the failure to bring Mengele to justice to a broader international public, Mengele's victims organized a trial in absentia in Yad Vashem, Jerusalem. On February 5, 1985, Shimshon Ovitz pushed his aunt Elizabeth's wheelchair out of the pouring rain and into the museum auditorium, while Sarah wheeled her sister Perla. *That day the sky was crying, too. I was sorry that Dr. Mengele was absent from his trial. The only reason I wanted him caught was so he could sit days and nights listening to what he did to us. I would have shown him the scars and ailments, told him about my weak heart and the legs that can no longer support me. I don't believe he would have apologized, but if the judges were to ask me if he should be hanged, I'd tell them to let him go. I was saved by the grace of the devil—God will give him his due.*

Since the dwarf sisters were wearing lookalike hats, raincoats, dresses, and handbags, the press mistakenly described them as fifty-nine-year-old twins. Elizabeth was in fact seventy-one, Perla sixty-four. To spare them the effort of mounting the podium, prosecutor Zvi Terlow came down to the first row to conduct the inquiry. As always, Elizabeth spoke out more than her sister; both she and Perla captured the imagination of the world press. *Newsweek*, for example, blended some fact with much fiction in describing how the Lilliputs "entertained their tormentors. On one hellish night, the entire family was stripped naked and marched on to a stage to perform for SS chief Heinrich Himmler"—it was not him; he's confused here with a minor Nazi official who strongly resembled him—"and 2,000 Nazi officers and soldiers. Mengele acted as emcee while Himmler sat in the front row, and recorded the fun with his movie camera."

The emotional impact of the 106 witnesses who testified at the trial stirred the governments of Israel, the United States, and Germany to make fresh efforts in the hunt for Mengele. Besides offering new and increased bounties of a million dollars and a million marks, officials from the three countries met in Frankfurt on May 10, 1985, to coordinate their efforts. They issued a warrant for the search of the Günzburg home of Hans Sedlmeier, a retired executive in the Mengele family firm, who was suspected of flying regularly to South America to deliver money to the fugitive. An address book found in Sedlmeier's flat led investigators to Brazil.

On June 7, scores of policemen and journalists gathered at Our Lady of the Rosary Cemetery on a hillside in Embu, ten miles from Sao Paulo. An incredulous Dina Gottlieb-Babbitt watched on television as the Sao Paulo assistant coroner Dr. Jose Antonio de Melo, standing above an open pit, presented a skull to the TV cameras and news photographers' blinding flashes. "I painted Mengele's portrait and know the shape of his skull," she says. "It was not like the one they showed. His face was much wider. My feeling was it was a cover-up by his family and associates to gain him extra time."

An international team of forensic experts examined the

remains. On the basis of the gaps between the skull's teeth—a subject Mengele himself had studied as a young physician— they declared that "it is . . . our opinion that this skeleton is that of Josef Mengele, within a reasonable scientific certainty." But many of Mengele's victims, as well as many others, were skeptical, and believed he was managing to live on as a free man into a ripe old age. In an attempt to quell such rumors, Mengele's son, Rolf, issued a statement on June 11, 1985 to the effect that on February 7, 1979, his father had suffered a stroke while swimming and had drowned. He explained that the family's subsequent six years of silence was a precautionary measure taken to ensure the safety of those who had helped the Auschwitz doctor hide for thirty years.

I cried all night when I heard that Dr. Mengele had died. He always insisted he was just obeying orders and I believed him. The streams of blood he took from us that sometimes spilled onto the floor would pass before my eyes, but still I cried. The heart is the stupidest human organ. Dr. Mengele had a heart of stone but mine is human, flesh and blood.

The doubts about Mengele's remains persisted until 1992, when Rolf and Irene Mengele both agreed to provide blood samples and undergo a DNA comparison with one of Mengele's bones. The bone sample matched. Mengele's dossier was closed.

For a while, the trial in absentia of Mengele brought the Lilliputs back into the limelight. For months, journalists and photographers courted Perla and Elizabeth, but eventually the fuss abated and the two Lilliput celebrities retreated again into anonymity.

As early as July 1951, the West German government had

approved a one-time grant to victims of Nazi medical experiments. Such grants, the government insisted, were not to be interpreted as compensation based on legal claims, but rather as donations to further the victims' recovery. For the most part, money was distributed among residents of Hungary and Poland; none of it reached Mengele's victims in Israel.

In 1985 Mengele's human guinea pigs in Israel, most of them twins who had testified in the trial, sued the West German government on the basis of the 1951 decision. One of the eighty-three claimants was Efraim Reichenberg, who had shared a barrack with the male dwarfs. He had arrived in Auschwitz with his seven siblings, all of whom were killed except for Laszlo, who was mistaken for Efraim's twin.

Laszlo had a resonant baritone singing voice and frequently entertained the SS, whereas Efraim could barely squeak out a tune. The differences between their vocal cords intrigued Mengele, who repeatedly injected substances into their throats. Laszlo began to have breathing difficulties and laryngeal swellings; his lungs became damaged. He died a year after liberation, at the age of nineteen.

Efraim himself was not spared. Over the years, his voice dwindled until he lost it completely. Eventually, he couldn't breathe or swallow food. He underwent twenty-two grueling operations to remove his mangled vocal cords, larynx, and part of his esophagus. He was totally mute until 1984, when a special microphone was implanted in his throat. His speech is slow; it sounds metallic, and a pause follows each word emitted from the voice-mechanism. "The Germans took my voice away in the camp and gave it back to me forty years later as installed equipment—'Made in Germany.' My case is anything but special, I am not unique. Many of us suffer kidney failure, different kinds of cancer, and cardiac problems. After Mengele's trial in Jerusalem we demanded our medical files be found so we could know exactly what was done to us and get the right treatment. We appealed to the Americans, the Russians, the Germans, and even to the Mengele family, but remain empty-handed, just dying painfully."

To avoid an embarrassing political and juridical debate, West Germany arrived at a compromise agreement with Mengele's Israeli victims, with each of the claimants settling for twenty thousand German marks. In the original 1951 offer, the minimum grant had been twenty-five thousand marks and the maximum forty thousand—for cases "where the victims' whole life has been ruined by the pseudo-medical experiments." The Ovitz family did not get grouped with the twins; nor did it get the belated compensation.

For two minutes, a siren is sounded throughout Israel on each Holocaust Memorial Day; for two minutes the traffic halts and everybody freezes in place. Shimshon Ovitz shivers as the siren carries him back to his childhood time in Auschwitz. Then comes anger. "They're whistling in our faces. It makes me furious that billions of German marks Israel got as reparation money have been wasted on extravagant public projects such as buying a fleet of fifty ships, trains, and industrial equipment, all made in Germany, while we were stuck in leaking barracks. Israel declares itself the sole heir of the six million, demanding that the money once belonging to them be channeled to the state. Nobody cares about the old and ailing survivors. They just need us as a tool to extract more money for projects."

In addition to the money it paid to the state of Israel, Germany allowed survivors to apply for personal compensation. Each member of the Ovitz family had to provide the German bureaucracy with evidence that they really had been interned in Auschwitz, that they had been assigned to the experimental barrack, that their health had been impaired. "I'm fifty-eight and much sicker than most people my age, all from the eight crucial months of my infancy when I was Mengele's lab rat," says Shimshon Ovitz. "Later I supported my family by selling clothes from a street-counter, but now I'm too ill to continue. Germany cannot buy itself out with the monthly eight hundred marks that I get, or even the thousand paid my helpless aunt Perla."

Shimshon had always flinched at the idea of visiting his native Rozavlea or returning to Auschwitz. With the passing years, however, he began to feel a need to see, just once, the camp that had tainted his life. He now plans to join one of the Israeli high school delegations that visit Auschwitz-Birkenau annually. "I was a toddler at the time, so I want to go there in the company of youngsters and see it from viewpoints of both child and grandfather."

TWENTY-ONE

Haifa, 1993–2001

Perla Ovitz's health prohibits her from embarking on any voyage, but not from recalling and recounting the one that brought her to her present time and place. *In Auschwitz I swore that if God let me stay alive I would tell my story again and again until my breath died out so that no one could say it never happened.* Perla does not hesitate to give interviews, to share her experiments with children writing essays about the Holocaust, or to lecture about her family history.

On Holocaust Memorial Day, all Israeli restaurants, cinemas, and theaters are closed by law. Official ceremonies are held in each town, and schools dedicate the day to remembering the victims and meeting the survivors. When we come to take Perla to meet schoolchildren, we find her all dressed up, sitting on the edge of her bed. In her tiny black handbag she has packed her cardiac pills, some cookies, and lipstick. She adds a photograph of Mengele. *I want the children to know his face,* she says. We cradle her in our arms and take her down the stairs and into the car. She is light as a feather.

In Yokneam, a small town a thirty-minute drive from Haifa,

she is wheeled into the school gym. The children stand up in silence to greet her. Six tall glass candles, a gigantic yellow star, and the slogan REMEMBER AND NEVER FORGET barely hide the ads for a local beauty parlor and mechanic's workshop. A ten-year-old boy dressed in the colors of the Israeli flag—white shirt, blue trousers—reaches up to the microphone. His voice is unwavering as he reads the special prayer for murdered children: "Let the Nation remember her beloved children, innocent and pure, snatched from the laps of their parents by human beasts. Tortured, beheaded, gassed, smothered, burnt alive. Babies and infants, smashed against walls, dropped from high roofs, suffocated in sacks, drowned in rivers."

The list of barbaric tortures and perverse methods of killing is repeated again and again by the children in their performances of dramatized readings, songs, and dances. The level of horror their program generates is so intense that it could carry the cinematic warning "unsuitable for children." The program ends with scenes of rebellion against shadowy forces, designed to imprint on the children's imagination the necessity of resistance in the event of another Holocaust: "Never again will we be led like lambs to the slaughter!" the chorus ceremoniously chants. "The Germans have come! Jews, take up arms! Better die on drawn swords—let's defend ourselves to the last breath! Death to the murderers!"

Perla Ovitz weeps silently; she wipes her tears with a checkered handkerchief. A class of nine-year-olds gathers around her.

"I didn't have a name, just this number." She rolls up the sleeve of her dress. All eyes are glued to her arm.

"How did they tattoo you?" inquires a boy with a punk haircut. "Did it hurt?" asks a skinny girl.

"I fainted twice, but that was the easy part." Perla doesn't spare them the gory details.

"Dr. Mengele was my boss, do you want to see him?" Without awaiting a response, she draws his photo from her handbag and passes it around.

The children glance at him with a mixture of amazement and repulsion.

"Did he make you a dwarf?" one of them asks.

"No, Dr. Mengele was a very powerful doctor, but even he couldn't make someone a giant or a dwarf." And she tells them the story of Shimshon Eizik and his two wives.

At the end of the meeting, the children draw out their pocket cameras and photograph themselves with her. Perla flashes the radiant smile of a film star. She signs autographs on pages torn from the young students' notebooks. Before they leave, the children pass in line in front of Perla's wheelchair; one by one, they kneel to shake her hand.

A fortnight later, the postman brings her a large brown envelope full of letters. One of them reads: "Dear Perla, I was so moved by your talk. You are so beautiful and I really love you. If you need anything don't hesitate to phone me and I'll immediately come to help you." The girl has written her home telephone number on the letter, which is decorated with flowers and two intertwined hearts: they bear her name and Perla's.

The factual fairy tale of the seven dwarfs who stuck together like peas in a pod began drawing to its close in the 1980s. In 1979 five of the surviving siblings and Elizabeth's husband moved into a stone house on the corner of a quiet street at the outskirts of the German Colony. They were now living just three blocks away from their cinema compound, which would stand deserted and crumbling for almost twenty years—eventually, an extravagant glass and marble shopping mall would emerge from its ruins.

Elizabeth and her husband took the largest bedroom, with a crescent-shaped corner balcony. Rozika and Franziska, inseparable as always, took the second bedroom, while Perla and tall sister Sarah shared the small one between the kitchen and the bathroom. *At night we tiptoed into our old sisters' room and stood by their beds to check that they were breathing.* Their late-found bliss proved to be short-lived. One by one they were plucked away, and with each death the survivors, confronted with loss and vulnerability, withdrew further into themselves. Franziska died in 1980, aged ninety-one. A year later, Elizabeth lost her darling Moshe Moskowitz.

The four sisters, in an attempt to fill the void each loss created, moved beds. *Life was frightening enough as it was, so I joined Elizabeth in her double bed so she wouldn't be so lonely after forty years of marriage.* Sarah moved in with the inconsolable Rozika, and they closed up a small bedroom.

In 1984 Rozika died; she was ninety-eight. Not many dwarfs reach such a ripe old age. According to the *Guinness Book of World Records,* the record holder is also a Hungarian showbiz personality, Susanne Bokoyni, stage name "Princess Susanne"— who died the same year as Rozika, but in the United States, aged one hundred and five. Rozika's death prompted Sarah to move a sofa into the large bedroom that Elizabeth was sharing with Perla, and the door to the second bedroom was closed.

Soon thereafter, the Ovitz sisters were again devastated—this time by the untimely death of Ariella, Shimshon's fifteen-year-old daughter, after a year-long battle with cancer. Ariella's heartbroken grandparents, Leah and Azriel, followed. In 1992 Elizabeth died of heart failure, and a year later, Sarah.

Perla, then seventy-two-years old, found herself alone. Since the day she was born, Perla had always been encompassed by her family. With her sisters and brothers gone, she felt so utterly abandoned that she joined them in the family plot:

> *Here lies the last of the family of dwarfs, Miss Perla Ovitz, daughter of Shimshon Eizik and Batia, who suffered every single day of her life.*

The epitaph on Perla's tombstone, which she sees whenever she visits the cemetery, does not strike her as bizarre or macabre; nor does she think that it conflicts with her abundant joie de vivre. *The stonecutter suggested it when I told him my story, and I thought it was an appropriate summary of my life. We were happy when we were together and even Dr. Mengele couldn't separate us. There in the cemetery we're together forever.*

In the city of the dead the Lilliputs dwell as if they had been set around the festive Sabbath table; Perla is on the far right, with Frieda to her left, and she's facing her sister Elizabeth and brother-in-law Moshe.

In the large, now mostly empty flat, their presence seems imminent. In part it's the photographs and the full-sized, sugary oil paintings of her and Elizabeth bedecked in clusters of dangling jewelry and long stage dresses. They make Perla feel less alone, as if they were still talking to her. On Friday afternoons, at twilight, when she lights her pair of Sabbath candles, Perla lights her dead sisters' candles, too. A special low railing in the stairwell tells of a time when she could go out on her own. Nowadays she leaves only rarely, to see her doctor or to visit the bank. A loyal taxi driver lifts her in his arms, carries her down the stairs carefully, places her in the backseat; her folded wheelchair goes in the trunk. Her arms have grown too weak to operate the wheelchair, so she must be pushed everywhere. She doesn't visit other people because she is swallowed up by normal-sized furniture.

Perla suffers terrible spinal pain due to the abnormal bone and cartilage formation typical of her type of dwarfism; her body weight presses down on her short, knock-kneed and bowed legs. As were the chests of her dwarf siblings, Perla's chest is narrow, and as a result she suffers from heart and respiratory problems. But in spite of such suffering, she is usually cheerful and welcoming. *The heart is crying, but the lips are smiling* is Perla's often-declared motto. She has always loved people, and since childhood *whenever I heard a voice in the other room I rushed to see who the guest was. And I've not changed.*

Perla was never offended when people called her "dwarf." *What else can they call me? I see myself in the mirror and it's a fact.* Still, she avoids using the term; instead she divides the world into *big people* and *we the little ones.* She most commonly refers to herself as a girl (*I'm a girl who . . .*), despite her womanly old age. *I could marry today if I wanted to!* she girlishly exclaims. *But I don't think that one should marry at any cost and I'm not sorry about never having had a man. I know love, I was in love many times, but not enough to get married. I didn't rush. My brothers and sisters were better than any husband for me. As I grew older, I realized that marriage turns a woman into a man's slave, and I didn't want to be one. I didn't need someone bossing me around. When a man is angry he always blames his wife. I would be an excellent wife for any man, but there's nothing a man can give me that I don't have already.*

Keeping to a strict schedule, Perla wakes up every morning at six, pours some water from the thermos near her bed, and swallows a cardiac pill. She then recites three daily psalms that a local rabbi has recommended and waits in bed. At eight, an aide sent by the social services arrives.

Look at me. I'm eighty and still have to be washed like a baby, Perla observes. Her bath done and breakfast on the way, Perla pulls a mirror from the drawer by her bed. She balances it on the stool—*I sat on this one in Auschwitz*—and, just like an actress about to face an audience, professionally applies her makeup, dabbing on the colors with her fingers. Once a month she dyes her hair raven black.

Perla's wardrobe is bursting with rows of identical, vibrantly colored dresses. *I instantly sense when the maid hands me one of Elizabeth's by mistake, but I never tell her to put it back since I like being in touch with my sister.* Perla prides herself on being an accomplished seamstress, and she still makes dresses, as well as bed linens and lingerie, with her Singer sewing machine. *We were like the dwarfs in fairy tales, always diligent and hard-working, better craftsmen than tall people.*

Perla watches with hawk eyes as the maid cleans the house, and she is not content until every crocheted doily and satin cushion is placed exactly at the right angle. The maid functions as Perla's legs. She does the shopping; she brings Perla her medication. Before she leaves at one o'clock, she serves Perla her lunch and places a napkin-covered supper on the low table by the window.

I maintain a rigid diet, eating very little, because we tiny people are in danger of being too heavy for our legs and lungs. Perla washes the plates herself, at her childlike sink in the corner. From one onward she's on her own. Her activity is confined mostly to her room, where everything she needs lies within reach: food, water, a telephone, a buzzer to open the front door. Behind a colored curtain is a low lavatory.

Self-reliant by nature, Perla tries to be as independent as she can. She would never ask a guest to fetch her something from the kitchen, for instance. A guest's first instinct is to sit on a low stool next to Perla's, so as not to overshadow her. But she always insists that guests take a more comfortable seat, one that is nearer their size. If it's not too hot or too cold, Perla drags herself into the shadows on the room's adjoining balcony for fresh air and a momentary escape from her prison. She slides the shutter open as if it were a stage curtain. She mounts her tiny armchair, and, just as she did in her childhood village in Romania, she watches the world go about its business.

This is her last podium.

Perla's regal emergence on the first-floor balcony attracts attention. Passersby stop on the pavement; they lift their eyes to greet Perla Ovitz, so theatrically dressed, so meticulously made up, and exchange a few friendly words.

I was an actress! she declares ostentatiously. She implicitly attributes every aspect of her life to her profession, but memories of the theater are painful. *It was the best part of my life, we were all together having fun, and it's all gone. When I think of those times I realize how lonely I am now and lose the will to live. Being alone is worse than being in a concentration camp.*

She can no longer go out to the movies or the theater, and since her last sister's death, she has not been in the mood to watch TV. Her most steadfast companion is an ancient red miniature transistor radio, and she sings to its music. When in an especially bad mood, she simply hums to herself. *Romantic Hungarian tunes are better than cardiac pills,* she advises. She cries when she sings her favorite song:

> *I'm going to the graveyard to talk to Mother.*
> *The forest is gloomy and the branches are crying.*

I would have told you, Mother, what troubles my heart,
how bitter is life without you.

She falls asleep with the radio on, but some nights she awakens with a scream. *In my dreams I am back in Auschwitz, although I rarely see Dr. Mengele. More often I'm in an* Appell, praying that no one is missing from the count—otherwise we'll all be killed.

While many Holocaust survivors boycott German products and object to Israeli orchestras playing Wagner, Perla Ovitz works hard at distinguishing the past from the present. Hannelore Witkofski, the historian and advocate for short people's rights, contacted Perla in the 1990s after hearing about her, and they soon began corresponding regularly. *Hannelore is hurt when people look at her as if she were a monster and make clear she should evaporate,* explains Perla indignantly. *She told me that even today in Germany, many people think that the life of dwarfs and people like her and me with disabilities is worthless and that the Nazis' idea of euthanasia was not bad after all. It's shocking.*

Accompanied by fellow advocates, Witkofski has flown to Israel several times to see Perla. Once she surprised Perla with a new, highly sophisticated wheelchair. *I asked Hannelore how much I owed her. She answered, 'You?! It's us who owe you everything!' She always wears trousers, and was intrigued to try on one of my dresses. It looked so nice on her that I used the same pattern to sew her a red sleeveless summer dress.*

It's January 10, 2001, Perla's eightieth birthday. In the stairwell, before pressing the doorbell, we light eighty candles and blow up colorful balloons. Perla is stunned to see us with Hannelore and other friends. Our birthday gifts symbolize the themes of her life: small diamond earrings, a guitar-shaped chocolate cake, a bottle of champagne, French perfume, a CD player, a child-sized walker. Perla is in a good mood and sings from her repertoire to the small audience gathered in the bedroom. She retains the glow of the girl, the chanteuse, the darling, the angel, when all of Romania was her stage.

Or perhaps it's the glow of her faith. Perla is steadfast in her religious practice. She keeps kosher, observes the Sabbath, and cooks the traditional meals from her childhood for herself on holidays. She puts on a festive dress and sits by herself to celebrate.

Auschwitz has shaken the faith of many survivors, but not hers.

It's beyond me to understand how he, who sees the whole world, could watch the flames coming out of the chimneys, devouring his children, and do nothing. There are rabbis who say that the Jews died in the Holocaust because of their sins. Although I'm Orthodox and have the utmost respect for rabbis, I totally abhor this explanation. Our friends and relatives were extremely religious and did nothing to deserve punishment of any kind. We are too small and lowly to comprehend God's intentions. The fire was his will, as it was his will that our whole family would survive.

If I were a healthy Jewish girl, one meter seventy tall, I would have been gassed just like the hundreds of thousands of other Jews in my country. So if I ever wondered why I was born a dwarf, my answer would have to be that my handicap, my deformity, was God's only way to keep me alive.

TWENTY-TWO

Rozavlea–Auschwitz, September 2000

O ur journey into the true story of the seven dwarfs who
were liege to no benevolent Snow White but rather to
a heartless beast started in 1994, when we came across this brief
comment in a history book: "In 1949, a troupe named 'The
Seven Dwarfs of Auschwitz' toured the cities of Israel in a song
and dance show." There were no individual or family names, no
further identifying details at all. But we were intrigued. We had
never before heard of this strange amalgam of death and amusement. That even we seasoned journalists, had missed this historical episode was not surprising. After all, half a million
Holocaust survivors, each with a separate ghastly and amazing
tale, had settled in Israel after the war.

Some sleuthing soon led us to the name "Ovitz" and the
family's hometown of Haifa. We did not expect to find any of
them alive after so many years, although we did discover nineteen Ovitzes in the Haifa telephone directory. Each call we made
seemed to confirm the futility of our mission. Then we chanced
on Perla.

She sounded suspicious over the phone, but then an elderly woman who lived alone in the city had reason to be. She opened up instantly, however, when she heard that we wished to learn more about the Lilliput Troupe and its travails in Auschwitz. Every fortnight since, we have traveled from Jerusalem to visit Perla. She greeted us always with a hearty smile, a kiss on both cheeks: *Oh, I've soiled you again with lipstick. Never mind, it's a proof of love.* We offer a box of chocolate pralines, occasionally a bottle of red wine: *Thank you so much, the doctor said it's good for my heart.*

One question is enough to set her sailing on the river of her memories. She describes her village, the main road, the houses she passed on her way to school, the yard where the geese and hens ran free. She takes us through the rooms of her childhood home. Her voice caresses the memory of furniture and curtains, and we get to know not just the house, but the texture of its happiness—as if we, too, had lived there. Her memory is startlingly vivid; she might have been there just last month, rather than fifty years ago.

She also remembers in gritty detail each of the barracks the Lilliputs inhabited in Auschwitz, and her mimicry of Mengele's speech and gestures brings his unsettling presence into her bedroom.

Still, we wanted to see the places with our own eyes; we wanted to find out whether Rozavlea and Auschwitz remembered the Lilliputs. So we flew to Bucharest, then took a one-hour flight north to Baia Mare, and from there a two-hour taxi drive to Sighet, the town closest to Rozavlea.

As Perla had stated with no uncertainty that the Lilliputs *always performed in the biggest, most luxurious halls,* we wandered around the town in search of the stages on which the famous troupe had performed. The largest public hall in town is the Teatrul Popular Sighetul Marmathei Sala de Spectacole Studio, across from the Piaza Libertace. The imposing name hangs over a shabby reality. The entrance has evidently fallen into disuse, as it is blocked by six heavy, brown iron doors, the type usually installed in warehouses. On the wall, a tattered poster dated eight months back announces a Laurel and Hardy–type pair of comedians and a *troupa de ballet*, the Romanian version of a Pigalle nightclub act. The illuminated sign on the second floor reads Discoteca No Comment.

"There's nothing to do here. There are no more theater shows, only once in a while a traveling troupe comes through," says twenty-year-old Ramona, a guide in the local ethnic museum; she favors tight blue jeans and speaks MTV English. Ramona leads us to the only other hall in Sighet, a cinema in a state of general deterioration. Its seats are torn and dirty; its program is mainly trashy American movies. Sixty years on, the town has lost virtually every shred of its former glory.

The street names, though, have not changed, and Bogdan Voda is still the principal road. Before the war, Sighet had a thriving community of ten thousand Jews. Today only a few dozen remain, most of them old. Half of the town's fourteen synagogues were destroyed by Horty's Hungarian Fascist regime, the other half by the Communists. Only one is still standing: the grand Sephardi synagogue. Elie Weisel's parents attended this synagogue, and it has recently been lavishly reconstructed with generous American donations. Yet it is not an active place of worship; rather, it is a monument to a dead community. Elie Wiesel's childhood home has been converted into a Jewish museum and a memorial—to "the first man from Sighet to be awarded the Nobel Peace Prize," as a tourist brochure declares. Wiesel is the local son who made good and attained international celebrity. However, the brochure does not mention the circumstances that preceded Weisel's success: his transport to Auschwitz as a teenager, along with the rest of the town's Jews; his settling in the United States after the mass extermination of European Jewry at the Nazi death camps.

Sighet, the northernmost town in Romania, lies close to the Ukrainian border. It has fifty thousand inhabitants but no car-rental agency. And there is still, a half century after the Ovitzes' days here, no train connection to Rozavlea.

We stop by the Jewish community center. We speak no Romanian and the clerk at the office understands no English. We try Hebrew, but the language of the prayer book provides no bridge in our communications, either. Luckily for us, a round, short, red-faced man with a raincoat and leather case happens to come in. Everyone calls Josef Tennenbaum "Professor," because he once taught Russian in high school, but in the eleven years since the demise of Ceaucescu and his regime, Russian has been out of style in Romania. So Tennenbaum has much free time on his hands. He agrees to be our translator—with his knack for languages, he's acquired a modest facility in English—and guide.

Tennenbaum does not own a car. Not many do in a country where 40 percent of the population earns as little as a dollar a day, and where a pound of meat costs $1.25, and a pack of American cigarettes, one dollar. But he does not want for resourcefulness. In a rush he leaves us, and half an hour later he returns with Berciu Petru, an unemployed technician whose ancient Delta—the Romanian version of a Renault 12—is in tip-top shape.

The following morning, the four of us drive to Rozavlea,

some twenty miles away. "They owned the first car in the village," is seventy-six-year-old Ivan Petrovan's first response when we ask him about the dwarf family. He remembers going to school with a dwarf girl (it was Perla). "They had nice clothes, but all the Jews dressed much better then the rest of us. Jews made more money than we did—the best land in the village belonged to the dwarfs. They were especially rich because they also made money from their shows. But now there are no Jews here."

Petrovan seems uncomfortable with the revelation. "We're not to blame," he adds hastily. "The Hungarians and Germans forced us to evict the Jews from their homes at gunpoint. I had a horse and a carriage and the militia gave me the name of a Jewish family to drive out of the village. The majority had to walk, and it was a sad sight to see them trailing along with their blankets and pillows over their heads."

When we mention that the Jews claim that their houses were looted, Petrovan grows defensive. "It wasn't us. It was the Gypsies who did that to them. I took nothing, not even a spoon. I do have some Jewish things at home, that's true, but I bought them with good money. A Jew returned from the war and sold me his family property before leaving for Israel. We were on very good terms with the Jews. I had many friends among them and I liked the special cakes they made at Easter."

Visovan Gheorghe, an agricultural engineer who switched to politics, is now serving his second term as *primar* of Rozavlea— he is the village principal. His office is located in a sizeable estate house that once belonged to one of Rozavlea's richest Jewish families; it is the only Jewish house that was not demolished. "When I was born the Lilliputs had already been gone for many years, but my aunt told me about them. Nothing is left of them now except memories that pass from generation to generation." The *primar* has a computer, a printer, a fax machine, a mobile telephone. And he has his own private toilet, to which he holds the key. It's a wooden shed in the yard, with no electricity; you crouch over a deep, smelly hole in the ground. The Ovitzes had the same type of toilet sixty years ago. In the absence of plumbing or a sewage system, the *primar*'s secretary is patiently waiting outside with a glass of water and a towel.

The 7,200 inhabitants of Rozavlea have had electricity since 1960 and automatic dialing since 1994; but in 2000 only half the population had running water. The other half continues drawing water from stone wells that are dug in their yards. As in the old days, the clean water of the Iza River is preferred for laundry. Daily life in Rozavlea is hard by modern standards, and the economic conditions are harsh—so harsh that they have caused a steep decline in the birth rate. In the Ovitzes' time, every family had eight to ten children; now most families have only two or three. "We cannot afford big families—simply cannot feed them," says the *primar,* a father of two.

Young people cannot find work in Rozavlea; their greatest dream is to leave the country. Twenty Rozavleans who have done "guest work" in Israel are the envy of the village. After just two years on the sun-scorched scaffolding, they returned to build the most beautiful villas in Rozavlea—for themselves. Visovan Gheorghe enjoys an extraordinarily high salary by Romanian standards, 150 dollars a month, but he is prepared to forsake it all if we can get him a government permit to work as a builder in Israel, where, he says, he could earn 600 dollars in a month. And could we tell all ex-Rozavleans in Israel that they are invited to the Roza-Rozalina, the Festival of Giants, celebrated every August?

Most of the houses in Rozavlea have been built along the main road. Perla's precise description leads us to the spot where the Ovitz family's big wooden house once stood. There is still no pavement, and the pedestrians share the street with the traffic— occasional cars and, more often, horses and carriages. Wooden fences shield the houses from the street, and—as in the old days—each family has a bench outside, where it can sit and watch the world go by.

The Ovitz house was demolished in 1969; some of its planks have been used to build a new shed in what was its yard. Even the synagogue next door, which had been refurbished with the Lilliputs' money, has been razed, and two houses have been built with wood stripped from the holy site. Ion and Maria Timis know that their house stands on the foundations of the Ovitz house. Ion Timis is a former *primar.* He takes us to a row of plum trees in the yard and points out the two oldest. He tells us that they were planted by the Ovitzes. His wife gives us a jar of her special plum marmalade, a gift for Perla.

"I remember their car," Timis says as we follow him to the spot where the garage once stood. "I was a child when they left, and for years the abandoned car was our Disneyland. Gradually it was dismantled piece by piece." Not much has changed over the years: the stone well still stands at the entrance; fragrant flower beds still brighten the front of the house; there are still vegetables growing in the backyard, two rows of beehives, cows in the shed.

A gate of climbing vines leads to the new house. The interior not only resembles Perla's description of the old one, but virtu- ally mirrors her current house in Haifa today! The Ovitz and Timis families are strangers to each other, yet like twins split by a twist of fate, they share an uncannily similar taste for plastic flowers, decorated cups displayed in a glass cabinet, little china animals and dolls, huge family photos hanging on the walls, embroidered red tablecloths. Only the tiny chairs and stools in Perla's Haifa flat mark a difference.

Of the hundred Jewish families living in Rozavlea on the eve of the war, only five returned after it, and the last of them left in 1964. Most surviving Rozavlean Jews now live in Israel. A few of them, those willing to forgive the hurt and put aside the anger over their expulsion from their birthplace, keep in touch with a former neighbor or schoolmate. Economically the Israeli Rozavleans fare incomparably better than their Romanian counterparts; before we leave for Romania, they give us parcels of instant coffee, bubble gum, cigarettes, stockings, and sweets, which we distribute on their behalf.

The cemetery is the village's only sign of a former Jewish existence. At an early-eighteenth-century wooden church—the pride of the village—we turn right. After warily treading the planks of a rocking, fragile, narrow wooden bridge slung across the Iza River, we pass a cornfield, and then an apple orchard. The ground is muddy and slippery. Then we see the stones standing erect at the foot of a green hill.

The cemetery plot is enclosed by a wire fence, and Rozka Gamber, who lives nearby, has the key to the gate. Our driver and guide happily stay with her in order to fill cotton sacks with ripe red apples to take to their wives. There are about a hundred tombstones. The graves of the prominent rabbis and leaders of the community are marked by solid monuments of white marble, which have fared well in the rough weather. Many of the more modest stones have simply crumbled away, their inscriptions now beyond recognition. We try to concentrate on our search for the name Ovitz, but find ourselves lingering by

each tombstone. We read aloud the Hebrew names and epi-
taphs, as if we were holding a private memorial service for each
of the deceased. For it has been decades since these graves were
last visited, and decades may well pass before the silence here is
broken again. We reach the outer edge of what is left of the
cemetery. Among the profuse weeds and the weathered headstones sinking into the soft earth, we spot the moss-covered
tombstones of the Lilliputs' parents.

The Jewish community of Rozavlea was so pious that it
buried men and women in separate rows. Even married couples
were not interred next to each other. But the Ovitz children had
managed to purchase a place for their mother in the women's
row directly behind their father, then seven years dead, in the
men's row. The Hebrew inscriptions, "an honest, virtuous,
learned man" and "the modest woman," bespeak a secret code
that only we can decipher. From the back of the tombstones we
carefully peel a splinter of each stone for Perla—Shimshon
Eizik's dark gray granite; Batia's lighter gray.

All that is left in Rozavlea of the Ovitz family's vibrant eighty
years here are two tombstones, two plum trees, and a smile on the
faces of the old people at the mention of the once-famous Lilliputs.

It is only a ten-minute drive to pastoral Dragomiresti in Berciu
Petru's Delta, but six decades ago, it took the convoy of weary
Rozavlean Jews, loaded down with their belongings, half a day to
walk the eight miles to the ghetto. Today, the sound of a solitary
violin from a late-afternoon music class spills from a window as
we stroll through the huge, empty schoolyard—and conjure up
the ghostly presence of 3,500 terrified people clinging to life and
their belongings.

We continue following the route that the deportees took into remote Poland. We wind through the hilly terrain. We edge past carts struggling under mountains of hay. Peasant women dressed in black stare at us from their yards, just as they might have stared at the ragged convoy of Jewish deportees on that hot day in May 1944; it is late afternoon, just as it was then. We get to the railway station of Viseul de Jos, and a stairway leads to a large waiting room with wooden benches; the walls are painted beige in a flowery pattern. The line for tickets is on the left. But this is not the way the deportees entered. They were led around the back of the building and pushed up toward the rails. There was no platform.

We step outside. The seemingly endless freight train standing in the station seems chillingly unreal, nightmarish, like a hallucination. We measure our height against that of a cattle car: the floor is over one meter high—for us, a strenuous climb; for the dwarfs, an impossible one.

You can't cross the border from this station. If you want to go to Auschwitz you have to take one of the two daily trains to Cluj, six sluggish hours away. There you change to the train to Oradea for an even longer, bumpier trip. A third train gets you to Budapest, and from there you take a night train to Kraków. It's a ten-hour trip, and comfortable as the sleeping compartments are, the unending clatter of the wheels, the tasteless coffee, the unpleasant odor from the private toilet are cause for mild complaint. It's impossible to imagine the conditions, mile after mile after mile, in that stuffy cattle car. The soft beds on the night train to Kraków somehow make us feel guilty of comfort, and we sleep under the burden of history.

There are police and customs checks all along the way. We give up trying to tell the uniformed guards one from the other;

they make themselves known with brisk commands and barking dogs. Repeatedly they wake us up. They bang on the door; they check our passports. Every frown or cough or momentary hesitation speeds up the beat of our hearts.

The train from Budapest to Kraków passes through Oswiecim. A rather nice hostel now stands at the site of the death camp, but as convenient as it would be, we find it too eerie even to consider sleeping in this place that once filled the sky with smoke every day. To say "we stayed a week in Auschwitz" seems a sacrilege. We also rule out several hotels in town. The Oswiecim tourist board will never be able to tempt visitors with slogans like "Come and enjoy our facilities" or "You'll have the time of your life in Oswiecim." As hard as it tries, the town cannot shed its ignominious history: its name is permanently contaminated. Dyskoteka System, with its weekend soft-porn performances, just two kilometers away from the former death camp, sparked international denunciation: "So near . . . so soon." In Oswiecim, time and distance will always be morally measured.

We decide to stay in Kraków. The receptionist at the Europeiski Hotel recommends the convenient one-hour train ride to Oswiecim, but we recoil at the idea of arriving by rail and decide to rent a car. For a week we shuttle between Kraków and Auschwitz, but somehow it always takes us twice the time to arrive there than it does to make the journey back.

It's free to pass under the sign *Arbeit macht frei* (Work Liberates) but you are charged at the parking lot. The visitors' center is like any such center anywhere in the world: a smiling hostess at the information desk, an auditorium, souvenir and book shops, public telephones, money exchanger, automatic drink machines, and Bar Smak—a self-service cafeteria. Each day we arrive early in the morning and leave in the late afternoon. We skip the cafeteria, which is always packed with famished tourist groups, because we cannot bear the thought of standing in line for a bowl of soup in Auschhwitz; we are afraid we might even find it palatable.

Among the half million annual visitors to Auschwitz is a steady stream of Polish high school students. They do not hide their delight at having the day off. Their exuberant puberty is ironically highlighted when they cavort next to the barbed wire. On the screen in the auditorium, in an endless loop every thirty minutes, exhausted, tiny Ludovit Feld again plods out of the camp gates on liberation day.

When you enter the barracks area, ambiguity assails you. Several tourist groups move through the site simultaneously; their languages—Polish, German, English—dissolve as they intermingle with each other. So that you do not lose your particular group, you are issued a special colored badge—ours is orange—to stick on your clothes. One cannot escape the feeling that with this identification of groups of people by shape and color the Auschwitz system is still effectively in operation.

Auschwitz, as opposed to Birkenau, is where the Lilliputs underwent special medical tests. In 1942, wooden shutters were installed on the windows of the notorious block 10 to prevent observation of the criminal experiments, mainly castrations and sterilizations. The shutters remain closed to this day, and block 10 is out of bounds to visitors. We move around the sealed site; we cannot find even a crack to peep through, and we wonder what horrors it must still harbor in its dark quarters six decades later.

Block 24 now hosts the camp archives. On the first floor the inmate-cards in the wooden boxes are all standing in *Appell*. These cards represent the lucky ones, since 90 percent of those who arrived to Auschwitz were extinguished immediately— their names unregistered, their arms not tattooed. For the many who were admitted but later sent to the crematoria, these registration cards are their only tombstones.

In an austere reading room on the second floor, the archivist allows us to handle the original medical documents regarding the Ovitz family. The information on the small pieces of paper is neatly typed or gracefully handwritten in ink by prisoners who hoped their clerical skills would save their lives. Whenever a new calligraphic style appears, we cannot help wondering what became of the previous prisoner-clerk. The forms carry Mengele's extravagant signature. The banality of clinical paperwork permanently renders our Perla an inmate-patient in Auschwitz.

Many of the archive's rooms are decorated with reproductions of Dina Gottlieb-Babbitt's portraits of Gypsies, and in block 12, four of her original paintings are on display. None of the seven souvenir shops on site sells her prints. They were removed when she began her legal dispute with the museum.

It is a short drive from Auschwitz to Birkenau, where over a million Jews were murdered and the Lilliput group was imprisoned. We enter by the same gates that the hundreds of death trains from all over Europe passed through with their human cargo. The clean air is the first thing that strikes us. Perla and all the other survivors we interviewed spoke of the smell—ever-present, smoky, nauseating—of burning flesh. The second thing we notice is the green sweep of the grounds—the blades of grass and small flowers now covering the muddy marshlands that once enveloped the camp. Nature has managed to heal itself or to restore to the land its innocence.

Then are we struck by the emptiness of the place. Of the 198 barracks that once stood in Birkenau BII, just 20 remain today. All the other buildings were leveled. The only traces left of them are the foundations and the forest of chimneys that rise like grim headstones in a horrific graveyard.

We peep into one of the remaining barracks. Signs on the wall in Gothic German letters read: "Cleanliness Is Your Duty!" "Quiet in the Barrack! Forbidden to Drink This Water—Dangerous for Health." The signs might have been painted by Dina Gottlieb, as such work was one of her first artistic assignments in Auschwitz.

Inside the barrack we verify the details of Perla's descriptions: the small room, like the one the Ovitz group shared at the entrance to the barrack; the wooden banks in three tiers; the moldy darkness. We see it all—where they slept, where they prayed—but we don't grasp any better how on earth they ever got through it.

A guide stops by with her group. "The lower bunk is the worst because of the cat-sized rats swarming on the floor," she explains, but her recitation sounds more like a tip for potential victims than a matter of historical fact. The huge toilet barrack has no partitions; it is made up of three long concrete banks with 174 toilet holes spaced so closely that the occupants were forced to sit next to each other, buttock to buttock, back to back.

On the ramp, you can stand on the exact spot where Mengele stood and, with the flick of a finger, determined the fates of thousands upon thousands of newly arrived Jews every day. At the side of the ramp, for those who cannot visualize easily, the museum has placed blown-up prints of black-and-white photos that were taken in the summer of 1944: columns of cattle trucks, rows of dazed human beings, lines of impassive guards. One of the photographs sums up the horror and the pity of it all. It shows a desperate old woman, her face wrinkled, her body stooped, as she hurries toward the crematoria with her three grandchildren. Afraid to lose them, she holds the youngest two tight, while the third grandchild, a girl no more than eight, trails behind, her head bowed down. You see it all. You understand nothing.

We bought a plan of the camp at the bookshop. Like devoted postmen, we call at every address the Ovitz group occupied: barrack 30 at the "Czechoslovakian Family Camp," barrack 14 at the male prisoners' hospital, barrack 9 at the women's camp, then the yard where Mengele held his concert perversely on Tisha B'Av. Near the kitchen is parked a bread cart similar to the one in which the Ovitzes and the Slomowitzes made their way to freedom. With our legs we measure the long and, for the Lilliputs, arduous distance from their barrack to Mengele's clinic; with our eyes we assess the height of the electrified barbed wire fence and the watchtowers. We slide into the deep, muddy ditches that were dug to separate the camp's sections. It's amazing the extent of the security precautions that were taken by the Nazis against people so helpless and feeble. We see it all, and understand nothing.

As if we were archeologists exploring an excavation site, we search the ground of a block where Perla once lived. Among the rubble we find a rusty, punctured white enamel soup bowl and a tin cup without a handle. We bend down to examine the artifacts more closely, but we refrain from touching these skeletons of memory.

Then, suddenly, we spot it. Something familiar: a large brown coat button.

We remember that Perla's sheepskin coat had buttons just like this, and we allow ourselves to pick it up. Tenderly, we rub the dust from it.

For a moment, we consider taking it with us and returning it to Perla.

For a moment. Then we lay it back down on the ground, to remain forever in the place where it belongs.

Perla Ovitz, the last of the Lilliput Troupe, died peacefully in Haifa on September 9, 2001.

Sources and Thanks

ARCHIVES:

Yad Vashem Holocaust Memorial Museum, Jerusalem, Israel
Auschwitz-Birkenau State Museum, Poland
Bundesarchiv, Ludwigsburg, Germany
International Tracing Service of the Red Cross, Bad Arolsen, Germany
The Public Prosecutor's Office in Frankfurt am Main, Germany
U.S. Holocaust Memorial Museum, Washington, D.C.

BOOKS:

Adelsberger, Lucie. *Auschwitz: A Doctor's Story.* Boston: Northeastern UP, 1995.

Astor, Gerald. *The Last Nazi: The Life and Times of Joseph Mengele.* New York: Donald Fine, 1985.

Braham, L. Randolph. *Genocide and Retribution: The Holocaust in Hungarian-Ruled Northern Transylvania.* Boston: Martinus Nijhoff Publishing, 1983.

Czech, Danuta (ed). *Auschwitz Chronicle 1939–1945.* New York: Henry Holt, 1990.

Enderle, Alfred, Dietrich Meyerhofer, and Gerd Unverfehrt (eds). *Small People, Great Art: Restricted Growth from an Artistic and Medical Viewpoint.* Hamburg: ArtColor Verlag, 1994.

Fenelon, Fania. *Playing for Time.* New York: Atheneum, 1977.

Gutman, Israel, and Michael Berenbaum (eds). *Anatomy of Auschwitz Death Camp.* Bloomington: Indiana University Press, 1994.

Hoedeman, Paul. *Hitler or Hippocrates: Medical Experiments and Euthanasia in the Third Reich.* Sussex: Book Guild, 1991.

Klee, Ernst. *Auschwitz: Die NS-Medizin und ihre Opfer.* Frankfurt: Fischer, 1997.

Kraus, Ota and Erich Kulka. *The Death Factory: Document on Auschwitz.* New York: Franklin Books Co., 1966.

Lifton, Robert Jay. *The Nazi Doctors: Medical Killing and the Psychology of Genocide.* New York: Basic Books, 1986.

Lingens-Reiner, Ella. *Prisoners of Fear.* London: Victor Gollancz,1948.

Lengyel, Olga. *Five Chimneys: A Woman Survivor's True Story of Auschwitz.* Chicago: Academy Chicago Publishers, 1995.

Mannix, Daniel P. *Freaks: We Who Are Not as Others.* New York: Pocket Books, 1976.

Matalon-Lagnado, Lucette and Sheila Cohn-Dekel. *Children of the Flames: Dr. Josef Mengele and the Untold Story of the Twins of Auscwitz.* New York: William Morrow, 1991.

Moskowitz, Elizabeth. *By Grace of the Satan: The Story of the Dwarves Family in Auschwitz and Dr. Mengele's Experiments.* Ramat–Gan, Israel: Rotem Publications, 1987.

Muller-Hill, Benno. *Murderous Science: Elimination by Scientific Selection of Jews, Gypsies and Others in Germany, 1933–1945.* Plainview, New York: Cold Spring Harbor Laboratory Press, 1988.

Nomberg-Pzytyk, Sara. *Auschwitz: True Tales from a Grotesque Land.* Chapel Hill, North Carolina, and London: The University of North Carolina Press, 1985.

Nyiszli, Miklos. *Auschwitz: A Doctor's Eyewitness Account.* New York: Fawcett Crest, 1961.

Perl, Gisella. *I Was a Doctor in Auschwitz.* New York: Arno Press, 1979.

Piper, Franciszek and Teresa Swiebocka (eds). *Auschwitz, Nazi Death Camp.* Auschwitz State Museum, 1996.

Posner, Gerald and John Ware. *Mengele: The Complete Story.* New York: McGraw-Hill, 1986.

Samuelson, Benjamin. *Abiding Hope: Bearing Witness to the Holocaust.* Los Angeles: Ulyssian Publications, 2003.

SELECTED ARTICLES:

Enderle, Alfred and Gerd Unverfehrt. "Die historische Bildpostkarte als Zeugnis menschlicher Wachstumsstorungen." *Osteologie,* 1999.

Koren, Yehuda. "Saved by the Devil: an interview with Perla Ovitz." *Telegraph,* February 27, 1999.

Muller–Hill, Benno. "The Blood from Auschwitz and the Silence of the Scholars." *History and Philosophy of Life Sciences* 21, (1999). 331–365.

Negev, Eilat. "They Say I Called Mengele 'Daddy': an interview with Shimshon Ovitz." *Yedioth Achronot,* April 28, 2000.

Seidelman, William. "The Professional Origins of Dr. Mengele." *Canadian Medicinal Association Journal,* vol. 133, December 1, 1985. 1169–1171.

Sinonius, L. "On Behalf of Victims of Pseudo-Medical Experiments." *International Review of the Red Cross,* no. 142, January 1973. 3–21.

FILMS:

Dood Spoor? Alexander Katan, film by Van Gennep, Roest and Scheren, Holland, 2001.

Liebe Perla, director: Shahar Rozen, Israel, 1999.

INTERVIEWS WITH EYEWITNESSES:

We are grateful to the members of the Lilliput group—Perla Ovitz, Shimshon Ovitz, Mordechai, Joseph, and Judah Slomowitz, Regina Ovitz, and Bassie Fischman-Glazer—who agreed to undergo with us the emotionally straining journey to their haunting past.

We are also deeply indebted to the other survivors of Auschwitz, who selflessly put aside their own tormenting experience to tell the tale of their co-prisoners, the dwarfs:

Dina Gottlieb-Babbitt, Kalman Bar-On, Peter Grunfeld, Efraim Reichenberg, Solomon Malik, Abraham Cykiert, Gitta Drattler-Budimsky, Isaac Taub, Eta Tessler, Zvi Klein, Leah Nishri, Ibby Mann, Arie Rubin, Zipora Schaps, Moshe Offer, Sarah Wirzberger, Yona Lachs, Sarah Angel.

Many ex-Rozavleans and inhabitants of Transylvania enriched us with reminiscences about life in the village before the war, and their colorful accounts were vital to rebuild the story: Haim Perl, Abe Glazer, Arie Tessler, Roza Stauber, Shoshana Glazer, Herman Szabo, Efraim Topel, David Giladi, Hanan Akavia, Ben-Zion Tessler, Israel Popowitz, Eliezer Stauber, Malka Solomonowitz, Dvora Pach-Kahana, Miriam Sheinberger.

INTERVIEWS WITH EXPERTS AND ADVISORS:

All the material that we assembled from the eyewitnesses, archives, books, and articles, was verified with a variety of experts, which does not diminish our responsibility for the accuracy of the text. We are grateful to historians Professor Israel Gutman, Professor William Seidelman, Dr. Daniel Nadav, Professor Isaac Peri, Dr. Gideon Greif, Helena Kubica, Professor Bezalel Narkis, Professor Alex Carmel, Professor Michael Harsagor, Amnon Weinstein, and Tuvia Friedman.

Thanks also to geneticists Professor Benno Muller-Hill, Professor Raphael Falk, Professor Zvi Borochovitz, Professor Avner Yayon, and biochemist Alexander Sharon.

RESEARCHERS AND TRANSLATORS:

Our researchers, Professor Ladisau Gyemant and Maria Ujvari in Romania, Gjorgi Szilagyi in Hungary, and Joseph Rosen, Miriam Shkedi, and Inbal Berner in Israel, furnished us with valuable findings.

We could not have made our way in the Babel of tongues without our small army of dedicated translators: from Romanian: Yehuda Gur-Arie and Joseph Tennenbaum. German: Miriam Ron, Michael S. Englard, and Nurit Carmel. Dutch: Effie Weiss. Polish: Michael Ben Avraham. Hungarian: Judith Berner. Russian: Haim Dobolpolsky.

We enjoyed the good assistance of Hannelore Witkofski, Moritz Terfloth, Mihai Armenia, Hari Markus, Eva Kor, Sylvain Brachfeld, Haviva Peled-Carmeli, Ferenc Katona, Shahar Rosen, Benoit Massin, Dr. Ute Deichmann, John Dollar, Debbie Perman-Brukman, and Professor Gustav Spann.

And special thanks to our good fairy and literary agent, Erika Stegmann, and to our editors, Philip Turner, Peter Skutches, and Keith Wallman, who made this the book we intended to write.

Index

About the Authors

Yehuda Koren, a journalist and author, was born in Israel. He studied Jewish History and Sociology at the Hebrew University in Jerusalem, and Television Drama Production in Britain. For many years he was a documentary editor, producer, and director at Israeli Broadcasting Authority (IBA), winning several awards for his programs. He has been a historical consultant for several British documentary films and radio programs, which were produced by Channel 4 and the BBC. Koren currently writes features for the British, Israeli, and German press, where his work has appeared in the *Saturday Times*, the *Guardian*, the *Daily Telegraph*, and *Die Welt*. *In Our Hearts We Were Giants* is his second book. He is currently working with Eilat Negev writing a biography of Assia Wevill, the lover of British poet laureate Ted Hughes.

Eilat Negev, a journalist and author, was born in Saratoga Springs, New York, to Israeli parents, and grew up in Israel where she studied English Literature and History of Art at the Hebrew University. She has Masters degrees in Translation and in Mass Communications. She was a documentary radio producer at the Israeli Radio, and had her own program featuring profiles of celebrated artists, writers, and musicians. For the past twelve years, she has been the senior literary correspondent of *Yedioth Achronot*, the major Israeli daily newspaper. She is frequently sent to assignments abroad, and has interviewed Salman Rushdie in hiding, Toni Morrison, Arthur Miller, Nobel Laureate Nadine Gordimer, Paul Auster, Iris Murdoch, Yevgeny Yevtushenko, Erica Jong, Shere Hite, and many others. Negev has published two books in Hebrew, *Intimate Conversations* and *Private Life*. A collection of her inteviews, *Close Encounters*, was recently published in the United States and Britain.